The Regulation Game

Strategic Use of the Administrative Process

Bruce M. Owen
Ronald Braeutigam

Ballinger Publishing Company • Cambridge, Massachusetts
A Subsidiary of J.B. Lippincott Company

International Standard Book Number: 0-88410-066-9

Library of Congress Catalog Card Number: 78-558

Printed in the United States of America

Library of Congress Cataloging in Publication Data

Owen, Bruce M
  The regulation game.

  Bibliography: p. 259
  Includes index.
  1. Industry and state—United States. 2. Trade regulation—United States. 3. Antitrust law—United States. I. Braeutigam, Ronald, joint author. II. Title.
HD3616.U4709   338.973   78-558
ISBN 0-88410-066-9

For our parents

※

Contents

✳

List of Figures

✳

List of Tables

Preface

We hope that students of economic regulation and administrative law will find one or two useful ideas in this book.

The main themes are set out in Chapter 1. The remaining chapters illustrate our themes with case studies of specific industries and specific regulatory decisions. The case studies are intended to have independent value.

Although this book is very much a joint effort, it may be useful to identify which author had primary responsibility for which chapter. Owen was primarily responsible for Chapters 1, 2, 4, and 5; Braeutigam for Chapters 3, 6, and 7.

We are indebted to many of our friends, students, and colleagues for helpful advice at various stages of the work reported here. A partial list of acknowledgments follows: Stanley Besen, Henry Block, Constance Dunham, Donald Dunn, Paul Goldstein, Joseph Grundfest, Sergiu Hart, J. Hilman, Michael Klass, Alvin Klevorick, Sebastian Lasher, John Ledyard, Roger McNitt, Charles Meyers, Bridger Mitchell, Roger Noll, John Panzar, Ed Park, Merton J. Peck, Owen Phillips, James Rosse, Antonin Scalia, F.M. Scherer, Sherrill Shaffer, Michael Spence, Leonard Weiss, and Robert Willig. In addition, we gratefully acknowledge useful suggestions from participants in various seminars at Stanford, Northwestern, and Duke Universities, and at the National Science Foundation. Marianna Scherrer, Florence Stein, and Alice Coldren provided, as usual, efficient and good-humored secretarial services.

Chapter 1

Introduction

This chapter will deal with two closely related but nevertheless distinct issues: The actual behavior of participants in the administrative process or what we have called "the regulation game," and the economic purpose of the process itself. We are interested in how the game works and in why it is played. We have also tried to provide an overview of the extensive but not very coherent literature on regulation.

The chapter is organized as follows. First, we put forward some suggestions as to the strategies that might be useful to a firm playing the regulation game. For purposes of exposition, we have chosen to write this as a "how-to" manual. This first section ends with some tentative hypotheses about the purposes of a regulatory game with the features that have been described, at least implicitly, by the strategic rules. The second section provides a brief overview of some of the literature on regulatory behavior. The third section is intended to address the question: Why does the regulation game exist and what economic purpose does it serve? We conclude with a brief discussion of the role of antitrust law and some normative speculations.

The two major conclusions can be briefly summarized. First, a major effect of the administrative or regulatory process is to attenuate the rate at which market and technological forces impose changes on individual economic agents; it is rational for voters to prefer such a mechanism for avoiding risk to a laissez-faire market system, even at the cost of some efficiency loss. The administrative process is "fairer" than the ungoverned market because it imposes due process requirements on any change in the existing set of goods, prices, and market structures. The result is to give individuals and firms some legal rights to the status quo. The second point is that regulated firms and industries operate within the administrative process just as they operate in the market; the environment provides opportunities for strategic behavior in pursuit of economic objectives. Given the first point, it must be emphasized that this strategic *use* of the administrative process does not necessarily constitute *abuse* of that process. Indeed, this chapter rather carefully avoids such normative judgments. Normative issues are discussed in the concluding section.

STRATEGIC USE OF THE ADMINISTRATIVE PROCESS

No industry offered the opportunity to be regulated should decline it. Few industries have done so. Railroads, airlines, telephone companies, radio stations, and most other industries have warmly embraced regulation when it was offered and have strenuously resisted efforts to remove it. With the exception of natural gas suppliers, whose prices have been held below competitive levels, every industry violently resisted the Ford administration deregulation program. Regulation protects such industries against competition from outsiders and from within the industry. It provides protection from antitrust attack. It provides a degree of protection from congressional investigation. Regulation greatly reduces the risk of bankruptcy from causes other than competition. And, while regulation may make very high rates of return difficult to achieve, it does virtually guarantee a steady stream of adequate profits.

Strategic use of the regulatory process is at least as important to many industries as the traditional decision variables: prices, entry, and innovation. In order to take full advantage of the process, it is useful to understand the motives and behavior of regulators, and the tools available to manipulate that behavior.

Government regulators are usually collegial bodies. The individual members are, on average, politicians. These politicians fall into two classes. The first, and by far the largest, consists of candidates who were not elected or reelected to office, and their former aides. As a group, they have strong political instincts but little imagination, and they regard their jobs as sinecures. The second and smaller group consists of not unsuccessful politicians, with larger ambitions, who are in their jobs in a temporary holding pattern. Their political instincts are even more sensitive since they are anxious to get ahead in the world. The members of the second group must walk a narrow line: they must build or maintain a reputation, and at the same time they must not make too many enemies. Generally speaking, they walk this line by being "efficient." They reorganize bureaus and try to make dockets move faster, and they make newsworthy but ultimately nonsubstantive speeches.

The behavior of a regulatory agency is guided by the nature of its commissioners, within the arguably very narrow constraints imposed by the statutory framework of the agency, the administrative process, and precedent. For this reason, it would be wrong to put great emphasis on the character and capability of the commissioners in explaining regulatory behavior.

The statutory framework which establishes the agency's charter should generally be regarded as a set of minimum constraints. Agencies can and do extend their charters when necessary to effectuate their "scheme" of regulation, and in doing so are regularly upheld by the courts [1]. The main reason for this is the broad injunction to protect the "public interest, convenience, and necessity" which nearly all the enabling statutes contain. This is a vague and open-ended license, and can be used to rationalize virtually any degree of intervention. (It cannot so easily be used to justify disengagement by the regulatory authority from some field, however [2]).

The administrative process is a set of procedures quite similar to those governing courts of law, which regulatory agencies follow in making decisions. Hearings are generally required to establish issues of fact, and there is usually ample opportunity for appeal within the agency, and then to the federal courts. All parties must be accorded due process. This jurisprudentially laudable set of constraints on agency behavior has an interesting side effect, which is the creation of substantial delays and legal expenses. Any party to a decision may impose these delays and expenses on the other parties. Thus, the administrative process provides important opportunities for strategic behavior by regulated firms.

Any established regulatory agency possesses a body of policies and past decisions that act as precedents for future decisions. Precedent is important because it has generally been sanctified on review by the federal courts. Even though some new departure may be legal, it must be tested on appeal, and thus carries with it certain doubts and risks. Finally, commissioners and especially agency staffs are often committed, intellectually or emotionally, to the previous policies and decisions of the agency.[a] This provides a significant constraint on behavior.

---

[a]Witness the FCC's stubborn commitment to UHF long after it was clearly a failure.

Strategies for Established Firms and Industries

Make Strategic Use of Information. The ability to control the flow of information to the regulatory agency is a crucial element in affecting decisions. Agencies can be guided in the desired direction by making available carefully selected facts. Alternatively, the withholding of information can be used to compel a lawsuit for "production" when delay is advantageous. Delay can also be achieved by overresponse: flooding the agency with more information than it can absorb. Sometimes, when a specific item of information is requested and it is difficult or impossible to delay in providing it, the best tactic is to bury it in a mountain of irrelevant material. This is a familiar tactic of attorneys in antitrust suits. It is also sometimes useful to provide the information but to deny its reliability and to commence a study to acquire more reliable data. Another option is to provide "accurate" information unofficially to selected personnel of the agency who are known to be sympathetic. If another party has supplied damaging information, it is important to supply contrary information in as technical a form as possible so that a hearing is necessary to settle the issues of "fact."[b]

In the context of a hearing, it is often useful to control access to information within the firm itself so that officials testifying for the company do not have knowledge of damaging facts. Thus, the internal information system of the firm must be carefully structured so that there are officials at various levels who can testify truthfully about various issues, and who are themselves ignorant of strategically important information. It is unwise to have a centralized management information system whose existence is known to many employees. Instead, information processing should be highly decentralized, and control should be exercised by careful personnel policies. It is always important that managers be loyal, and promotion policies should select this quality. The American Telephone and Telegraph Company has over the years made masterful use of information strategies, some of which are described in Chapters 2 and 7.

Make Strategic Use of Litigation. Litigation costs are usually small compared to the stakes in a regulatory decision for an established firm or industry. On the other hand, they are likely to be proportionally much more important to new firms, prospective entrants,

---

[b]An example is the FCC's newspaper-TV cross-ownership proceeding, in which the NAB commissioned a study by a private consulting firm to counter evidence submitted by a public interest intervenor regarding economic effects. The result was that the FCC saw the economic experts "cancel out."

and public interest advocates. If the established firm has correctly manipulated agency policy, then the status quo is a state congenial to the firm, and the strategic use of administrative procedure can prolong the status quo. A demonstration of willingness to do this may even forestall efforts by outsiders to engage in the process. The delay which can be purchased by litigation offers an opportunity to undertake other measures to reduce or eliminate the costs of an eventual adverse decision. These measures include strategic innovation, legislative proposals, and lobbying activity. If the administrative process goes on long enough, it is even possible to ask for a new hearing on the grounds that new and more accurate information may be available. The agency usually cannot resist the effort to delay through exhaustion of process because this would be grounds for reversal on appeal to the courts.

Make Strategic Use of Innovation. It is extremely useful to have available a well-managed research and development activity whose output of inventions can be controlled for strategic purposes. This is not applicable to many regulated industries, but for those involving developing technology it can be a crucial element in winning the regulatory game. A well-timed announcement of an innovation or technological breakthrough can moot a difficult issue which threatens to go against the firm. At a minimum, the terms of the debate may change sufficiently to require the decision process to begin anew. The optimal timing of innovation is affected by the presence of regulation. Examples include AT&T's invention of "SG" underseas cable (Chapter 2), cellular mobile radio systems, and "data under voice" digital communications capacity (Chapter 7).

A steady stream of cost-reducing innovation is useful to the maintenance of high profits in the face of rate of return regulation. A firm in this situation can continuously lower prices at a rate less than the rate at which costs decline, and thus avoid regulatory review that is either strict or frequent.

Produce More than One Product or Service, and Price Some Below Cost. An extremely successful strategy is to provide below cost service to classes of customers who are favored by redistributional policies of the government. Rural, residential, and poor customers are ideal subjects for this treatment, as opposed to urban, business, or wealthy consumers. It is important to have this policy recognized and endorsed by the regulatory agency. Most federal regulatory agencies, with strong lingering New Deal traditions, welcome the opportunity to engage in redistribution. The existence of cross-subsidization is an extremely powerful barrier to entry. The agency will not allow competition to affect profits if it is convinced that those profits are necessary to continue the cross-subsidy. Local airline service is an important example. It is not always necessary to actually cross-subsidize in fact, if the cost allocations are sufficiently complex and if the regulated firm claims the subsidy exists with sufficient conviction and frequency. Sometimes it is useful to give these subsidies in kind, if no opportunity for price subsidies is available. Public service expenditures endorsed (or, preferably, mandated) by the regulatory agency are as useful as cross-subsidies. Public service programming on TV stations is a good example of this.

Another reason for producing more than one product or service is that in doing so one has the opportunity to shift assets, profits, and costs (for accounting purposes) from one to another as the occasion demands. It is particularly useful to participate in one or more markets that are not regulated, at least by the same agency. For years the TV networks have played this game, with profits shifting from the network operation to the owned and operated stations.

Use the Agency as a Cartel Manager.   One of the worst fears of a regulatory agency is the bankruptcy of the firm it supervises, resulting in "instability" of service to the public or wildly fluctuating prices. Thus, it is in the interest of the agency to prevent price competition among the firms it regulates. The ideal strategy is to get the agency to endorse "self-regulation" by the industry so that the industry cartel can manage things under an umbrella of antitrust immunity. Transportation and insurance rate bureaus and the NAB code (limiting quantities of advertisements in TV and radio) are excellent examples of this strategy. The cartel rates or practices thus determined are immune from the usual tendency toward cheating because they carry the force of law, or at least the threat of direct intervention by the agency.

Lobby the Agency Effectively.   Effective lobbying requires close personal contact between the lobbyists and government officials. Social events are crucial to this strategy. The object is to establish long-term personal relationships transcending any particular issue. Company and industry officials must be "people" to the agency decisionmakers, not just organizational functionaries. An official contemplating a decision must be led to think of its impact in human terms, and not in institutional or organizational terms. Officials will be much less willing to hurt long-time acquaintances than corporations. Of course, there are also important tactical elements of lobbying, of which not the least is information gathering at low levels of the agency staff. Each contact must be carefully tailored to the background and personality of the official being lobbied. For this reason, it is useful to keep files on the backgrounds of agency officials, and to maintain a diverse and well-informed lobby staff as well as one not too remote from the corporate organization so as to maintain loyalty.

Coopt the Experts. Regulatory policy is increasingly made with the participation of experts, especially academics. A regulated firm or industry should be prepared whenever possible to coopt these experts. This is most effectively done by identifying the leading experts in each relevant field and hiring them as consultants or advisors, or giving them research grants and the like. This activity requires a modicum of finesse; it must not be too blatant, for the experts themselves must not recognize that they have lost their objectivity and freedom of action. At a minimum, a program of this kind reduces the threat that the leading experts will be available to testify or write against the interests of the regulated firms. AT&T has made a major investment, for instance, in very high grade economic talent over the past decade. It is not entirely accidental that this group of economists has produced a formidable new theory of multiproduct natural monopoly that may serve as a powerful argument in favor of barriers to entry and the exclusion of competitors in AT&T markets [3]. The only other apparent beneficiary of the normative implication of this theory is the postal service.

A special case of cooption applies to Washington law firms. The Washington law firm is essential to success in the regulatory game. Thus, it is useful, at a minimum, to deny potential competitors access to the best firms by keeping them on retainer. It is not possible, of course, to do this with all of the firms; those with particular expertise and influence in the fields of interest should be selected.

Trade-off the Agencies. The established regulated firm will find opportunities to play one agency against another. The most common instance of this occurs with respect to geographic jurisdiction: state versus federal, or one state versus another. The interests of these agencies often diverge, and one can court the assistance of one agency in dealing with another, particularly in the event of an appeal to Congress or public opinion. In matters of rate regulation, it is as useful to be able to transfer assets, costs, and profits among jurisdictions as among product lines.[c]

---

[c]The telephone industry has an extremely complicated set of "separations" principles, which have been manipulated to the advantage of intrastate service rates and to the political advantage of AT&T with state public utility commissions.

Strategies for New Firms and Industries

A firm or industry which is new to the economy must be able to take wise action with respect to regulation. If the firm produces something that competes with the products of a regulated firm, then regulation is a sine qua non of existence. But this is no matter; any firm with aspirations to steady but not spectacular profits should embrace regulation willingly. A prospective entrant with a new technology or service not identical to that provided by existing regulated firms should try very hard to be regulated by a different agency or at least by a new bureau of the old agency. This is useful in countering the powerful establishment forces that will be put in the path of entry. The airlines took advantage of this strategy in the thirties. What might have happened to the airlines at the tender mercies of the ICC beggars the imagination. Another example is the creation of the FCC's cable television bureau to promote cable interests within the FCC. An industry or firm which is not providing a service that threatens an existing regulatory protectorate should strive to be regulated by an agency that has other and more important responsibilities. The ideal situation is to have the protection of the regulatory machinery and its immunities, but to be sufficiently obscure that the agency spends little effort in trying to regulate. Examples here include the international telegraph companies, title insurance underwriters, and small independent telephone companies, discussed elsewhere in this book.

The newly regulated firm should arrange, if possible, to be regulated by more than one agency, or in several jurisdictions. This creates administrative problems in the short run, but in the long term it provides a helpful degree of flexibility in dealing with any one of the agencies. The charter of one or more of these agencies should include the power to grant antitrust immunity.

Strategies for Conflict

Regulated firms face the most serious financial threats, not from their regulators, but from potential competitors. Regulation is an excellent device for eliminating competition within the industry and for preventing direct entry. It is not as foolproof in dealing with competing technologies, especially ones not reachable by the agency under its statutory charter. In order for the agency to control the threat it must first assert jurisdiction over it. In itself, this implies only that the established regulated industry must be prepared to give up something to the new industry, but under carefully controlled and gradual circumstances. The more serious case occurs when the new technology manages to become regulated by a different or new agency. In this case, as with issues affecting the regulated firm arising from other quarters such as public interest intervenors, the stage is set for a major conflict. Such conflicts generally end up in the halls of Congress and in the White House.

It is important to understand that the politicians who will decide such issues are seldom interested in the technical details; they are certainly not concerned with sophisticated analysis. They are interested in appearances and in the political power and influence of the parties. Any halfway significant industry which claims loudly enough that it will be irreparably harmed by another can usually succeed in blocking the decision, often indefinitely. Congress, like the agencies of the executive branch, much prefers to sanctify a compromise endorsed by the warring parties than to make a hard decision. Thus, the party with the most to gain from the continuance of the status quo is in a position of power in the negotiations for a compromise. The party making the challenge must acquire sufficient political influence to be able to block decisions on some other issue where delay would harm the established firm. Eventually, in a kind of logrolling environment, the conflict is resolved.

The Regulation Game

The regulation game has not been effectively modeled. One of the major reasons for this is that it has been very difficult to produce convincing arguments to justify workably specific objective functions for the agency itself. However, it is worth asking whether the regulatory agency does have an objective function at all, or whether it is better modeled as a passive mechanism, reacting according to simple rules derived from its constraints. In inventing the collegial form for most administrative agencies, Congress has virtually guaranteed that agencies will not have consistent decision-guiding objectives. And even if agencies do have objectives, they have little freedom of action within the constraints of process, precedent, and charter. Thus, it seems best to regard the regulatory agency as an endogenous force whose behavior can be strategically manipulated by the firms it regulates.

THE LITERATURE ON REGULATION: A BRIEF OVERVIEW [4]

The literature on regulation is so extensive and eclectic as to defy any neat taxonomy. We provide here brief reviews of the hypotheses associated with a few individual scholars, followed by a partial categorization. The Chicago school of economists and lawyers—George Stigler [5] and Richard Posner [6] in particular—are associated with the idea of agency "capture" by organized interest groups, either by initial design or as a result of subsequent machinations. Sam Peltzman [7], also of the Chicago school, has recently generalized this model to the point that it can no longer be called a "capture" model. A leading political science theory of regulation is provided by Marvar Bernstein's [8] "life cycle" hypothesis. The notion that agencies are in fact creatures of the interest group being regulated is now implicit in much of the political science literature [9]. Roger Noll and Morris Fiorina [10] provide a political-science-based model of congressional demand for administrative activity based on the voters' demand for congressional facilitation services. Finally, because of its novel perspective, we will review Victor Goldberg's idea of regulation as contract [11].

Until the 1960s, the prevailing view of regulation was that it provided, or at least was intended to provide, a degree of protection for consumers from the depredation of monopolists, from shoddy and dangerous fly-by-night operators, or that it protected producers from the harmful effects of certain fundamentally unstable markets. Classical case studies, for instance, insisted that the purpose of the Interstate Commerce Commission was to protect farmers from the discriminatory pricing practices of railroad cartels [12]. The initial intention of the Pure Food and Drug Act was to deal with the fake drug remedies marketed by marginal operators [13]. And the primary purpose in creating the Civil Aeronautics Board was to bring about and insure a stable air transport market [14].

During the 1960s, the economics profession at least came to hold contrary (and sometimes inconsistent) views of regulation. We came to believe that regulation was ineffective in restraining monopoly power, that regulatory agencies were often captured by industry groups and used as cartel managers, and that regulation introduced potentially serious distortions in the resource allocation process, particularly by causing utilities and other industries with heavy capital investment to select inappropriate factor proportions [15]. We came to believe that public utility commissions did something other than make natural monopolies behave as if they were competitors.

Averch and Johnson made the study of regulation respectable by snatching it from the institutional and bringing it into the mathematical realm. Unfortunately, most of the tractable models of regulated behavior require that the constraints be exogenous. The notion that regulated firms interact with their regulators, or that the regulators themselves may be trying to do something more complicated than limiting rates of return, causes difficulties for these models. This fact has never gone unnoticed. Economists, lawyers, and political scientists have tried to cope with the problem of endogenous regulation, a task which must at least begin with institutionalism. If regulation is endogenous, the problem is much more complicated than maximizing a profit function subject to some set of constraints. The complications are of the same sort as those encountered in the study of oligopoly behavior, with the added difficulty that the objective function of one participant, the agency, is unknown, if indeed one exists at all.

Capture Theory

There are two versions of the capture theory (or what Posner calls the "economic" theory) of regulation. In the first, regulatory agencies are established for "public interest" purposes, but subsequently they become the tools of the industry they regulate. This version of the theory is really indistinguishable from the life-cycle hypothesis to be discussed below. The other version of the theory is that regulatory agencies are in fact *created* to serve the interests of the industry they regulate, as a direct response by congressmen to the demands of industry for cartel management. That industries might have such a demand is obvious. But it was not until Peltzman's 1976 paper that the capture theory enthusiasts had any explanation of the supply side of the market for regulation. Peltzman provides a supply side by assuming that politicians and agencies desire to maximize vote margins, and by using the redistributive powers of regulatory agencies to benefit groups that can supply these vote margins. The theory is thus a special case of the general proposition that government will seek to redistribute income to benefit majorities of the electorate. The capture theory model is a framework in which the purpose of regulation is to redistribute incomes in favor of groups that will supply electoral rewards to the politicians who engineer the redistribution. The regulatory agency is only one of the tools available for this purpose. Various direct tax and expenditure programs, of course, may be used, and presumably are used, to similar effect. Peltzman's model is by far the most sophisticated, formal, and testable statement of the capture or "economic" theory of regulation.

Life-cycle Theory

The political science literature reaches roughly the same conclusion about the effect of regulation as the capture theory—that it favors industry groups at the expense of consumers, even though its initial purpose and effect may have been different. Bernstein's life-cycle theory suggests that short-lived coalitions of consumer interest groups are formed to pass regulatory legislation that is intended to benefit consumers, but that the machinery thus established subsequently becomes captured by the industry. The consumer interest coalition fades in potency as the issue loses political salience. The loss of salience is due in part to the perpetuated myth that the agency is acting to protect consumer interests. This is what Edelman calls "symbolic politics" [16]. The symbolism is useful; the myth of consumer protection reduces the potential for political protest and alienation by evoking the symbols and rituals of the state.

Edelman's position that regulation is a useful symbolic charade must be assessed in light of the fact that the activity involved, however symbolic, is not costless. A very large part of the legal profession is employed in its operation, and there are numerous additional costs imposed by the process, quite aside from the substantive transfer from impotent to potent political groups. Indeed, as Posner has suggested in another context, much of the gains from the transfer process may be competed away by expenditures on the process of maintaining a politically or economically potent position [17]. One is left with the question whether both groups have not ended in a "low level equilibrium" trap, with lawyers, lawmakers, and consulting economists as the only beneficiaries.

Another early hypothesis describing regulatory behavior resulted from attempts to explain the political decision-making process. Writing in 1953, Robert Dahl and Charles Lindblom pictured regulatory agencies as one among many competing interest groups [18]. For example, the Food and Drug Administration (FDA), the medical profession, the pharmaceutical industry, and various consumer groups are all viewed as special interests attempting to influence policies affecting the development of new drugs. In such a context, decisions eventually handed down by the FDA are more the result of bargains and compromises than independent deliberation.

It must be emphasized that agencies are not to be mistaken as passive tools yielding to the strongest pressure of the time. Presumably they too have an identifiable interest, whether it be to satisfy a congressional mandate, an administrator's personal goals, or something else. Most writers adhering to the bargaining hypothesis are hesitant, or simply unable, to identify the specific interests of the regulators [19]. They prefer to interpret these interests within the context of case studies, which is tantamount to saying the bargaining hypothesis does well with hindsight, but is short on foresight. The hypothesis also suffers from the same problem of generality present in the life-cycle hypothesis; specifically, too many different kinds of behavior are explainable as outcomes of compromises, while no particular behavior is predictable, aside from being the result of a compromise. In short, the hypothesis lacks a basis for testing. Moreover, the hypothesis cannot adequately explain why some interests are more effectively represented than others, or under what conditions some groups succeed and others fail. As a consequence, since the writing of Dahl and Lindblom, the bargaining hypothesis has undergone continual refinement.

Interest group interaction in the administrative process is of increasing importance as the courts have steadily expanded the scope of interest group representation, a trend documented by Stewart [20]. Recently James Q. Wilson has tried to give the hypothesis more substance by speculating on what the most likely regulatory behavior will be under three contrasting interest group settings [21]. He argues that if the benefits of regulation are distributed over a large cross-section of the population while the costs are concentrated (for example, automobile safety standards), then regulatory policy will be stalled in the administrative process. Or secondly, if the benefits go to a small group and the costs are diffused, as in the case of milk price regulation or occupational licensing, the regulator tends to serve the interests of the smaller group. And finally, if both costs and benefits are concentrated between competing groups, the regulator will act as an arbitrator. The structure of the problem will be familiar to those who have read Olson's *Logic of Collective Action*. Note that Wilson's arguments still spring from the original interest-group hypothesis: the fundamental determinant of regulatory behavior is the political context of the regulating agency, a position clearly consistent with Peltzman's more formal model. The principal difference lies in the perception of the degree of control exercised by the political decisionmakers.

Regulatory Goals

Porter and Sagansky [22] argue that the key variable in understanding the phenomenon of regulation is the set of *goals* of the regulatory agency. This emphasis on agency goals contrasts with emphasis on agency *decisions* or the efficiency and welfare *impacts* of agency decisions that are the primary concern of most students of the regulatory agencies. Porter and Sagansky assert that one cannot infer agency goals from an examination of agency decisions or from the effects of such decisions on the economy because there are likely to be intermediating constraints and information-related mistakes.

The importance of this distinction between goals and decisions can be seen through an example of two alternative, competing hypotheses of agency goals: (1) the agency pursues the public interest, (2) the agency seeks to promote the welfare of the group it regulates. Porter and Sagansky contend that the socially inefficient agency decisions that are observed can be consistent with both hypotheses, not merely with the second. It is consistent with the first hypothesis, for example, when there are constraints such as limited information or limited analytical capacity. The distinction between goals and decisions becomes extremely important when remedies for economically inefficient results of regulation are sought. One cannot assume that the agency's actual goal is to protect regulated firms and then prescribe an appropriate restructuring of the agency's incentives. It is entirely possible that the agency's actual goal is to protect the public interest, in which case a sufficient remedy would be the removal of constraint by increasing agency resources for gathering data or for enforcing decisions.

The distinction between decisions and goals also becomes important in the choice of data that describe regulators' behavior. If there is an unconstrained relationship between agency goals and agency decisions, then it is sufficient to examine the decisions themselves; studying the actual process of decision-making is unnecessary. Indeed, studying the decision processes themselves may be misleading in the event that the administrative process is a charade, masking the agency's true intentions toward the group disadvantaged by its actions. However, if there are constraints which prevent one from making inferences about goals simply on the basis of decisions, then studying the decision-making process assumes critical importance.

Porter and Sagansky argue that the agency is best viewed as optimizing a multi-argument objective function subject to multiple constraints. They contrast this with the pre-Peltzman capture theory which implies that the agency has one unambiguous goal (serving the regulated firms) that is pursued subject to no binding substantive or procedural constraints.

Joskow suggests that regulatory agency behavior can be, at any one time, characterized as in one of two modes: (1) the agency in equilibrium with its interest group environment and (2) the agency in a period of innovation [23]. In the first case, there is a well-established organizational structure for the regulatory agency and well-defined regulatory procedures and instruments which the agency uses repetitively and predictably. This is the period during which the agency has attained its goal of minimizing conflict and criticism from the industry and consumer groups, subject to its legislative and judicial constraints. Once procedures with satisfactory results have been adopted, decision rules emerge and agencies operate relatively independently of economic conditions. These particular decision rules will withstand moderate changes in the economic environment. However, severe hardships such as those caused by inflation beginning in the late 1960s can lead to a disequilibrium situation—the innovative stage.

The period of innovation is essentially dynamic: a period during which the agency's rules are no longer satisfactory to the interest groups it faces. Because of the ensuing conflict, the agency is pushed into a search process for new rules which will eliminate conflict. Typically, in the case of state regulatory commissions, several "leader" commissions can be identified that initiate most of the development of the new rules. (In the case of electric utility regulation, these states are New York, Wisconsin, and California.) Through a process of trial and error, new principles are developed, many of which have "struck at the heart of long accepted administrative principles viewed from 'inside'." Each new attempt at a set of rules which might quell the criticism of interest groups is applied to a few firms at a time. When a successful system has been devised, it is then rapidly diffused throughout the nation by imitation by the "follower" regulatory agencies.

Joskow's model of the regulatory agency bears a strong family resemblance to the so-called cybernetic approach to modeling bureaucratic behavior [24]. The idea is to recognize the agency not as an economic "rational actor" maximizing some objective function, as Peltzman would have it, but as an organization with bounded rationality, conflicting goals, and limited information. While this is a sensible idea, it is not clear whether it can be useful outside of the context of replicated tasks, such as budget-setting and rate of return regulation.

Bureaucrats and Legislators

Although market competition does not compel bureaucrats to maximize net revenue, or minimize costs, as the case may be, they still have preferences that influence the behavior of their bureau. Therefore, economists have sought to model these preferences as a means to study and predict regulatory behavior. While the interest group hypothesis views bureaucratic preferences as merely one factor among the many that determine regulatory policy, the utility maximization approach focuses on these preferences, and more exactly on the maximization of the administrator's satisfaction subject to certain constraints, such as opposing interests and legal restrictions.

William Niskanen bases his model on what he considers two critical characteristics of bureaus [25]. First, bureaucrats strive to maximize the total budget of their bureau, and second, bureaus exchange a specific output for a specific budget. This second characteristic gives the bureau's sponsors, for example, the House appropriations committees, a take it or leave it choice—implying that bureaus wield some monopoly power. Underlying the first characteristic is the maximization of the administrator's utility function with arguments such as salary, office space, power, and public recognition. Niskanen's model leads him to conclude: "For different reasons . . . both monopolies and bureaus operate in output regions that are inherently nonoptimal. The substitution of a bureau for a monopoly to provide some product or service . . . solves no problem" [26]. The chief criticism of Niskanen's model is that its assumptions are strong. For instance, budget maximization may be a poor proxy for bureaucrats' real objectives.

Roger Noll and Morris Fiorina [27] provide the essential link between Niskanen-type bureaus and voters. The link is forged by demonstrating the importance of "facilitation" services provided by congressmen to their constituents who must deal with the federal bureaucracy. The role of a congressman is not merely, perhaps not even primarily, to legislate public services, but to facilitate their delivery. Modern congressmen function as ombudsmen for their constituents, and they do so because it contributes to electoral success, and provides an important advantage to incumbents. Congressmen have become increasingly aware of this role. There has been a steady increase in effort devoted to their home office. For instance, between 1960 and 1974 the percentage of all congressmen's staff devoted to district offices increased from 14 to 34 percent, and the proportion of congressmen listing multiple offices has risen by 43 percentage points! Hence it appears to be in the interest of both bureaucrats and congressmen to have bureaucracy grow, while it is not necessarily in their interest to be efficient.

Regulation as Contract

Victor Goldberg [28] proposes a novel approach. He observes that "relational contracts" (long-term contracts between parties with a continuing economic relationship) have many of the features of administrative regulation. Such contracts may give suppliers a right to serve and consumers a right to be served as a result of a process in which both parties voluntarily limit their future options in order to minimize costs or uncertainty. Long-term contracts may not specify prices so much as procedural mechanisms for determining prices, and so on. There is a striking analogy with regulatory procedures. Goldberg goes one step further and suggests that a regulatory body may usefully be treated as if it were the "agent" of the consumer group in negotiating and administering such a relational contract. This is an interesting idea, although it seems inconsistent with the theory of administrative law, wherein the regulator is supposed to be an impartial arbiter of the public interest (where "public interest" includes the interest of the firm being regulated). Goldberg is not very explicit about this, but it is possible that the correct view is that the agency is a sort of court administering a "contract" in which consumers are represented by a fictitious agent. Then the regulatory body "estimates" the negotiating position of the fictitious agent and, as a court would, helps administer the contract. Whether or not this is plausible, Goldberg's main point is that the deals that would be made by such an agent might well include, say, restrictions on entry of competing suppliers. The reason for this is that in public utility type industries, consumers want to avoid the increased capital costs that would result from risky heavy investment under free entry. If this were a theory of administrative agency behavior, it might easily explain both the traditional behavior of the agencies in acting like cartel managers and the otherwise anomalous behavior of agencies in promoting competition, such as the FCC's policy toward AT&T. Unfortunately, it is far from obvious that this is an acceptable theory of the behavior of such agencies, although it may very well be a useful normative framework. One difficulty with testing the theory is that contrary evidence may simply be interpreted as "mistakes." Bounded rationality and uncertainty are the motivation for relational contracts in the first place.

Goldberg's approach is critical of the standard objections to agency behavior, which use static analysis of "discrete transactions" to condemn stability-augmenting policies such as entry barriers. The proper question, according to Goldberg, is whether the policies of the agency are different from those that would be freely negotiated by an agent entering into a long-term supply contract on behalf of a consumer coalition, and whether such a long-term contract is itself desirable in preference to a spot market. The areas where agency behavior can be viewed most sympathetically from this perspective are the heavily capitalized public utilities, such as electricity and telephone service.

An Assessment

Within the range of discretion left by the operation of administrative procedure, the problem of predicting agency behavior is about as difficult as the problem of predicting oligopoly behavior. When the number of actors is small, and the variety of contexts large, general models are extremely difficult to construct. At best, given the current state of knowledge, we can hope to predict behavior only within a rather constrained set of circumstances, or to show that individual agencies behave in internally consistent ways.

We have a grab bag of theories, but there are a number of tantalizing links among them. Clearly the political scientists' interest group approach to agency decision-making can be linked up with Peltzman's model of regulatory income redistribution. Goldberg's notion of regulation as contract may provide the insights necessary to construct a formal normative model of the "public interest" theory of regulation in a way that allows us to distinguish empirically between "good" and "bad" agency behavior. Noll and Fiorina provide the all-important link between agencies and voters through the electoral process.

The various ways of thinking about the process of regulation that have been described in this section can be sorted very roughly into three broad categories. The first is the old "naive" public interest notion that regulators in fact do what they are supposed to do—protect the consuming public from the effects of a variety of market imperfections. Goldberg's approach perhaps comes closest to making this notion operational and testable. The second category includes the various "rational actor" models, such as those of Peltzman, Noll and Fiorina, and Niskanen. In these models rational regulators with well-defined objectives seek their own ends. Generally, such models regard regulators as politicians seeking essentially political rewards by use of the government's power to redistribute income. These models tend to be cynical, or probably appear so to noneconomists. The third general category of models tends to emphasize the limited information and bounded rationality of organizational decision-making bodies with perhaps conflicting internal goals. Approaches such as those of Joskow, Porter and Sagansky, and the "cybernetic" or organizational theorists fit into this category.

It should be clear at once that these approaches need not be mutually exclusive. A really general theory of regulation would include elements from each. But all of these theories fail to explain some regulatory phenomena and, in particular, they fail to explain why administrative regulation takes the special form that it does. Why should the benefit-distributing regulators of Peltzman's model bother with the forms and awkwardness of due process? Why not redistribute by fiat? Why do some powerful interest groups sometimes not get their way in regulatory proceedings? The answer to these questions may lie in a better understanding of the actual process of decision-making imposed upon regulators by administrative law.

TOWARD A THEORY OF REGULATION

In this section we put forward the notion that the effect of administrative procedure, the legal rules that constrain the forms of regulatory decision-making, is to slow down or delay the operation of market forces. From this observation we deduce that the effect may be intentional, and look for a reason why it may be intended and a mechanism by which the intention is carried out. The result will be a hypothesis about the "cause" of regulation that may provide a useful framework into which the various ideas explored in the previous two sections can be fit. The effort is motivated in part by the inability of any of these older models to explain the existence and peculiar form of administrative procedure, and partly by the existence of obvious counter-examples to the predictions of these theories.

It seems unreasonable not to begin with individuals. At least, the choice of any alternative "primary actor" requires greater justification. Thus, it seems sensible to assume, at least at the outset, that on average and over the long-term Congress reacts to voters' preferences and that regulatory agencies behave the way Congress wants them to act. Of course, it is possible that voters are continually frustrated with the behavior of congressmen (or that voters do not care about this sort of policy issue), or that Congress in turn is continually frustrated by the behavior of regulatory agencies but has no better alternative. These are serious objections to the proposition that regulatory agencies tend to behave the way voters want them to behave. The objections are serious because there is a substantial amount of evidence and a mass of literature that support them. As to the link between voters and particular congressional policy-making on individual regulatory *issues*, the objections simply cannot be assumed away. But the objections to assuming that long-term consistent policies covering a wide range of similar issues reflect the attitudes of median voters are not so serious. The second part of the objection, that regulatory agency actions may not be used to infer congressional objectives because the agencies may act to frustrate those objectives, is easier to assume away. Congress has too many controls over the behavior of the agencies, their budgets, and the law under which they operate to make this objection plausible as a long run characterization of behavior. The continual establishment, over the years, of new agencies with the same form and the same rules is strong evidence that Congress is reasonably content with their behavior. Other tests of this hypothesis are possible, and we will return to the issue later.

So, at some risk, we are going to infer the objectives of Congress (and therefore of median voters) from generalizations about the behavior of regulatory agencies. This approach appears to leave no room for agency discretion, and is therefore in itself no theory of agency behavior. Surely administrative agencies have some range of choice in policy-making, within and consistent with the broad objectives of congressional intent. This is precisely where those theories of agency behavior discussed in the previous section come into play.

The present hypothesis provides an explanation of some sources of broad consistency in the decision-making process. These consistencies are related to the single element that guides all agency decisions, namely, administrative law. Within the framework of administrative law, and consistent with its imperatives, agency policy-making may follow one or more of the hypotheses that have been constructed to explain it. The important point is that certain important aspects of the policy-making process are constrained to follow rules that bias the outcome in predictable ways, and that these rules have a plausible explanation in individual preferences. In contrast to much discussion of regulatory behavior, this is not necessarily a theory of pathology.

The idea put forward here is simple. The courts and Congress have collaborated in constructing a law of administrative procedure that has certain economic implications. Congress has simultaneously expanded the range of economic decisions that are subjected to the forms of this process. We should therefore be willing to accept the implication that Congress (and voters) intend this result. Examining the nature of the result gives insight into the objectives sought. The objective is economic justice or fairness. This is quite explicit; this is what law is all about. There are two features of the administrative process that are of interest. The first is delay. The second is derivative: the grant to individuals and their interest groups of equity rights in the status quo.

Delay is inherent in any decision-making procedure that is formalized. But the peculiar nature of the administrative process is to accentuate that delay and to make the period of delay responsive to the actions of the parties. In particular, any party disadvantaged by the prospective decision is granted the right to delay that decision for many years. The extensive delay is not automatic. The easing of standing criteria and the promotion, by the courts, of interest group representation have increased the importance of this right [29].

The argument that it is an intended and rational policy depends on the assertion that voters agree that the victims of economic change should not be placed at the mercy of the impersonal market, but should instead be protected by a mechanism that provides economic justice.[d] A very primitive, minimum response to this desire is the

---

[d]The words "justice" and "fairness," with certain exceptions made obvious by the context, are used synonomously in this chapter. Legal fairness or justice, is sometimes said to mean treating equals equally, as opposed to giving each what he deserves. Both definitions are fuzzy at best. However, in this chapter the central concern is with procedural fairness, a concept that implies the ability to rank economically identical outcomes on the basis of the manner in which they were attained. If the representative voter prefers one such manner or method to another, we shall call it "fairer," or more just.

grant of a period during which adjustment can take place and useless fixed costs amortized. Noneconomists are great respecters of sunk costs; the transformation of useful physical and human capital into an irrelevant sunk cost by market or technological forces is a process that is easily viewed as unjust and even inhumane. In addition, substantive policy decisions are affected: people cannot be deprived of existing services at existing prices without due process. Examples of this abound: cable television, radio formats, local service airlines, passenger railroads, natural gas.

The Noll-Fiorina theory predicts increasing use of administrative procedure because of congressmen's desire to increase the demand for their facilitation services. There is no contradiction. But congressional facilitation services are not as effective in the regulatory area as in the normal executive bureau precisely because administrative law protects the process from them. The facilitation model works best (or most plausibly) for social security and veterans' benefits matters, and is least plausible for the sorts of decisions governed by the strict form of administrative law (e.g., in non-rulemaking procedures). Indeed, the major impact of Congress in individual *regulatory* agency processes is not facilitation but rather increased delay, and then mostly in policy (rulemaking) matters.

What needs to be supplied to complete the model? First, we need to show that individual voters may prefer that all economic changes be subjected to administrative procedure. One way to do this is to assert that people prefer the forms of justice to the forms of the marketplace simply because courts are fair and markets are not; but this is tautological. Can it be demonstrated that it is in people's economic interest to prefer judicialized decision-making to economic decision-making? The second step is to analyze the efficiency and distributive consequences of replacing markets with courts. The third step is normative: can the objectives defined in step one be achieved more efficiently with alternative procedures?

The Search for Procedural Fairness

It is easy enough to find examples of agency behavior that contradict at least the simpler versions of the capture theory of regulation. Certainly neither the telephone company nor natural gas suppliers would agree with the proposition that its respective regulators were sympathetic cartel managers. Nor would stockbrokers or passenger railroads. Each of these industries has reason to complain about the behavior of its regulators. The FCC has been trying to encourage other firms to enter AT&T's previously monopolized markets. Natural gas prices have been held not merely below monopoly levels, but below market-clearing levels. Stockbrokers have been forced by the

SEC to decartelize their rates. Passenger railroads have been forced into bankruptcy by the ICC's insistence on continued service.

The hypotheses that predict agency capture by or identification with the industry being regulated are thus not wholly consistent with the evidence. Of course, there is also a great deal of observable behavior that is consistent with these theories, such as regulation designed to "stabilize the market" (federal agricultural policy, occupational licensure, and early airline regulation). Roger Noll's review [30] of the Ash Council Report provides many other examples.

Until the Great Depression, regulatory agencies were severely circumscribed by direct judicial review of their decisions affecting prices and profits [31]. The judiciary saw a clear conflict between the role of administrative agencies and the due process guarantee of the Bill of Rights. Accordingly, the fairness of rates of return and the like could only be settled by courts of equity. As the scope of regulation increased with the altered climate of opinion in the New Deal, the judges ceded much of their substantive decision-making power to the agencies, reserving for themselves only the right to review decisions for comformity with accepted standards of fairness in the agencies' procedures. This gave at least the appearance of increased administrative power in the agencies, and the Congress reacted by codifying the rules of procedural fairness in the Administrative Procedure Act of 1946.

The essence of administrative law is that the decision-making process must conform to reasonable standards of fairness, which in practice means that decision-making is judicialized. Within each agency factual issues must be resolved in hearings that are in fact trials employing the traditional adversary process before an "administrative law judge." The judge's decision is appealed to the commissioners themselves, and then to the courts. There are rules of evidence, rules against ex parte contacts, discovery procedures, and subpoena powers; in short, there is a wholly judicial process. Even "rulemaking"— broad policy decisions—is increasingly forced into this mold [32].

The purpose of this process is to give every interested party a day in court, to ensure that all relevant information is adduced and scrutinized, and to ensure that secret, fiat decision-making is eliminated. The reviewing courts have acted to strengthen the integrity of this process, and to enlarge the scope of interest group representation.[e] Recent "sunshine" laws underscore the intent of Congress.

The effects of judicialization are well known. Decision-making is, or can be, extensively delayed by the process of hearings and appeals.

---

[e]The demonstration of this tendency and its evaluation are Stewart's main theses.

Parties with superior resources have an advantage in being able to sustain heavy litigation costs, but even parties with few resources can use them strategically to delay resolution of the issue. The advantage lies with those who gain from the status quo, which can in many cases be perpetuated for years. For example, it is commonly known that the 1962 Kefauver-Harris Drug Amendments have operated to impede the introduction of new drugs. The administrative process is so lengthy and involved that it now takes five to seven years before a new drug can reach the market, usually several years after the same compound has been introduced in Europe. Needless to say, the amendments work to the advantage of those drugs already established [33]. That this advantage does not always lie with the regulated industry is a point well illustrated by the Alaska pipeline controversy and the problems of electric utilities in an age of environmentalists and inflation [34].

Legislators and successive democratically elected administrations, reacting to the preferences of voters, or median voters, have been steadily replacing markets with courts. We can reject the notion that this is done because markets are inefficient compared to fiat allocation. The regulatory agencies are almost never told what sort of allocational criteria they are to use. Legislators, and therefore presumably median voters, are concerned that the *process* of resource allocation be fair, and are apparently prepared to accept the outcome so long as the procedure is fair. From this, it is possible to infer that people dislike the very process of free market allocation, no doubt because its outcome is regarded as risky and therefore unfair. Alternatively, we might say that voters prefer a system that provides some leverage when the market confronts them with an economic loss, particularly one that is unexpected. This is hardly inconsistent with producers' demands for cartel management, and it explains why the political system does not react favorably to the economist's calls for deregulation.

Market forces, particularly those associated with innovative activity, necessarily pose a threat to human beings with less than instantaneous adaptive capabilities. It is not merely that investments in physical capital with few alternative uses may be threatened, but also investments in human capital: specialized skills, knowledge of an industry or a firm, and the like. Political activities designed to protect these investments from sudden, unexpected reductions in value may be indistinguishable from actions designed to achieve an increased return on investment through monopoly. But to the extent legislators see the proposals for regulation as being principally an attempt to obtain the benefits of due process, with its slow deliberation, in order to protect human investment, they may reasonably be sympathetic. This point of view, when coupled with the symbolic political usefulness of the notion that regulation is to protect the consumer from monopoly prices or unsafe practitioners and products, may be quite persuasive. In a sense, then, regulation is not much different from unemployment insurance and agricultural price supports, both of which are intended to protect human as well as financial interests from the shocks and blows of market forces.

It is, however, an open question whether the effect of the administrative process is merely to soften, to draw out, the effects of underlying market forces, or whether a fundamentally *different* result is achieved. Can we predict the likely direction of structural changes in the absence of regulation? Did the railroads merely fail later than they otherwise would have? Will cable and pay television arrive in due course, twenty or thirty years late?

It is worth mentioning again that process delay is available not just to vested regulatory interests, but to others as well. The delay is beneficial to those who wish to preserve the status quo. In the normal regulatory context, therefore, the beneficiaries are the existing regulated firms and the "victims" are new entrants and consumers. But there are other contexts in which the regulated firms are the victims of process delay: electric utilities seeking to build new power plants of any type are a dramatic example. Relatively small organized environmental groups have successfully delayed construction of such plants for years. This supports the point, that the effect (if not the purpose) of the administrative process is to slow down the rate at which things *change*, but it must be admitted that the evidence is equally consistent with the proposition that the point is to make sure that the change is "fair." Thus, even when the policy of the agency is to deprive the regulated industry of some power or benefits, that policy can only be enacted with painful and frustrating deliberation. The FCC's pro-competitive policies have been in existence for years, but AT&T has used the administrative process to delay their realization. The SEC was not able to end fixed exchange rates quickly.

The search for fairness in the economic decision-making process is attended by the persistent myth of the free enterprise ideal, and the fundamental conflict between this ideal and the interest of every actor in the economic system. The myth has substance, for it is embodied in the laws of private property so that there is a contradiction between the reality of intervention and the legal basis of economic activity. Once we see that individuals no less than business enterprises desire the intervention of the state to provide shelter from the free market, we see the necessity for judicial constructions that seek to preserve both myth and reality. But the veil of administrative due process with which the judiciary has shrouded this contradiction has its own substantive implications. In effect, it provides a new set of rules for resource allocation.

A Preference for Stability

In choosing among those policies by which they wish to be governed, voters are moved by personal interests as well as abstract principles. If there is any single ideological principle governing regulation, it is that free markets should be left alone because government is not competent to improve them. But if there is any general statement that can be made about regulation over the past fifty years, it is that the scope of administrative regulation has steadily increased. How are we to reconcile these observations? They must be reconciled by examining the incentives of voters with respect to their own interests.

It is well known that free market economies are subject not merely to the greater or lesser periodic booms and busts of the various cycles of macroeconomic activity, but also to sudden and total dislocation of particular micro-sectors as a result of shifts in technology and demand. The free market is, in a word, risky. It is reasonable to suppose that most people wish to reduce the risks that they face, and even that they will pay something to reduce those risks, at least when the risk of a very great loss is present. In other words, voters may be expected to be risk averse.

If the effect of regulation is to reduce the risks faced by individuals (by delaying change and subjecting it to a judicial process that is "fair") then it is easily demonstrated that voters in a society of risk-averse individuals will prefer a regulated economy to a free market economy, even if it costs something (see the Appendix to this chapter).

On the surface, at least, it would appear that the newest regulatory agencies—the Environmental Protection Agency, the Consumer Product Safety Commission, the Occupational Health and Safety Administration—have been created not to impede change but to accelerate it. But a closer look suggests that this need not necessarily be true. Of course, it would be silly to argue that the *only* purpose of regulation is delay. Congressmen do indeed want to clean up the environment and improve safety conditions. But they choose a mechanism for achieving these ends that is perhaps much less direct than such feasible alternatives as improved liability rules. And in *operation*, a major impact of environmental and safety regulation often is to delay economic growth and change. But there are exceptions. The Consumer Product Safety Commission was not given the power to hold up marketing of all new products until their safety had been demonstrated. (The EPA has such power for pesticides, as the FDA has for drugs.) Does legislation to provide the CPSC with such power lie in the future?

Even though the facilitation-services model of congressional candidate success be valid, congressional candidates will still take positions close to those of median voters on policy issues. Thus, we have a clear link between voters and congressional policy in establishing regulatory agencies and in setting the rules by which they operate. The intention is to attenuate the rate at which income is redistributed in society as a result of market forces and technological progress. This is achieved not so much by the substantive policies of the agency as by its mere existence in the context of the administrative process. The contrast between this model and Peltzman's should be clear: regulation exists in Peltzman's model because it is a device whereby the politician achieves electoral success by redistributing income. Regulation exists in the present model in order to slow down the rate at which the free market redistributes income, thus reducing the market risks faced by voters. Unfortunately, at least for purposes of testing, delay is consistent with both models.

As Mordecai Kurz [35] has persuasively argued, income redistribution must be regarded as an endogenous part of any democratic society. The relative stability of the shares of middle-income groups in the American economy is evidence consistent with the view that those who are most likely to be risk-averse are those who enjoy real political power.

With this statement of the hypothesis, it is possible to inquire into the behavior of the agencies themselves, using some of the theories reviewed earlier. It is the procedure as much as the ultimate outcome that matters. Or rather, the procedure *is* the outcome. It is nevertheless instructive to ask whether Congress is generally satisfied or frustrated with the behavior of regulatory agencies, since evidence of general frustration might suggest that the agencies were acting contrary to the wishes of median voters. The most powerful tool of congressional control is the budget process. A budget committee that was dissatisfied with the behavior of a regulatory agency might either increase that budget (to allow the agency to get on with the job) or cut the budget (to punish the agency for bad performance). In either case, the variability of regulatory agency budgets would be greater than that of other agencies. The evidence is that the budgets of regulatory agencies over the last twenty years have not behaved differently from the budgets of nonregulatory independent agencies [36].

The model of regulation proposed here is derived from a generalized observation about the *effect* of regulation, an argument that it would be rational for voters to wish for this effect, and a political link between voters and the legislated procedures, charters, and budgets of agencies. As such, the model does not in any important sense compete with the rational actor models of Peltzman and others, or with the "cybernetic" models of scholars like Joskow and Allison. There is room within the present paradigm of regulation as a filter for the other two approaches. The cybernetic theory explains how rules of thumb develop to guide decisions in an environment of limited information and bounded rationality, but it does not explain why this particular organization of means and ends came into being, or why it resists rationalization. Thus, the theory of administrative procedure as micro-market stabilization provides a framework within which the cybernetic approach makes even greater sense. Similarly, while rational actor models of the Peltzman type abstract from the frictions and imperfections of the real world, they too can be fit into the model in order to explain policy decisions that lie within the set left feasible by administrative procedure and judicial delay. It would be foolhardy to argue at the end that administrators, active agency chairmen, and their related congressional committees have no power whatever over policy choices. Models such as Peltzman's are entirely appropriate to explaining the use of that power.

Equity in the Status Quo

The stress on procedural fairness and judicial forms breeds a preference for fairness in substantive outcomes. The ideal court of equity determines, on the basis of fair procedure, the parties' substantive *rights*. The outcome may well be one in which one of the parties loses substantial amounts of money or property which "rightfully" belong to another party. But in the world of regulation, there is no body of substantive rights, or at least not a well-developed body of rights. Consequently, there is a tendency to seek outcomes which appear distributionally fair, according to prevailing social norms. This results in market-splitting arrangements, for instance, in cases where competing firms or industries are regulated by the same agency. Economic survival is one fundamental index of fairness. Ensuring the survival of all parties requires entry barriers, price fixing, and the like. Surely regulators who were striving for the most efficient industries would not be embarrassed by the exit of marginal firms. Yet when the Penn Central Railroad filed for bankruptcy in the early 1970s, the ICC found itself in a very difficult position. The commission was forced to explain why Penn Central should be bankrupt and not other railroads. In other words, why was Penn Central treated unfairly? It is predictable that agencies will reject economists' efficiency-oriented solutions if these fail to take account of equity considerations. Regulated firms have, in effect, a legal right to their market shares, and their customers have, in effect, legal rights to the existing prices and quality of services. And it is important that regulatory agencies recognize these rights. The Federal Trade Commission was brought to this realization in its first major confrontation with big business. In 1917 the FTC issued a report stating there was "only artificial show of competition among the largest five meatpackers" [37], and that the Big Five had formed unlawful combinations to control the livestock market. This convinced the Justice Department that the industry should be more competitive. However, when charges were brought against the meatpackers there was such an uproar in Congress that the case never got to court. Senator James Watson of Indiana held the FTC responsible for the indictments and sponsored a resolution to investigate the commission which reportedly was invested with Bolsheviks. The resolution did not pass, but regulatory jurisdiction over the meatpacking industry was soon transferred to the Department of Agriculture where the competitiveness of the industry went unquestioned.

The case of radio formats serves as another example. In large cities there are dozens of radio stations, comprising a highly competitive industry. Changing consumer tastes and other factors lead these stations, from time to time, to alter the nature of their programming. But the D.C. Circuit Court of Appeals has recently held that stations are not free to do so at will. In particular, "unique" programming formats (and what format is not in some sense unique?) may not be abandoned without a formal adjudicatory proceeding before the FCC. In effect, listeners have been granted a legal right to their present level and type of service, of which they may not be deprived without due process. The economic effect of the due process requirement is that an expensive blockade stands in the path of change, and the status quo achieves a more substantial stability. It is worth noting that this is the court's idea, and that the FCC is actually opposing it [38].

The point can be further illustrated by returning to the FCC's common carrier regulation. Economists have generally welcomed the commission's pro-competitive entry policies in this field, not so much because it is well known that competition is optimal in this industry (a proposition in current dispute) as because we do not know that monopoly is optimal. A policy favoring free entry and exit of competitors looks like a good way to find out, although it requires a fairly high prior estimate of the probability that competition will turn out to be the right policy in order to offset the costs of wasted investment in the event that it is not. Nevertheless, everyone is very nervous about the possibility that entry that turns out ex post to be unwarranted will not be followed by exit because the FCC will artificially preserve these entrants, as it has with Western Union over the years.

In a laissez-faire economy agents vote with units of purchasing power. The status quo in such an economy can be disturbed by a technological change or by a change in tastes. Exogenous shocks in such an economy set off forces which move the economy from one position on the Pareto frontier to another position on the frontier or to a new frontier. It will not always happen that such changes will move the economy to a position which is Pareto superior to the old position (even if the effect of the change is to move the frontier outwards) in the sense that no agent is hurt by the change. The principal effect of the proposition that our economy is now controlled by administrative law is that the voting power of such harmed agents is significantly increased. In effect, they are granted some legal rights in the status quo, of which they cannot be deprived without "due process." Compensation may take the form of an outright bribe or subsidy, or it may take the form of a substantial delay in implementing the change which threatens. Sometimes compensation cannot be paid and the change is effectively vetoed. This observation is not novel. Political economists interested in public policy issues have traditionally accepted the necessity of paying off politically effective groups that stand to lose from a policy change. The difference here is that compensation is not limited to groups that are politically effective, since the courts insist on interest group representation even when there is no effective representative. This allows self-styled public interest advocates to wield influence in directions that may in fact be contrary to the interest they nominally represent. For example, despite its newness and apparently strong mandate, it is not entirely clear just whose interest the Consumer Product Safety Commission (CPSC) serves. Recently, in the interest of "public safety," the CPSC, aided by the trade association for American bicycle manufacturers, developed bicycle safety standards which included some designs that would have effectively excluded foreign-made bicycles from the market. However, due to protests from the bicyclists' lobby the designs were never used [39]. In the more traditional political system, interest groups wield political power only if they can be effectively organized, and this necessarily results in a representation that is attuned to the real interests of the group. When consumer groups, for instance, are represented by proxy advocates, it may be much more difficult to design or even conceive of compensation schemes that unblock the proposed allocation. Political reality confines the policymaker to the task of finding the least costly compensation mechanism, and the effect of administrative procedure is to severely limit the available options. Finally, the nature of administrative law makes it virtually impossible for one important interest group to be represented—that group which does not exist until the proposed change has been made, and which could be organized or even identified only after the change. Decentralized market systems do not discriminate against such groups.

Formal analysis of the effect of administrative fairness could presumably proceed on a very abstract level by constructing a general equilibrium model of an economy with agents who, individually, have legal right to the status quo. Such a model would doubtless show that compensation schemes are necessary to achieve any reasonable definition of efficiency. *The* problem then may be seen merely as an excessively inflexible menu of compensation options. But this may be inaccurate if people view money transfers as inherently inferior ("distasteful") to economically equivalent compensation in the form of delay, outright blockage, or alternative concessions.

Models of resource allocation under various rules of fairness are apparently extremely sensitive to assumptions that are difficult to make realistic. Consider an economy with three agents, starting out with the unequal allocation 10, 1, 1. This economy is subject to exogenous shocks that are cyclic over three periods. In period 1 we alter these allocations by +1, +1, −1. In period 2, the alteration is +1, −1, +1, and in period 3 it is −1, +1, +1. In a laissez-faire economy this sequence proceeds without hindrances. After eighteen periods, the allocations are 16, 7, 7. An economy, subject to rules of procedural fairness that simply delay all allocations (that hurt anyone) by one period, will lag one period behind the laissez-faire economy. After eighteen periods, the allocations are 17, 6, 6, which is equivalent to the seventeenth period of the laissez-faire economy. A second possible model of procedural fairness would block permanently any change that lowered aggregate social welfare. We define a garden variety social welfare function, $w = \sum_i \sqrt{\alpha_i}$, where α_i is the resource allocation of agent i. If a change is blocked, the allocation of the previous period remains in force. After eighteen periods, such an economy has allocations of 10, 7, 7 and a welfare number of 8.45, which is *lower* than the welfare of either the laissez-faire economy or the simple delay model. Finally, we might consider a myopic Rawlsian rule that permanently blocks alterations that reduce the allocation of the poorest agent. Such an economy after eighteen periods has allocations 6, 7, 7. The Rawlsian rule results in a drastic trend toward equality, but when equality is reached, it proceeds as if it were laissez-faire. The period required to attain equality is extremely costly to the total wealth of the economy, however, and it never recovers. (Note that the poorest agent in the Rawls model after eighteen periods has the same wealth as the poorest agent in the laissez-faire model.)

The changes in the preceding examples (+1, +1, −1, etc.) are very mild ones, in which poor agents gain disproportionately. One might wish to consider changes that are proportionate to initial endowments, one drastic version of which is the pattern:

period 1	+20%	+20%	−20%
period 2	+20%	−20%	+20%
period 3	−20%	+20%	+20%

After eighteen periods of this, the economy that is unconstrained by procedural fairness has allocations of 23.38, 2.34, 2.34, and welfare of 7.89, while the economy in which changes that reduce w are blocked forever has allocations of 89.19, 0.78, 0.78, and welfare of 11.21. A myopic Rawlsian rule results in a quick move toward equality followed by the same pattern as the laissez-faire economy. The results of all these alternatives are summarized in Table 1−1.

It is clear that the comparison of these rules is sensitive not only to the rules themselves but to the assumptions made about the initial conditions and the nature and size of the exogenous changes. In particular, the pattern of changes in the first few periods (which may each be a generation long) is very important. It is very far from obvious what the proper set of assumptions is from the point of view of realism. This suggests that it will be difficult not only to build a reasonably comprehensive model of the actual procedural rule (the examples above are very primitive) but to say what the implications of that model will be. One thing that this exercise has shown is that procedural fairness may be extremely costly in terms of total societal wealth, and that it does not necessarily result in a global pattern that satisfies its own myopic criteria.

Table 1–1.   Summary—18th Period Allocations and Welfare

	Resources				
	#1	#2	#3	Σ	w**
A. *(+1, +1, –1) etc.*					
Delay 1 period	17	6	6	29	9.02
Block if $w\downarrow$	10	7	7	24	8.45
Laissez-faire	16	7	7	30	9.29
Rawls*	6	7	7	20	7.74
B. *(+20%, +20%, –20%) etc.*					
Block if $w\downarrow$	89.19	.78	.78	90.75	11.21
Laissez-faire	23.38	2.34	2.34	28.06	7.89
Rawls*	2.62	2.99	2.99	8.60	5.08

Source: See text.

*After equality is achieved, Rawls economies are laissez-faire.

**Welfare in the first period in each case is 5.16.

THE ROLE OF ANTITRUST LAW

Antitrust law is an obvious candidate counterexample to the proposition that markets have lost political legitimacy. But the counterexample will not stand up to scrutiny. First, much antitrust policy historically has protected competitors, not competition. The whole notion of "unfair" competition and its regulation is consistent with our hypothesis. Second, antitrust law is not concerned with competition in the efficiency sense, but with competition in the fairness sense. Small firms are better than large ones. Economies of scale are no defense. All mergers are bad. Despite a good deal of wishful thinking on the part of economists, antitrust law, and usually antitrust policy, has little to do with the legitimacy of the price system. A gloss on antitrust law might, with only slight exaggeration, read "in those markets where courts do not directly control allocation, market actors must be fair to each other."

There is a second aspect of antitrust which is of interest here. This is the conflict between antitrust and regulation, involving antitrust attack on regulated firms and even regulatory agencies. Within our present system, there is a clear and long-standing antagonism between the regulatory statutes and the antitrust laws, and their respective agents. This antagonism is reconciled at times in statutes granting antitrust immunity to regulated firms, but there remain two areas in which direct interaction takes place. The first is in actual antitrust litigation involving regulated firms, where the courts must decide issues of implied immunity, exclusive and primary jurisdiction, and state action. The second is in the policy-making process, where the Antitrust Division is frequently a party to rule-making procedures of the regulatory agencies. The division has been particularly active in banking, communication, and airline issues. Both of these areas of antitrust activity, however, involve traditional issues of industry structure, entry, and competition, rather than the interaction of agencies with their industries and strategic anticompetitive use of the administrative process.

The law of antitrust in the area of regulated industries is very far from being settled. Recent decisions swing both ways, with such cases as the Detroit Edison Company's sale of light bulbs [40] and the preliminary jurisdictional ruling in *U.S.* v. *AT&T* [41] on one side, and *U.S.* v. *NASD* [42] on the other. These cases really turn on statutory construction. A more interesting approach from the present perspective is the use by regulated firms of the administrative process itself to achieve ends repugnant to the antitrust laws. The notion here is that such firms may "abuse" the administrative process. The resolution of this issue by law is important, since we have argued that the behavior involved, far from being an abuse of process, is precisely the behavior for which the process is intended. It is therefore worthwhile to examine the cases which deal with this issue.

First, there is some common law and some patent case law dealing with abuse of judicial process. An example of abuse is the initiation of a law suit to compel payment of a debt which is not the subject of the complaint, accompanied by an express offer to terminate the suit if the debt is paid [43]. The use of process to intimidate others, or to preclude their own access to process, is a tort, provided that the transgressor has taken specific collateral actions which prove intent. Inquiry into subjective motives is generally insufficient. "Acts which in themselves are legal lose that character when they become constituent elements of an unlawful scheme" [44].

Second, there is a line of patent cases in which infringement suits by the patentee were viewed as abuse of process because their intent was proven to stem from a pattern of behavior designed to eliminate competition in violation of the antitrust laws [45].

Third, when abuse of process comes squarely up against the First Amendment rights of persons to petition public officials for redress of grievances (i.e., to lobby for special interest treatment by government), the activity is protected. Two cases in this area severely limit actions for abuse of process. They are *Eastern Railroad President's Conference* v. *Noerr Motor Freight*, and *United Mine Workers* v. *Pennington* [46]. For a time these two cases seemed to eliminate anticompetitive abuse of process as a Sherman Act violation by reason of First Amendment immunity. In the *Noerr* case, a group of railroads conducted a publicity and lobbying campaign to influence state of Pennsylvania officials to the detriment of the trucking industry. They were successful. The Supreme Court unanimously upheld the railroads' right to "attempt to influence the passage or enforcement of laws . . ." [47]. In *Pennington*, the court said, "*Noerr* shields from the Sherman Act a concerted effort to influence public officials regardless of intent or purpose" [48].

The *Noerr-Pennington* doctrine was applied and extended by the lower courts in a long series of cases in the 1960s [49]. But there were exceptions. One court refused to grant *Noerr* immunity to a knowing submission of false data to a regulatory commission [50]. In two cases involving the D.C. Circuit, attempts were made to "balance" the antitrust policies of the nation with the defendents' First Amendment rights [51]. Generally, the effect of these decisions was to widen an exception written into *Noerr* by the Supreme Court: that "sham" conduct is nonimmunized abuse of process.

The pendulum swung back from *Noerr* in two recent cases where abuse of process was found to be an antitrust offense. In the first, *California Motor Transport* v. *Trucking Unlimited* [52], a group of truckers joined in an announced plan to exhaust process in opposition to each and every new application for certification by the California PUC, and to share the expenses of doing so. The Supreme Court found an antitrust violation in this because the effect was to deprive entrants from having "free and unlimited access" to the agencies and the courts by means of the conspirators' massive, concerted, and purposeful activities.

The crucial distinction seems to be between the right of a group to seek its own advantage from the government and a program of action which prevents another group from doing the same. This is a narrow and awkward distinction, and one wonders whether it can be a viable tool in deciding future cases. On the other hand, it is consistent with the hypotheses put forward in the preceding section. The second case, *Otter Tail Power Co.* v. *U.S.* [53], involved efforts by Otter Tail to discourage municipalization of power service by entering into litigation with the cities, thus hampering the sale of "litigation-free" revenue bonds. The district court found that "repetitive use of litigation by Otter Tail was timed and designed principally to prevent the establishment of municipal electric systems and thereby to preserve defendant's monopoly. . . . The litigation comes within the 'sham' exception to the *Noerr* doctrine . . ." [54].

These cases pretty clearly leave the legal issues undecided. If our characterization of the purposes of administrative regulation is sound, one should expect that the courts will eventually strike down the use of antitrust law to prevent anticompetitive *use* of process, and to strengthen procedural norms in order to deal with *abuse* of process. In doing so, the courts will be bound to further strengthen the role of interest group representation, and may be forced, in effect, to protect the agencies from "excessively" powerful interest groups.

CONCLUSION

When there is a sudden shortage of gasoline or natural gas, or water, an overpowering instinct in favor of rationing and price controls seems to motivate both public opinion and political action. The market system, at least when it responds to abrupt changes, is regarded as an unfair allocation mechanism. The first instinct of an economist is to say that this behavior reflects dissatisfaction with the distributional effects of a price system, and that an efficient and also just result could be achieved by using some compensation scheme in conjunction with market prices. Such schemes are seldom used. Perhaps the reason is that distributional effects in the usual sense are not the real issue. The medium is the message. *The fairness of the allocation mechanism itself is the real economic issue.* People are willing to trade off some efficiency for increased procedural fairness. In other words, compensation schemes that preserve the preexisting distribution of wealth may nevertheless be regarded as inferior to rationing schemes with lower economic efficiency. This is essentially the point that Robert Nozick makes in *Anarchy, State & Utopia* regarding means and ends in economic choice.

The climate of intellectual opinion regarding regulation has essentially reversed itself since the days of the New Deal. Government activities that were then thought to be humanistic and liberal are now "known" to be illiberal and regressive. But perhaps we have gone too far in our criticism of the behavior of regulators and regulatory institutions. It is easy enough for economists to get caught up in the fantasy of assuming that the world cares or should care about some narrowly defined notion of efficiency, and we have apparently persuaded other disciplines to the same view. Too little attention has been paid to the implications of the institutional framework of procedure in the administrative process. When we do focus on this process, it becomes at least arguable that regulation, at the cost of some efficiency and of some progressivity, may have provided substantial benefits to individuals by protecting them from some of the risk they would otherwise face from the operation of the efficient but ruthless free market. Whether this is so is a question that must be addressed by further research; it is certainly not self-evident. The hypotheses that we have been discussing in this chapter do not yet have normative implications; we do not regard the phenomena of regulation as either good or bad. Future research that is aimed at normative conclusions must consider, first, whether the administrative process does provide people with a means of avoiding risk in the market system, and second, whether it does so at acceptable cost or whether it is superior to alternative means of achieving economic security and justice. We do not know the answers to these questions. Nevertheless, we are reminded of Edward Gibbon's comment on the fall of Athenian democracy: "In the end they valued security more than they valued freedom, and they lost both."

Appendix

The proposition stated on page 25 of the text is trivial in mean-variance analysis with one good. In the following note Mr. Sherrill Shaffer demonstrates its validity under somewhat more general conditions.

To motivate the discussion, we note that, whenever parties can forestall or diminish a threatened loss through regulation, the uncertainty of their endowment in the next period is reduced on the downward side. However, since blocking such losses also involves blocking corresponding gains to other parties, the regulatory process may be expected to reduce endowment uncertainty on the upward side as well.

NOTATION

Consumers: $i = 1, \ldots, H$

Goods: $j = 1, \ldots, G$

Endowments: $\overline{w}_i \in \mathfrak{R}^G$ date 1 to consumer i. ($\mathfrak{R}^G$ is the G-dimensional real Euclidean space).

$\tilde{e}_i \in \mathfrak{R}^G$ date 2 to consumer i, a G-vector of continuous random variables

$e_i \in \mathfrak{R}^G$ a realization of $\tilde{e}_i$

Consumption: $w_i \in \Re^G$ date 1 to consumer i

          $\tilde{x}_i \in \Re^G$ date 2 to consumer i, a G-vector of bounded, continuous random variables

          $x_i \in \Re^G$ a realization of $\tilde{x}_i$

Trades: $t_{1i} = w_i - \overline{w}_i$ date 1, net to consumer i

          $t_{2i} = x_i - e_i$ date 2, net to consumer i

Noise: $\tilde{z}_i \in \Re^G$ date 2 to consumer i, a G-vector of bounded continuous random variables

Utility: $U_i = U_i(w_i, x_i) \in \Re$

Regulation: The superscript r on a variable indicates that the variable is being considered in a state of the economy in which one, several, or all goods are regulated; absence of the superscript denotes an unregulated economy. Alternatively, absence of the superscript may be taken to mean a partially regulated economy, in which case the superscript will denote regulation of an additional good or goods.

ASSUMPTIONS

1. Regulation affects only date 2 variables.

2. $\tilde{e}_i$ has the same distribution as $\tilde{e}_i^r + \tilde{z}_i$ for all i. This assumption expresses the filtering effect of the regulatory process. Note that it allows the possibility of different effects on different people; also, it does not require that $\tilde{e}_i = \tilde{e}_i^r + \tilde{z}_i$.

3. $E(\tilde{e}_i^r) = E(\tilde{e}_i)$. This assumption will be relaxed slightly.

4. $E(\tilde{z}_i | e_i^r) = 0$, for all e_i^r.

5. Regulation does not alter date 2 prices. This simplifying assumption may be regarded as a Nash condition: each consumer in evaluating regulation examines only his own expected endowment change and realizes that it alone has a negligible influence on prices when there are many consumers. It is necessary in this interpretation to assume that prices have no stable joint distribution with $\tilde{e}_i$ for any i (e.g., one could assume that $\tilde{e}_i$'s are distributed independently over consumers), since otherwise consumers

could learn the distribution over time and predict prices with and without regulation.

6. $t^r_{2i} = t_{2i}$ for all e^r_i and e_i. This assumption will hold in expectation given assumptions 3 and 5, with price-taking, utility-maximizing consumers.

7. $U_i(w_i, x_i)$ is continuous, weakly concave, bounded, and monotone increasing for all i.

RESULT

$$E\{U_i(w_i, \tilde{x}^r_i)\} \geq E\{U_i(w_i, \tilde{x}_i)\} \quad \text{for all } i. \tag{1}$$

That is, regulation is unanimously, weakly preferred.

Proof: By Assumptions 1 and 6 we can take w_i, t_{1i}, and t_{2i} as given, so that

$$E\{U_i(w_i, \tilde{x}^r_i)\} = E\{U_i(\bar{w}_i + t_{1i}, \tilde{e}^r_i + t_{2i}) \mid \bar{w}_i, t_{1i}, t_{2i}\}$$

which is a function of $\tilde{e}^r_i$ only; and similarly for the unregulated economy. Assumptions 2, 3, and 4 allow us to apply to $\tilde{e}_i$ and $\tilde{e}^r_i$ the ordering $\leq_a$ defined in Rothschild and Stiglitz [55]. Assumption 7 and our definition of $\tilde{e}_i$ and $\tilde{z}_i$ as vectors of real, bounded, continuous, random variables enable us to apply the generalized ordering $\leq_u$ of Rothschild and Stiglitz [56]. The equivalence of the two orderings mentioned in Rothschild and Stiglitz [56] and proved in Strassen [57] proves (1). Q.E.D.

COMMENTS

(a) Note that it has not been necessary to assume a fixed relation between $E(\tilde{e}_i)$ and $\bar{w}_i$. The model thus allows for expectations of growth or recession, which may change over time (e.g., set $E(\tilde{e}_i) = \bar{w}_i + \alpha$, where α may vary and assume either sign). What is required is that $E(\tilde{e}_i) = E(\tilde{e}^r_i)$.

(b) The result of weak regulation preference was obtained for consumers who are either risk averse or risk neutral. A more interesting result is obtained when consumers are risk averse (U_i is strictly concave): then, for all z_i not identically equal to the zero vector, $E\{U_i(w_i, \tilde{x}^r_i)\} = E\{U_i(w_i, \tilde{x}_i)\} + \delta_i$, $\delta_i > 0$, for regulation of some good or goods. This implies that, holding w_i constant, there is some nonrandom, compensating variation of the date 2 endowment, Δe_i, such that

(i) $\Delta e_i = \Delta e_i (\delta_i)$, a rising function of δ_i, and

(ii) $E\{U_i(w_i, \tilde{x}_i^r - \Delta e_i)\} = E\{U_i(w_i, \tilde{x}_i)\}$,

by Assumption 7.

Thus we may construct a new, random, date 2 endowment $\tilde{\epsilon}_i^r$ such that

(i) $\epsilon_i^r = e_i^r - \Delta e_i$ for all e_i^r (where ϵ_i^r is a realization of $\tilde{\epsilon}_i^r$), and

(ii) $E\{U_i(w_i, \tilde{\epsilon}_i^r + t_{2i}) \mid w_i, t_{2i}\} = E\{U_i(w_i, \tilde{e}_i + t_{2i}) \mid w_i, t_{2i}\}$

That is, regulation may incur a real cost of Δe_i (i.e., reduce the expected date 2 endowment by that amount) and still be weakly preferred. Reductions by less than Δe_i will leave regulation strictly preferred. This, then, is the promised relaxation of Assumption 3: instead of requiring that $E(\tilde{e}_i) = E(\tilde{e}_i^r)$, we only need the weaker condition that $E(\tilde{e}_i) \leq E(\tilde{e}_i^r) + \Delta e_i$. Note that, for any given δ_i, Δe_i is a G-manifold.

(c) Assumptions 3 and 4 are not necessary in modeling regulation as a noise filter, but they are necessary to the above proof of unanimous regulation preference. However, unanimity is a much stronger result than that required for the theory of regulation established in Chapter 1.

(d) Assumption 7 is not necessary for unanimous regulation preference. The result would still hold if, for instance, we omitted Assumption 7 and replaced assumptions 2, 3, and 4 by

(2a) $(\tilde{e}_i + t_{2i})$ has the same distribution as $(\tilde{e}_i^r + t_{2i}^r) + \tilde{z}_i$ where t_{2i} is a function of $\bar{w}_i$ and e_i, and t_{2i}^r is a function of $\bar{w}_i$ and e_i^r;

(3a) $E(\tilde{e}_i + t_{2i}) = E(\tilde{e}_i^r + t_{2i}^r)$; and

(4a) $E\{\tilde{z}_i \mid (e_i^r + t_{2i})\} = 0$.

Interpreting these new assumptions, though, is not straightforward.

(e) Note that quite general distributions of $\tilde{e}_i$ are allowed. In particular, examine the case of $G = 1$, so that the endowment consists of one good, say income. We may treat the notion of unemployment of a consumer, even though no production or labor market has been modeled, as follows:

(1)   Assume that without regulation there is a probability π that a given consumer will be unemployed in date 2.

(2)   Assume a unimodal distribution $f_i(\tilde{e}_i)$ of $\tilde{e}_i$ given that consumer i is employed:

$f_i(\tilde{e}_i)$

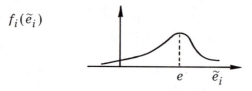

where e is the mean of $f_i(\tilde{e}_i)$.

(3)   When consumer i is unemployed, assume that his endowment follows a unimodal distribution $g_i(e_i)$ with mean less than that of his "employed endowment":

$g_i(e_i)$

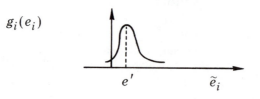

where e' is the mean of $g_i(\tilde{e}_i)$.

(The variances of $f_i(\tilde{e}_i)$ and $g_i(\tilde{e}_i)$ may take any finite values.)

(4)   Thus the distribution of $\tilde{e}_i$ unconditional on i's employment, $h_i(\tilde{e}_i)$, is given by $\pi g_i(\tilde{e}_i) + (1 - \pi) f_i(\tilde{e}_i)$ and is a bimodal distribution with mean $\bar{e}$:

$h_i(\tilde{e}_i)$

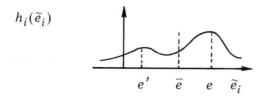

Now, one may approach the effect of regulation on this distribution in several ways.

(1) Our mechanism of risk reduction (Assumptions 2–4) may (a) leave $h_i(\tilde{e}_i)$ bimodal but shrink e and e' toward $\bar{e}$; it may, alternatively, leave e unchanged, but raise e' and π ; (b) it may leave e' the same but lower e and π (c); or it may convert $h_i(\tilde{e}_i)$ into a unimodal distribution (d):

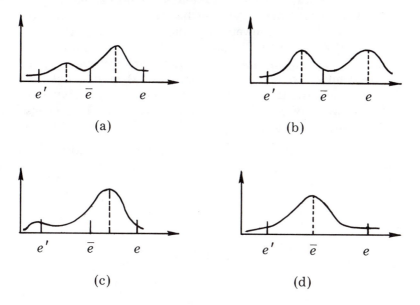

(a)   (b)

(c)   (d)

(These four outcomes are representative, not exhaustive.)

(2) Approaching the issue from a fairness perspective, one expects regulators to be concerned with a consumer's right to a maintained value of his human capital, or more simply with his right to work. Thus we would expect effective regulation either to lower π (alternatives (c) and (d) above, where (d) is interpreted as a full employment economy) or to raise the mean endowment of an unemployed consumer (alternatives (a) and (b)). Alternative (d) does not necessarily imply a full employment economy; but as long as $f_i(\tilde{e}_i)$ and $g_i(\tilde{e}_i)$ remain unimodal, the only other interpretation is that in (d) the mean endowment of an individual is the same whether he is employed or not, an unlikely outcome.

There are several interesting points about all this:

(1)   The risk reduction approach in this simple example gives the same result as a fairness approach, and is therefore empirically indistinguishable.

(2)   The result in alternatives (c) and (d) is to lower the expected endowment of a working consumer below that obtained without regulation. Therefore, if people compare outcomes using e rather than $\bar{e}$ as a reference point (as seems likely), it will appear that regulation has cost something in cases (c) or (d); but, by the very construction of our model (Assumptions 2−4), regulation has zero cost in this example.

(3)   The illusion that results (c) and (d) are costly may create an incentive to regulate by methods (a) or (b). But fairness considerations may offset this incentive, since a "right to work" may appear fairer than a "right to be compensated for not being allowed to work."

(f) Systematic transfers to each consumer under regulation, τ_i^r, may be incorporated into the model. Let

$$x_i = e_i + t_{2i}$$

$$x_i^r = e_i^r + t_{2i}^r + \tau_i^r$$

τ_i^r positive, negative, or zero

$$\sum_{i=1}^{H} \tau_i^r = 0 .$$

Assume here that regulation is costless. Then regulation is at least weakly preferred by all consumers i for whom $E(\tilde{e}_i) \leq E(\tilde{e}_i^r) + \tau_i^r + \Delta e_i$ (or $\tau_i^r \geq -\Delta e_i$ for $E(\tilde{e}_i) = E(\tilde{e}_i^r)$; see Comment (b)).

The significance of such a transfer scheme is obvious: suppose a group of individuals were to increase their wealth through balanced-budget transfers alone. They would find no one willing to support the scheme, as it demands contributions (in our notation, $\tau_i^r < 0$) from persons outside the benefiting group. On the other hand, if the group combines the transfer scheme with a costless, risk-reducing regulatory plan, the transfers may be designed so that the complete package is preferred to nonregulation without transfers, even by persons for whom $\tau_i^r < 0$. If the Δe_i's may be observed or inferred then any group of consumers may thus explicitly maximize the redistribution to itself subject to retaining unanimous (or majority) preference for the plan.

Chapter 2

Regulation of Oligopoly: International Communication

In this and subsequent chapters we begin to illustrate some of the phenomena described in Chapter 1. The aim is to present actual examples of the strategic use of the administrative process, and to shed further light on the issue of whether regulation achieves the goals it seems to have been designed for.

The example in this chapter is the international communications industry in the context of a particular decision faced by the FCC in 1971: whether or not to approve AT&T's application for permission to build a new transatlantic telephone cable facility called "TAT−6" using a particular technology called "SF−type" cable. There are important lessons to be learned from the FCC's and AT&T's behavior in this decision-making process as well as from the regulatory framework that provides the backdrop for the decision. We will review these lessons after the story has been told.

BACKGROUND

The Industry

The international communications industry consists of five important firms: American Telephone and Telegraph Company (AT&T), Communication Satellite Corporation (COMSAT), Western Union International (WUI), RCA Globcom, and ITT Worldcom (see Table 2−1). There are, in addition, several minor companies. The history of these companies is recited elsewhere [1].

The products or services provided by the industry consist of (1) international telegraph (or "record") communications made up of

Table 2-1.   International Communication Revenues by Company (1969)
(millions of dollars)

Company	Total Revenue	International Communication Revenue
AT&T	16,053	186
COMSAT	47	47
WUI	37	37
RCA Globcom	4,067*	78
ITT Worldcom	3,106*	59

Source: FCC, *Statistics of Communications Common Carriers* (annual).
*1968.

message service (ordinary telegrams), telex service, and private line services; and (2) international telephone (or "voice") service made up of message (ordinary telephone) and private line services. The remarkable growth of revenues from each of these services is given in Table 2-2 [2].

The technologies of communication have changed considerably over the past 100 years (see Table 2-3). Each technology has had a number of generations of improvement. The principal technologies today are underseas telephone cable and communication satellites. There are, in addition, a number of techniques that expand the nominal capacity of existing facilities by "compressing" the messages transmitted [3].

The industry is characterized by an extremely high rate of growth of demand (illustrated in Figure 2-1), by a fairly rapid rate of technological change, by economies of scale, and by extremely "lumpy" investments. Prices charged for service have declined steadily over the years (see Figures 2-2 and 2-3). A three-minute call from New York to London cost $75 in 1927, but the price has now fallen to about $3.50 for a direct dial call. Less dramatic price decreases have taken place in the other services, usually at the request of the FCC and timed to coincide with the introduction of new capacity with lower average costs. Variable costs are very small compared with fixed costs, and average total cost is very sensitive to the degree of capacity utilization.

As a result of regulatory decisions to be discussed below, the industry is highly compartmentalized. Only the three "record carriers" (RCA, ITT, WUI) can offer nonvoice service; only AT&T can offer voice service.[a] AT&T is vertically integrated, as are the record car-

[a]There is a special type of service called "alternate voice/data" from the provision of which AT&T was excluded by the FCC after a long struggle by the record carriers.

Table 2–2.   International Communication Revenues *(millions of dollars)*

Year	Telegraph				Telephone			Grand Total
	Telex	*Message*	*Private Line*	*Total*	*Message*	*Private Line*	*Total*	
1951	—	42	2	44	12	—	12	56
1960	7	57	7	71	42	7	49	120
1965	21	50	20	91	101	16	117	208
1969	55	53	45	153	234	17	251	404
1972 (est.)	—	—	—	294	—	—	529	823
1980 (proj.)	—	—	—	950	—	—	4200	5150

Sources: FCC, *Statistics of Communication Common Carriers* (annual); U.S. Dept. of Commerce, *U.S. Industrial Outlook* (1971).

Table 2-3. International Communication Technology

Year	
1866	first transatlantic telegraph cable
1901	low frequency radio service
1927	high frequency radio (first voice service)
1956	first voice-grade transatlantic cable (TAT-1)
1962	first communication satellites (experimental)

Transatlantic Facilities

Name	Year Installed	Capacity (voice circuits)
Existing		
TAT-1 cable	1956	51
TAT-2 cable	1959	48
TAT-3 cable	1963	141
INT-I satellite	1965	240
TAT-4 cable	1965	138
INT-II satellite	1967	240
INT-III satellite	1968	1500
TAT-5 cable	1970	825
Authorized		
INT-IV satellite	1971	6000
Proposed		
TAT-6 cable (SF technology)	1973	825
TAT-7 (SG technology)	1976	3500

Sources: Kurt Borchardt, *Structure and Performance of the U.S. Communications Industry* (Harvard, 1970); Jack E. Cole, *International Telecommunications: Policy, Planning and Regulation* (Comsat Corp., 1971); Asher Ende, "International Communications," *Law and Contemporary Problems* (Spring 1969); OTP Staff Paper, "International Facilities Study" (1971).
Note: Capacity data do not include TASI.

riers, in the sense that they possess a collective monopsony on the demand for international communication facilities and are also the owners of cable facilities. COMSAT possesses a statutory monopoly [4] of international satellite services but is allowed to sell its services only to AT&T and the record carriers, not to the public (or even to the government) directly [5].

Underseas cables are owned jointly by AT&T and the record carriers at one end, and by foreign governments at the other. The unit of ownership is "half-circuits" (one-half of a circuit from the mainland to the middle of the ocean and back), and each participating entity has an "indefeasible right of use" in the half-circuits it owns.

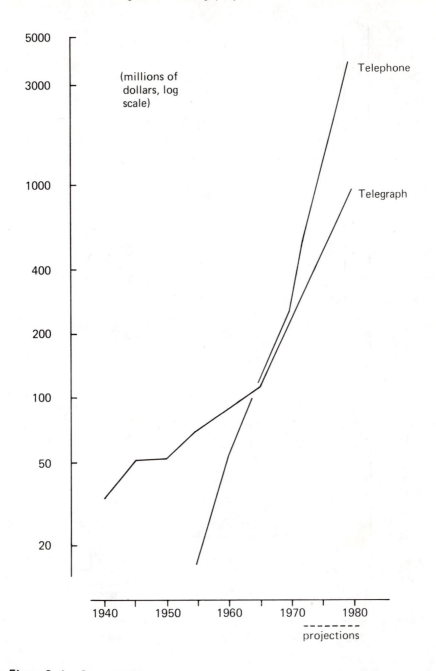

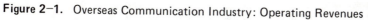

Figure 2-1. Overseas Communication Industry: Operating Revenues

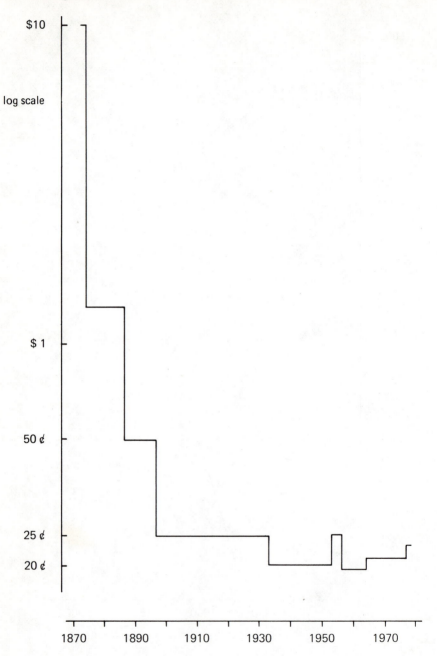

Figure 2-2. Overseas Telegraph Rates *(Per word, New York to London)*

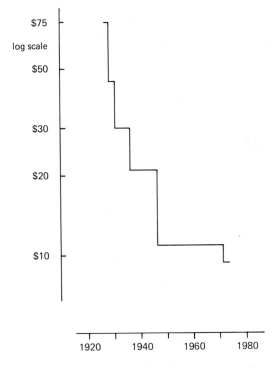

Figure 2–3. Overseas Telephone Rates *(3-minute call, New York to London)*

Satellites are owned, not by COMSAT, but by an international consortium (INTELSAT) in which COMSAT has an equity interest equal to its proportional usage (roughly 50 percent). Satellite earth stations are owned, in this country, 50 percent by COMSAT and 50 percent by AT&T and the record carriers. Half of the equity stock in COMSAT itself was originally owned by AT&T and the record carriers, but this ownership interest has now been dissolved.

The compartmentalization of services and technologies among companies has the effect of fixing market shares. Aside from postal service and personal travel, there are no close substitutes for the services provided by these firms or the production processes they employ. Entry is subject to regulation by the FCC, and is not an important factor in industry structure. The only significant events involving entry have been (1) AT&T's entry in 1927 when voice service first became possible, and (2) COMSAT's entry, by statute, in 1962.[b]

---

[b] In 1972, the FCC did allow Tropical Radio, a minor record carrier, entry into the Atlantic market.

Regulatory History

The statutory framework of regulation in this industry is found in the Cable Landing Act of 1921 [6], the Communication Act of 1934 [7], and the Communication Satellite Act of 1962. The industry differs from most other regulated oligopolies in the respect that the Departments of State and Defense, and the executive office of the president, all have significant interests in the performance of the industry.

Traditional rate and rate of return regulation have played only a minor role in recent years. There was a rate case involving increases in rates in the 1947–50 period [8], and a case involving decreases for some carriers in 1958 [9]. There had been no formal rate case since 1958, but there was an ongoing investigation of COMSAT's rate of return, and the FCC had occasionally ordered broad percentage rate reductions in connection with new investments, such as the TAT–5 cable [10], or structural decisions favorable to the cable owners, such as the Authorized Use Decision [11].

Most of the regulatory activity in this industry has concerned market structure, intercarrier competition, and new investments. The concept of allowing the three record carriers to "compete" (but not in price) for telegraph service business had to pass the hurdle of a skeptical Supreme Court: in *FCC* v. *RCA* [12], the Court found that a regulatory commission cannot rely on an abstract national policy in favor of competition in an industry "so regulated" as this one, but must instead find, on the basis of the evidence before it, that there was a "reasonable expectation of tangible benefit" [13]. The practical effect of this was not great, since the commission could always certify, on the basis of some sort of evidence, that benefits would probably result from competition, and the Court generally bows to the "expertise" of the commission in such cases.

COMSAT came into being as the result of legislation resolving a conflict between AT&T and the nation's major aerospace firms. AT&T had pioneered in the development of the *Early Bird* satellite, which utilized a nonsynchronous technology of the type later used by the Soviet *Molnya* system. The aerospace industry feared that AT&T would obtain a monopoly of communication satellite service, and that it would follow its general policy of manufacturing its own equipment, including launch vehicles, "in-house." The industry was successful in persuading Congress to deny AT&T its monopoly, partly by arguing that the synchronous, geo-stationary satellite system was of acceptable quality and vastly cheaper.

The initial structure of COMSAT was a result of political compromise. COMSAT has gradually developed into a more normal relationship with its rival carriers, the government, and foreign governments. The anomolies which surrounded COMSAT initially included its tripartite role as U.S. representative to INTELSAT, manager of INTELSAT operations, and U.S. monopolist of satellite communications; its ownership structure, which included the other carriers; and members of its board of directors appointed by the president of the United States. The FCC's "authorized user" [14] and "earth station ownership" [15] decisions carried this structure to its present state, the first by giving AT&T and the record carriers a legal monopsony of COMSAT's trade (barring COMSAT from offering direct service to consumers), and the second by giving AT&T and the record carriers one-half interest in COMSAT earth stations.

The advent of high capacity satellites and cables in the 1960s occasioned concern with the market shares of the respective carriers and the allocation of the traffic among the various facilities. The FCC evolved a rule to deal with this problem and an enforcement mechanism. The rule was the "proportional fill" rule by which traffic was allocated to facilities (cable or satellite) in such a manner that each facility would reach 100 percent utilization at the same time [16]. This was enforced by an FCC rule requiring permission from the commission for the "activation" of previously unutilized capacity on a "circuit by circuit" basis.

The preceding set of rules allocated growing traffic among existing facilities, but did not prevent the carriers from competing for market shares by proposing *new* capacity investments. Investments in new capacity (say, by means of a new transatlantic cable) would increase the market share of cable owners under the proportional fill rule. Actual customers, or users, have no choice as to which type of facility their message is carried on, and the same "composite rate" is charged for the two services. Since the price is the same, users would have preference for one medium over the other only to the extent that there are quality differentials between the two media.

Since investment in new capacity is necessary in order to meet rapidly growing demand, the carriers can use the investment process as a device for allocating market shares. Not surprisingly, this results in considerable controversy whenever a new cable or new satellite is proposed. This is in marked contrast to domestic investments by the carriers which generally receive *pro forma* approval. The first major crisis of this sort occurred in connection with AT&T's request for permission to lay TAT−5, a transatlantic cable which was, according to some observers, considerably more expensive than commensurate satellite capacity [17]. The FCC finally approved the new cable [18], but undertook a search for a decision rule to follow in future cases of this type [19]. Almost simultaneously, AT&T applied for permission to construct another cable (TAT−6) employing the same technology as TAT−5.

THE TAT−6 DECISION

There were two separate but related issues to be resolved in the TAT−6 controversy: what sort of decision rule should be used in authorizing new facilities, and whether to approve AT&T's investment in TAT−6.

TAT−6 was to be an 825-circuit cable between the United States and France. It would be owned by AT&T, the record carriers, and foreign governments in the usual manner. Its investment cost was to be about $86 million. It would last for twenty-four years, and the present value (at a 10 percent discount rate) of operational and maintenance (O&M) expenses over this period would amount to $22 million [20]. O&M expenses are not sensitive to capacity utilization rates.

The FCC had already authorized construction of sufficient satellite capacity to supply demand (as projected) in the Atlantic Basin through at least 1977. Traffic projections available at the time suggested that 1977 capacity requirements would justify 14,183 circuits at year-end 1977 in the Atlantic region [21]. These "official" demand projections were based on simple projections of historical trends, and as such were highly unsophisticated. On the other hand, recent historical trends did reflect significant price reductions and other influences of the sort that might be expected to continue. Thus, although the demand projections were unsophisticated, there was no reason to suppose that they were biased in one way or another. Most importantly, the FCC apparently believed these estimates. Cables and satellites already in existence or authorized by the FCC for this region would, by 1977, have exactly the required number of circuits: 10,417 on satellites, 3,293 on cables, and 473 on other facilities, mostly HF radio [22]. When account was taken of various "compression" techniques for increasing facility efficiency, there was clearly sufficient capacity to handle projected traffic through 1977. The justification for a new cable had therefore to be found somewhere other than in the need for raw capacity. On the other hand, existing cable capacity would be fully utilized long before 1977, and new traffic would have to be allocated entirely to high capacity satellites, thus reducing the share of cables (and their owners) in total traffic.

AT&T justified the need for a new cable on the grounds that the cable would be necessary in order to maintain an "optimal mix" of facilities in the Atlantic; AT&T's idea of an optimal mix of facilities was 50 percent cables and 50 percent satellites (in terms of capacity). If TAT−6 were not authorized, the actual mix would deviate substantially and quickly from this norm. Moreover, AT&T argued that the revenue requirements of the new cable would be lower than the rates presently charged by COMSAT to the carriers for satellite service. At the time of the decision, COMSAT's price to the carriers for a half-circuit year was $45,600. AT&T estimated the revenue requirements of its proposed SF cable at $8,600 per half-circuit year.

The concept of an optimal mix cannot be justified on the basis of cost since cost minimization would require 100 percent of whichever technology were cheaper. The justification for an optimal mix comes in terms of "reliability of service." Reliability increases as a function of redundancy. For a given level of redundancy, reliability also increases as a function of "diversity" of facility types. This is due to the fact that the probability of failure of redundant facilities of the same type is not independent, whereas failure probabilities for facilities of different types may be independent. If, for instance, sunspot activity causes one satellite to fail, it may act similarly on redundant satellite capacity while not affecting cable capacity.

The reliability characteristics of cables and satellites differ sharply. Cables are subject to infrequent failures of long duration (when broken by fishing trawlers, for instance) whereas satellites are subject to much more frequent failures of very short duration. When combined with the construction of capacity-augmenting "compression techniques," a 50−50 mix would imply the ability to restore *all* satellite capacity on cables or *all* cable capacity on satellites in the event of total failure of either mode.

There are two economic problems associated with this controversy. The first is to determine the optimal degree of reliability, in terms of its costs and benefits, and the second is to minimize the cost of attaining any desired level of reliability. Unless redundant facilities of the same type are subject to a high covariance of failure, diversity will be a more expensive means of achieving a given level of reliability than redundancy of the cheaper technology. Engineering opinion is divided on the point of failure covariance in the case of satellites. (There have been no instances of simultaneous satellite failure from a single cause.) Its value for cables is probably negligible. The evidence available at the time of the decision in 1971 suggested that, overall, cables and satellites had virtually identical total "downtimes" [23]. From the point of view of optimization, the central factor is the effect of facility mix on the distribution of customer waiting time caused by stochastic failures. This distribution is affected by the mix of facilities since satellites tend to fail relatively frequently but for short periods, while cables fail less frequently but for longer periods. The benefit to the public of reliability must be a function not merely of expected waiting time for a connection, but of the entire probability distribution of waiting times. (For instance, customers may prefer a distribution which has a lower probability of very long delays to one which has a greater probability of frequent short delays, given equal expected values of the delay.) There is simply no evidence available which would help to determine the demand for various distributions of waiting times, but an analysis by the Office of Telecommunications Policy indicated that "sufficient" reliability could be achieved by using redundant satellite capacity, provided that fast automatic restoral equipment were installed. The same study suggested that the costs of the proposed TAT−6 cable, at capacity utilization rates appropriate for 1977, were between four and six times the costs of satellite capacity of comparable reliability.

The cost comparison is summarized in Table 2−4, which shows the costs of two different kinds of cables ("SF," that which was proposed for TAT−6, and "SG," the next generation of cable technology) under each of two sets of assumptions, and of the present satellite generation (INTELSAT IV) under each of two sets of assumptions.

Of the two sets of assumptions for the cables, one is designed to be "reasonable" (columns 2 and 4 in Table 2−4), while the other is designed to be "conservative" (columns 1 and 3). "Conservative" means that the various assumptions discussed below were selected to make a best case in favor of cables. The reason for doing this is that information available prior to the analysis suggested that cables were more expensive than satellites, and it was therefore useful to ask whether an extreme set of assumptions would be sufficient to reverse this judgment. The two sets of assumptions regarding satellites also correspond to "reasonable" (in column 6) and "conservative" (anti-satellite, in column 5) conditions, with one exception. The exception is that in column (5) a "point-to-point" antenna configuration is assumed. This is discussed below.

In cost comparisons of this kind, there are literally thousands of possible combinations of assumptions. The analyst must select those that seem more or less reasonable, and then check the results by performing a "sensitivity analysis" to see how much difference it makes if certain assumptions are changed. An informal sensitivity analysis

Table 2–4. Comparative Costs of International Facilities, (1971) *(millions of dollars)*

	Facility					
	SF Cable		SG Cable		INT. IV Satellite and Earth Stations	
	(1) Conservative	*(2) Reasonable*	*(3) Conservative*	*(4) Reasonable*	*Pt.-to-pt. Beam (5)*	*Global Beam (6)*
Discount rate (%)	10	10	10	10	10	10
Time Horizon (yrs.)	24	10	24	10	24	10
% Redundancy	0	0	0	0	100	50
Sat. Failure Rate	—	—	—	—	1 in 4	1 in 3
Investment Cost ($m.)	86	86	94	94	148	50
Operation & Main.($m.)	22	15	26	18	24	52
Administration ($m.)	0	0	0	0	28	0
Terrestrial Tails ($m.)	0	18	0	18	0	0
Scrap Value at Horizon ($m.)	0	(1)	0	(5)	0	(4)
Total Cost ($m.)	108	118	120	125	200	98
Capacity (circuits)	825	825	3,500	3,500	8,500	4,800
Cost/circuit ($)	130,909	143,030	34,286	35,714	23,529	20,417

Source: Based on Office of Telecommunications Policy Staff Papers, *International Facilities Study* (1971) (National Technical Information Service accession number PB 208670).

was applied to the cost comparison in Table 2–4. Unless otherwise noted, the result that cables are more expensive than satellites is not sensitive to the assumptions chosen.

The comparison is constructed as follows:

1. All values are discounted present values, with a discount rate of 10 percent.

2. Cables last twenty-four years, satellites, seven. Satellite costs include replacement at appropriate intervals with new satellites of the *same* technology. (In fact, satellite technology is apparently changing rapidly, and becoming cheaper and more capacious.)

3. Redundancy levels are set at zero for cables. For satellites, two levels of redundancy are posited: 100 percent in column (5) and 50 percent (the actual plan) in column (6). This redundancy includes both duplicate satellites and duplicate earth station antennas.

4. Satellites come in two types—high capacity "point-to-point" configurations with spot beams, and lower capacity "global beam" systems, serving dozens of different points simultaneously. The point-to-point mode is strictly comparable to cables, which do the same thing. But global beam configurations are those actually employed. This makes the comparison of cables and satellites troublesome. The very cheapest way of serving heavy traffic between two points is with a spot-beam satellite, as in column (5). The global beam configuration actually used makes it possible to serve light traffic routes (Africa to South America) for which a cable would be unthinkable. But the effect is to reduce the efficiency (capacity) of the satellite—in this case from 8,500 circuits to 7,200 circuits. In column (6), all costs are allocated to the satellite's twelve "transponders," eight of which, containing 4,800 circuits, would be used for U.S. to Europe traffic.

5. Satellite costs depend on rocket launching failure rates. One failure in four was the historical rate in 1970, but there was reason to suppose that this would decline.

6. Investment cost includes the present value of all facility fixed costs over the time horizon. For the cables this is simply the initial investment cost. For satellites this is the cost of satellites and earth stations replaced at appropriate intervals, including redundant facilities and satellites which blow up on the pad. In column (6), with the global beam configuration, there are ten earth stations, eight in Europe. These data are taken from AT&T and COMSAT filings with the FCC.

7. Operative and maintenance expenses (discounted to present value) are taken from FCC filings. The high O&M figure in column

(6) is due to the large number of earth stations. It is worth noting that the figures for satellites are probably inflated since newer earth stations proposed for the U.S. domestic system by AT&T have fewer operating personnel.

8. Administration costs for cables are unknown. Reasonable estimates of these costs would not change the basic result.

9. "Terrestrial tails" are the costs of those facilities necessary to connect traffic centers with cable landing points. Satellite terminals can be located at or near the traffic centers.

10. The global beam satellite employs a large number of earth stations, but has lower total capacity.

One possible cost attributable to satellites has been overlooked—the opportunity cost of the electromagnetic spectrum used in satellite communication. It is, of course, extremely difficult or impossible to calculate this cost, given U.S. and international spectrum allocation policies, which do not allow a free market to operate in this area. However, the value of this resource in international communication is arguably negligible at present, since there is little or no "crowding" of the relevant region of the spectrum, or of "orbital slots" suitable for international communication. Much higher utilization rates for both resources are planned for U.S. domestic satellite systems. In the distant future this may be a problem worth serious consideration, particularly with regard to the tradeoff between a satellite's cost and its spectrum utilization efficiency, and especially for global beam satellites.

The result of the preceding cost analysis is that SF—type cables cost about six times more, per available circuit, than the satellite capacity which the FCC had already authorized. SG—type cable, because of its higher capacity, costs only about 50 percent more than satellite capacity. In the model comprising columns (1), (3), and (5) of Table 2—4, the absolute cost of the satellite system is higher than either cable system, and the cost comparison is thus dependent on projected utilization rates. This is not the case, however, for the "reasonable" comparison comprising columns (2), (4), and (6), where the satellite is cheaper for any level of utilization.

While not admitting that this cost comparison was accurate, AT&T pointed out that the projected revenue requirements from the TAT—6 (SF) cable were *lower* than COMSAT's present charges for satellite circuits ($8,600 vs. $45,600). In other words, AT&T, as a buyer of communication services, could obtain additional capacity more cheaply by building the cable than by buying more satellite circuits.

This point deserves special attention. COMSAT rates to the carriers were higher than the costs of its newest facilities because (a) it rate averaged high and low density routes, (b) it had a low utilization rate on its high-capacity satellites, (c) its rates were based on historical, not future, costs, and (d) its then current return on investment was upwards of 25 percent.

The effect of rate averaging was to raise rates on high density routes, such as the North Atlantic, from 14 percent to 53 percent over nonaveraged rates [24]. This rate averaging is purportedly a policy promoted by the U.S. State Department. The low utilization rate for COMSAT satellites was due to historical FCC decisions authorizing new cables, timing of investments in relationship to traffic growth, and COMSAT's penchant for replacing satellites which were neither full nor inoperative with new ones of higher capacity. Both cable and satellite prices are extremely sensitive to capacity utilization rates, given the major role of fixed costs. Finally COMSAT was at this time "making up" for its early operating losses, and thus earning higher rates of return than it might try to justify over the long term.

The dichotomy between COMSAT rates and the costs of new facilities, either cable or satellite, poses what may be a serious problem: Is it possible that rates to the public may actually be lower, or even "second best" through authorization of expensive new cable capacity, given COMSAT's various failings? The answer, as it turns out, is no. Future rates, for both satellites and cables, must ultimately depend on investment decisions which affect future costs. Whether or not FCC profit regulation is effective, a reduction in costs must ultimately lower prices, even for an unregulated monopolist, and even for a rate-averaging monopolist. The AT&T proposal was not merely to authorize TAT−6 (SF) but to embark on a program that would result in a "50−50 mix" of cable and satellite capacity. Given traffic projections, one can calculate the effect of this on average cost per circuit in use. For instance, for 1975 traffic levels, using the cost data from columns (2), (4), and (6) in Table 2−4, a "satellite only" policy results in costs which are lower by a factor of 3 than a 50−50 mix policy (see Table 2−5). Thus, unless one believes that some drastic change for the worse is due to take place in COMSAT's behavior with respect to rate of innovation, profit levels, rate averaging, etcetera, FCC authorization of least-cost investment alternatives must ultimately be the second-best policy, taking account of the arguments previously proposed for service homogeneity. This conclusion requires the assumption that the interrelatedness of international and domestic communication markets does not present a

Table 2–5. Cost Per Circuit for Alternative Investment Policies

Year	Demand[a]	*Average Total Cost Per Circuit in Use in Thousands of Dollars*		
		SF Cables Only[b]	Satellites Only[c]	50–50 Mix[d]
1971	701	168	139	308
1972	1104	213	89	196
1973	1582	149	62	137
1974	2125	167	46	157
1975	2812	168	35	119

Source: See text.

[a] Demand is expressed in projected circuit requirements in excess of existing cable capacity, United States to Europe (see text).

[b] The "cables only" policy requires SF technology through 1976 when SG was to become available. In this calculation, SF cables are added as needed, resulting in five cables by 1975. Costs from column (2) in Table 2-4 are used to derive these figures by dividing the discounted present value of the total cost of the facilities by the actual quantity demanded in each year.

[c] Costs are based on column (6) in Table 2-4.

[d] Here the 50-50 policy is taken to mean a 50-50 split of *traffic*, not capacity. This lowers the cost of the 50-50 policy.

perverse offsetting effect on least-cost investments in the international market. Adoption of a least-cost policy would have required the commission to deny authorization of TAT–6 (SF) and possibly TAT–6 (SG). The effect of a contrary decision, of course, would be to ensure that COMSAT's capacity utilization rates would remain low, both because traffic is diverted to cables and because prices to customers are kept high by being averaged with cable costs, and thus to keep COMSAT prices high relative to its full capacity rates and cable costs.

It is not irrelevant to this discussion that payments by the carriers for satellite capacity, and the revenues therefrom, have no investment or "rate base" associated with them, and thus present no possibility of a return if the rate of return constraint were binding. It is not clear, however, that there is a binding rate of return constraint in this industry. Data on AT&T's rate of return on its cable facilities are not available.[c] The three record carriers, in 1969, earned 20.7 percent before taxes on sales, and 11.4 percent after taxes on stockholders equity. Are these relatively high (for public utilities) profit

[c] On March 15, 1977, Richard Hough, president, AT&T Long Lines, testified before the Communications Subcommittee of the House Interstate and Foreign Commerce Committee that AT&T did not know what rate of return it earned in international services, but that "revenues from international services help to hold down domestic telephone rates."

levels consistent with the dramatic rate reductions mentioned earlier? Probably they are, since the rate reductions were accompanied by drastic cost reductions and increased traffic levels on facilities with high fixed costs and rapid technological improvement. Even an unconstrained monopolist reduces prices when his cost curve shifts down. Moreover, FCC rate regulation has generally taken the form of mandating rate reductions corresponding to the improvement in "revenue requirements" alleged by the carrier when each new facility is applied for. Since the FCC does not seem to independently calculate the actual projected cost reduction, the carriers have been free to suggest reductions which seem reasonable to themselves.

The record carriers and AT&T, then, wanted a 50−50 mix of facility capacity between cables and satellites, and wanted TAT−6 (SF) authorized in order to implement this policy. The implications of such a policy, as compared with a policy of authorizing no new cables, and allocating all new traffic to satellite capacity already authorized, would be to make future costs and rates higher and to create considerable excess capacity. Such a policy would also probably increase overall reliability of communications, but obviously at considerable cost. COMSAT, naturally, opposed the idea of authorizing TAT−6, although their attitude toward the 50−50 policy was somewhat ambiguous. A "fair" market splitting arrangement protects COMSAT as well as AT&T.

There were other forces at work besides the industry itself. The secretary of defense sent a letter to the FCC endorsing the authorization of TAT−6 on the grounds that national security would be enhanced by increased diversity of routes and facilities for defense communications.[d] No doubt this was (and is) true. There remained a serious question about the value of this increased security, and the cost to be paid for it. The OTP study suggested that there were about 130 circuits in the North Atlantic which could be regarded as "priority requirements" for defense purposes. Without TAT−6, there were then 1,203 cable circuits and 1,687 satellite circuits available in an emergency for defense use. The 130 defense circuits could be thus obtained on any one of three separate cables (TATs 3, 4, 5) or, in the future, three different satellites, supplemented by the older cables, compression techniques, and the various military communication systems themselves. The national security rationale for TAT−6 was not overwhelming since the added reliability created by the addition

[d]A curious statement in view of the fact that at the time there was a Defense Department policy against routing security communications through France, where the cable was to land.

of still more redundancy must be small. As to facility vulnerability to hostile action, there is even less of a case for additional cable capacity. Attacks on a satellite require massive jamming or even nuclear explosions, while cables can be cut by fishing trawlers, and the latter can be perceived as accidental while the former cannot.

Most of the European governments also favored both TAT—6 and a 50—50 facilities policy, and their views were of great concern to the Department of State, which had an important role to play in the decision. It is not clear why the Europeans favored more cables, except for the same reasons put forward by the U.S. carriers—that is, present satellite rates and increased reliability. Communication in most European countries is a state monopoly run by Ministries of Posts and Telecommunications.

The final source of pressure on the FCC was the White House Office of Telecommunications Policy (OTP), which argued that TAT—6 (SF) was far more expensive than already authorized satellite capacity, was not required to meet traffic growth projections, and should not be approved. OTP also argued against using any "predetermined mix" of facilities as a decision rule in authorizing new investments, but favored "least cost" as the proper investment criterion. AT&T, which had already invested a large sum in preliminary manufacturing of TAT—6 (SF) amplifiers, stated that if its TAT—6 authorization were denied, it would abandon the cable business entirely on the grounds that it was too risky a business for a public utility to pursue.

The FCC issued its decision in June 1971, one year after announcing its inquiry [25]. The decision was to deny AT&T permission to construct TAT—6 (SF), but to grant instead, *in advance of application*, permission to lay TAT—6 (SG) as soon as possible. The commission said that while it was unable to determine what an optimal mix of facilities would be, it would nevertheless in the future take steps to ensure that there was "reasonable parity" of facility types in the North Atlantic. Soon after this decision was announced, AT&T found itself able, through improved technology, to increase the capacity of its SG—type cable from 3,500 circuits to about 4,000 circuits, thus adding capacity that was lost through denial of TAT—6 (SF). A cable landing license was issued by the FCC in March 1972.

One factor that weighed heavily in the FCC's decision was AT&T's threat to abandon further research on cable technology if its application were denied. That threat was specific to the TAT—6 (SF) application, and in a sense the FCC called AT&T's bluff by denying authorization of that particular cable. But the advance authorization of the SG—type cable was apparently irresistible. The FCC felt that if AT&T abandoned the cable business, future technological progress in cables might be forestalled. The industry has clearly benefited from rapid technological progress, and one branch of this progress might be cut off by implementation of the AT&T threat. It is obviously difficult to assess the future costs of cutting off one avenue of R&D effort in order to weigh these costs against those incurred by the FCC's actual decision. Indeed, AT&T's threat may very well have been a bluff. It is worth noting that AT&T would have no *incentive* to cut off research in cable technology, even if its application were denied. It is also worth noting that even if a "least cost" rule were followed, there would certainly remain some routes (shorter ones) for which cables would be the cheaper medium. While the economic choice on a particular route must be either all cable or all satellite, there are in fact many routes, of varying lengths and traffic density, where cables are cheaper whether or not AT&T "abandoned" the business. For these reasons, the FCC's concern may have been rather naive.

BEHAVIOR

The salient facts about the international communication industry are that it is subject to regulation, rapidly changing technology, rapidly growing demand, lumpy investments, and economies of scale. All of its firms but one (COMSAT) are vertically integrated, supplying both facilities and retail service to the public. The structure of the industry is such that competition is not possible except through investment policies that affect market shares (and, in the case of the record carriers, sales effort). In this framework, it was not irrational for the carriers to support TAT−6. Its costs would not be higher than satellite rates unless the INTELSAT consortium abandoned rate averaging. AT&T and the record carriers wanted, in effect, to "creamskim" the lucrative North Atlantic market. TAT−6 would enter their rate base, and satellite investment would not. Most important, TAT−6 and the 50−50 policy would guarantee the carriers a 50 percent share of the rapidly growing market.

The FCC's behavior is less easy to rationalize. From the point of view of consumers, a policy of "reasonable parity" is very costly indeed. It is very difficult to find any benefit for the public in such a policy, except that of maintaining stability in the industry. One hypothesis which seems to fit the facts is that the FCC is engaged in performing the role of a cartel manager. In doing so, it is concerned that each member of the industry obtain its "fair share" of business. The process by which this fair share is determined and implemented turns out to be extraordinarily costly to consumers.

Regulatory decisions are, of course, always couched in terms of public interest considerations. But the FCC sees the public interest here as being coincident with a stable, healthy industry within the structural framework determined by previous decisions. Radical restructuring is extremely difficult, perhaps impossible, to carry out because the commission does not have the policy tools to compensate the losses which such restructuring would occasion.

What is the rationale for regulating an oligopoly? By the traditional logic, one or the other of the words in the phrase "regulated oligopoly" is inconsistent. If the conditions for regulation (say, great economies of scale) are present, then oligopoly is inefficient. But if these conditions are not present, some degree of competition is possible, and regulation is no more necessary under the traditional rationale than in other oligopolistic industries with a similar degree of concentration and market power, such as automobile or steel manufacturing. It is difficult to imagine a convincing conventional argument for *ab novo* regulation of an oligopolistic industry, especially if one object of the regulation were to preserve each of the participants in the oligopoly. What generally appears to have been the case is that technological change has resulted in the addition of new firms to previously monopolized industries. The invention of substitutes for the products (or processes) of regulated monopolies could be used, by regulators, as an opportunity for competition and deregulation. Instead, the new technology and the new firms are generally embraced within the preexisting regulatory framework, with the objective, among others, of protecting the interests of the older monopoly or its customers.

Since the object of embracing new firms and technologies within the regulatory fold is precisely to prevent competition, the regulatory agency must take measures to thwart the natural instincts of the members of the industry. In this role, the regulatory agency becomes in effect a "cartel manager." The role of cartel manager has two functions—to maintain industry profits at a satisfactorily high level, and to prevent encroachments by one firm on the market shares of its rivals. Such encroachment can take place in a number of ways— by price cuts, by variations in the quality of service (or advertising), and by investment decisions. The regulator must set up rules and procedures for preventing any of these forms of competition. Both of these cartel management functions are presumably at variance with the role of the regulator as protector of the consumer. Accordingly, the objective of regulation in such cases is often stated as protection of consumers from "destabilizing competition," and particular emphasis is placed on that group of consumers (usually rural) who would in fact be disadvantaged by the demise of one competitor.

The international communications industry can only be characterized as an obscure one, far from public attention. In this regulatory backwater, we may be seeing the face of regulation undistorted by public relations and symbolic politics [26]. The FCC's view of the efforts of OTP to promote cost minimization policies was that it was either absurdly naive or engaged in an effort to aid COMSAT interests. The bureaucrats of the commission understood that economic efficiency simply was not on the policy agenda.

The behavior of AT&T in the struggle illustrates superb command of the strategic manipulation of process, particularly in its utilization of a cynical Defense Department and cooperative European allies. COMSAT was inept. Nothing much was made of the fact that AT&T was "creamskimming" the North Atlantic market, a practice AT&T was simultaneously condemning in other contexts. AT&T was similarly successful in making strategic use of innovation. The promotion of TASI as an automatic restoral device rather than as a cheap source of capacity and the sudden "breakthrough" that accelerated the development and increased the capacity of SG cable were brilliant strokes. But perhaps the most important strategic success of all was scored, much earlier in the story, not by AT&T but at its expense. The Communications Satellite Act of 1962 was a major victory by the aerospace industry, particularly by the Hughes interests, in preventing AT&T from monopolizing the communication satellite equipment supply business.

The FCC's policy of sharing the wealth and preventing "ruinous" competition was underscored during this same period in its *domestic* satellite decision [27]. The "DOMSAT" decision was undertaken in the light of considerably greater publicity. The parties that stood to gain or lose from that decision were able to delay the process for about a decade while they jockeyed for position. The final policy supposedly favored "open skies"—that is, free entry. But this was symbolic rhetoric. In fact, the commission carved up the market, and prospects for "free" entry are remote indeed. But more of this in Chapter 7.

※ *Chapter 3*

Regulating a Depletable Resource: The Natural Gas Industry

INTRODUCTION [1]

Natural gas is a clean burning fuel that represents a vital part of the energy supplied in the United States. In 1920 it provided only 4 percent of our total energy. Today about 30 percent comes from natural gas (see Table 3—1). Approximately a quarter of the yearly gas supply goes to residential use, and almost half of it is consumed by American industry (see Table 3—2).

During recent years there has been a shortage of natural gas, particularly during the heating season when the demand is greatest. Since 1970 some users have not been able to purchase all of the gas they want at prevailing prices. The shortage has increased sharply

Table 3—1. Percentage of Total Energy Furnished by Source by Year

Source	1920	1950	1974
Gas	4	18	30
Oil	14	39	46
Coal	78	38	18
Other	4	5	6
	100	100	100
Total Energy Consumed (Quadrillion BTU)	20	35	73

Source: House of Representatives, Report No. 94–732 (94th Congress, 1st Session), p. 35.

Table 3-2. Uses of Natural Gas by Sector, 1974

Use	Percentage by Use
Residential*	24.5
Commercial	11.6
Industrial**	46.2
Electric Generation	16.5
Other	1.2

Source: House of Representatives, Report No. 94-732 (94th Congress, 1st Session), p. 52.

*Over 70 percent of residential use is for space heating, and about 20 percent is for water heating.

**Of the industrial use, about 24 percent goes to chemical and allied products, 16 percent is petroleum and coal products, and 13 percent to primary metal industries.

over the last six years. Importantly, in every year since 1968 we have consumed more natural gas than we have added to our proven reserves by discoveries of new fields and extensions of existing ones.

The central issue raised by the natural gas shortage has been whether the Federal Power Commission (or its successor established by the Department of Energy Organization Act of 1977, the Federal Energy Regulatory Commission) should continue to regulate the prices at which producers sell gas to the pipelines in interstate commerce. The mechanism for regulating these prices (called wellhead prices) has changed form noticeably over the last ten years. The administrative process has attempted to establish a procedure which controls the wellhead prices so that (1) the prices are not set at levels which are "unreasonably high," (2) the prices lead to "adequate" supplies of gas, and (3) the process is reasonably expedient in handling the cases for the thousands of producers who sell into interstate markets. While the Federal Power Commission had some success in expediting the administrative process, it was not able to satisfy the first two objectives simultaneously during this decade. It has supplemented wellhead price regulation with other controls, but the shortage persists.

A historical examination of the regulation of natural gas shows that the debates generated by the shortage are only the latest in the controversy over wellhead price controls. The struggle surrounding this regulation has been accompanied by interesting behavior on the part of the regulators, the producers of gas, the individual states, and the courts. In this chapter we analyze certain aspects of the behavior of these agents and suggest several lessons that can be learned about the administrative process itself.

BACKGROUND

The use of gas in this country began in the nineteenth century. At first it was employed primarily to operate gas lighting systems in the streets of large cities. Most of the gas used in these systems was manufactured from coal. In the last part of the century gas became even more widely used. One of the reasons for this was the development of "water gas" which was obtained by passing steam through hot coke. It was not until the turn of the century that "natural" gas, which was extracted directly from the earth rather than manufactured in some way, attracted attention as an economically viable source of energy.

As the nineteenth century drew to a close, electricity replaced gas as the primary fuel for artificial lighting. The transition to electricity followed the development of the incandescent lamp by Thomas Edison in 1878. The contraction of the market for gas resulted in a number of mergers among local gas companies which had previously competed vigorously with one another. For example, the six companies that existed in Baltimore in 1871 had merged to one firm by 1888. In New York and Chicago similar mergers occurred [2].

The gas industry searched for a new market to serve, and was successful in replacing coal as the primary fuel for domestic cooking. But another, more important change was occurring that helped local gas companies turn a stagnating economic picture into a prosperous one. This was the transition from manufactured gas to natural gas, made possible by the construction of gas pipeline systems capable of transporting natural gas from producing fields to the major cities. By 1931 Chicago was using gas piped from the fields of Texas, and more long distance construction followed. The network continued to expand after World War II as gas became the preferred means of space heating.

Natural gas contains approximately twice the potential heating value of an equivalent volume of manufactured gas. This is one reason that consumers began to favor natural gas. By 1945, 45 percent of gas customers used natural gas, a figure that increased to 98 percent in 1967 [3].

The Natural Gas Act

Natural gas is produced either from a reservoir which primarily yields gas, or from fields which produce both gas and oil. Gas found along with oil is called associated gas. Gas gathered at the wellhead is transmitted by pipeline to various markets, either directly to an end user (such as an electric utility) or to a local distribution company which in turn sells it to end users (primarily residential and commercial customers).

The local distribution of gas has been regulated for over a century in some cities, even before natural gas replaced manufactured gas as the primary fuel supplied by the industry. Before the 1930s there was very little interstate transmission of gas. Most of the activity associated with it, including its manufacture and distribution, was intrastate.[a]

In the 1930s several large hydrocarbon reservoirs were found in regions of the country far away from major cities, especially in the Southwest. Improved exploration and drilling techniques facilitated production. However, the transmission of gas required well-engineered compression systems and pipelines which were less prone to leak than the older welded type. Technical advances in compression, along with the development of seamless pipe, combined to make long distance transmission feasible at a cost low enough to compete with other energy sources in major cities. Natural gas transmitted across state lines became an important source of energy.

Before 1938 state and local regulators were powerless to control the price which local distributors paid for imported gas. The Supreme Court had ruled that interstate pipelines were outside the jurisdiction of these regulators [4]. Thus, state and local authorities could regulate the prices which local distributors charged their customers, but these prices were affected greatly by the uncontrolled prices which distributors paid for imported gas. Alfred Kahn suggests this as the major reason for the regulatory legislation of the time.

> For example, as the progress of technology in the 1920's and 1930's made increasingly feasible the interstate transmission of electricity and natural gas, local and state commissions found an increasingly large component of the cost of service of the companies under their jurisdiction—namely the electric current or the gas imported from out of state—falling outside their reach. This growing gap was filled by the Federal Power Act of 1935 and the Natural Gas Act of 1938, which conferred on the Federal Power Commission regulatory authority over those wholesale rates [5].

In 1938 Congress "declared that the business of transporting and selling natural gas for ultimate distribution to the public is affected with a public interest, and that Federal regulation in matters relating to the transportation of natural gas and the sale thereof in interstate and foreign commerce is necessary in the public interest" [6]. The

---

[a] One notable exception was the transmission of gas by an early pipeline from Indiana fields to Chicago, beginning in the 1890s.

Natural Gas Act brought the interstate transmission of natural gas and its sale for resale under the control of the Federal Power Commission. The act exempted the gathering of gas and its retail distribution, a point which will be discussed in detail below.

Under the act, rates for transmission and sale were to be "just and reasonable" and without "undue" preferences. Pipelines were required to publish tariff schedules, to adhere to them, and to give advance notice of proposed tariff changes. The commission was given a standard set of administrative powers, including those to conduct hearings, suspend proposed rate changes, order refunds to consumers when warranted, and issue orders to insure that rates were reasonable [7]. The act also authorized the commission to establish and enforce a set of accounting procedures. As amended in 1942, the act required companies to obtain certificates from the commission for the construction of interstate facilities, extensions, acquisitions, and abandonments.

Regulation at the Wellhead

After World War II the issue of wellhead price regulation became increasingly important. Before pipeline networks were built, associated gas was often produced as a virtually valueless by-product of oil. It was often flared (burned) at the wellhead. However, as gas pipelines reached the wellhead, the value of gas went up markedly. Prices for gas already in production rose as a result of "favored nation" clauses, which stipulated that a buyer (pipeline) would pay a producer a price equal to the highest price paid to any other producer in the area, or in some cases, by any other pipeline in the area. The pipelines viewed the higher prices they paid for gas as representing higher costs of operation, and filed requests with the commission for higher prices on the gas which they in turn sold to local distributors and industrial customers.

Until 1954 the commission had assumed that it did not have jurisdiction over wellhead prices, although there was much debate on this point. This belief rested on a clause of the Natural Gas Act, stating that the act "shall not apply . . . to the production or gathering of natural gas," even though gas sold to a pipeline would be resold by the pipeline [8].

The issue came before the Supreme Court in 1954 in a well-known case, *Phillips Petroleum Company* v. *Wisconsin et al.* [9]. Phillips was the largest of the independent gas producers at the time, and had raised its wellhead price for natural gas. The state of Wisconsin, along with the cities of Milwaukee, Detroit, and Kansas City, complained before the commission. Their objection to the increase in price was typical of the regional disagreement of the time; the gas-consuming states of the North wanted low wellhead prices (regulated if necessary), while the gas-producing states of the Southwest opposed the control of wellhead prices. When the FPC declined to act on the complaint registered by Wisconsin and her partners, the case was taken to court.

The testimony in the Phillips case delineated the battle lines clearly. The Wisconsin consumer representatives argued that Phillips had monopoly power in the market for natural gas sales to pipelines, and were concerned that the exercise of this power would result in wellhead prices, and ultimately consumer gas prices, that were excessively high. Phillips vigorously denied the existence of monopoly power, pointing out that as of the late 1940s approximately 2,300 independent producers or gatherers supplied gas to the pipelines. With such a competitive industry, Phillips argued, federal regulation was unnecessary to protect consumers against excessively high prices [10].

Ultimately the Supreme Court concluded that although the actual production and gathering activities of Phillips were exempt from regulation, the sales of gas to pipelines intending resale did fall within the scope of the act. The Court assigned the commission the duty to determine the reasonableness of the price of gas sold by Phillips in interstate commerce. The Court supported its decision by noting that the primary aim of the act was to protect consumers from exploitation by natural gas companies [11].

The ruling was controversial for two reasons. As already described, it was not clear that Congress intended the law to include the regulation of wellhead prices. It could be argued that these controls did regulate quite severely the actual production and gathering activities in fact if not in law. Second, the nature of any market imperfection which warranted regulation was never clearly established. Did producers have sufficient monopoly power to justify the control of wellhead prices to protect consumers from exploitation? While assertions in the affirmative were plentiful, hard analysis was not.

The Administrative Logjam
The Supreme Court decision left the FPC in a difficult position. The commission was not faced with the "usual" task of a public utility regulator with only one or a few firms under its jurisdiction. Between 1954 and 1960 it was inundated with requests for rate increases. By 1960 "there were 3278 producer rate increase filings under suspension and awaiting hearings and decisions" [12]. The commission was confronted with an impossible task, particularly if

the traditional cost-based pricing methods of public utilities were to be applied in each case. The commission itself estimated that it would not finish its 1960 caseload until the year 2043 [13].

In 1960 the FPC took its first step in attempting to expedite the administrative process for its wellhead price case backload. It divided the nation into twenty-three geographic areas, and then began to determine uniform ceiling prices in each area based on prices observed in the 1956–1958 period. This became known as area rate-making.

A central feature of area rate-making was the designation of a two-tiered rate schedule. There were two ceiling prices, one for gas already being produced (called "old gas") and for gas associated with oil, and a second (higher) price for gas not associated with oil which was classified as "new gas." New gas was defined as gas which was either discovered or committed to interstate commerce after a date specified by the FPC. Alfred Kahn describes the reasoning behind this scheme, saying that it was thought to be "both undesirable and unnecessary to extend that higher price to old gas—undesirable because to do so would confer windfalls on the owners of reserves discovered and developed at lower costs in the past (a noneconomic argument), and unnecessary because the investments in the old gas had already been made (an economic consideration)" [14].

The first of the geographic areas to be considered was the Permian Basin of western Texas. The old gas ceiling was based on cost and investment data for all producers in the area for gas wells already in production. The new gas ceiling was based on industry averages of costs arising from the production of new unassociated gas.

The FPC order for the Permian Basin was issued in 1965. It was ultimately appealed to the Supreme Court, which upheld the FPC area rate-making approach in 1968 [15]. In later orders the commission has continued its system of multiple (sometimes more than two) tiers in its rate schedules.

As the first part of 1970s passed, it became apparent that the area rate-making approach would not be sufficiently expedient to allow the FPC to react promptly to changing conditions in wellhead markets. By 1974 the commission had set rates in only seven of the twenty-three areas, and rising costs and increasing shortages had made it necessary to issue a second ruling for the Permian Basin. The time had come for a second step in breaking the logjam. Instead of setting rates by areas, the FPC decided to establish a new policy, one which would determine nationwide price ceilings. On June 21, 1974, the commission established "a uniform just and reasonable national base rate of 42 cents per thousand cubic feet at 14.73 psia [pounds per square inch, absolute pressure], for interstate sales of natural gas" [16]. This rate was to apply to new gas, at the time designated as gas which was first committed to interstate commerce after January 1, 1973. At the same time the FPC was deciding upon an appropriate nationwide rate for old gas. It also intended to review nationwide rates every two years, with adjustments to be made for changes in exploration and production costs.

In proceedings in July and November of 1976, the commission established the following five-tiered rate schedule: [17]

1. Gas from a well whose production was commenced prior to January 1, 1973, which was also contracted for sale prior to that date (sometimes referred to as "old flowing" gas), has a ceiling price of 29.5 cents per Mcf (thousand standard cubic feet).
2. Gas from a well whose production was commenced prior to January 1, 1973, which was contracted for sale after that date, has a ceiling price of 52 cents per Mcf, plus 1 cent per year escalation.
3. Gas from a well whose production was commenced after January 1, 1973, but before January 1, 1975, has a ceiling price of 93 cents per Mcf plus 1 cent per year escalation.
4. Gas from a well whose production was commenced after January 1, 1975, has a ceiling price of $1.42 per Mcf plus 4 cents per year escalation.
5. Gas, the sale of which continues in interstate commerce under a renegotiated contract, upon the expiration of the contract term which occurs after January 1, 1973 (sometimes referred to as "roll-over" gas), has a ceiling price of 52 cents per Mcf plus 1 cent per year escalation.

The Structure of Wellhead Markets

As testimony in the 1954 *Phillips* case indicated, there are thousands of natural gas producers nationally. Since oil and gas are often found in the same formations, it is not surprising that major producers of gas are also major producers of oil (see Table 3—3). The largest producer of natural gas sold into interstate commerce in 1971 served less than 10 percent of the national market, with the largest four, eight, and twenty firms supplying 26.7, 45.4, and 69.6 percent respectively (see Table 3—4). These figures by themselves do not say very much about the degree of competition in the production of gas, so to put them in perspective we consider the following items.

The concentration figures are somewhat higher if we look at major gas-producing regions instead of the national market. In Table 3—4 the regional concentration numbers are for gas sold under new

Table 3–3.   Ranking of Largest Companies in the Petroleum Industry (1970)

Natural Gas Producers	Liquid Hydrocarbon Production (1)	Petroleum Refining	U.S. Refined Product Sales	Natural Gas Sales to Interstate Pipelines
Exxon	1	1	1	1
Texaco	2	2	2	7
Gulf	3	5	7	2
Shell	4	7	3	3
Chevron	5	4	5	11
Amoco	6	6	4	4
Atlantic-Richfield	7	8	8	8
Mobil	8	3	6	6
Union Oil	9	10	11	9
Getty	10	15	17	17
Sun	11	9	10	12
Phillips	12	11	9	5
Continental	13	14	14	10

Source: *Natural Gas Survey* (FPC, 1975), Volume I, Table 3–1, p. 55.

(1) Ranking is by volume of domestic production.

Table 3–4. Selected Concentration Ratios for Producers

Concentration Ratio, Including This Number of Largest Firms	Percentage of Annual Volume under New Sales Contract, 1969			National Sales of Natural Gas to Interstate Pipelines, 1971
	Southern Louisiana	Permian Basin	Texas Gulf Coast	Percentage of Total Sales
1	11.1	21.1	21.9	9.8
4	38.4	57.8	62.6	26.7
8	63.7	71.5	71.5	45.4
20	—	—	—	69.6

Source: *National Gas Survey* (FPC, 1975), Vol. I, pp. 57–58.

sales contracts in 1969. No single producer dominates any of the three regions in the table, although by some standards the concentration ratios are high enough in the Texas Gulf Coast and Permian Basin areas to appear oligopolistic. It should be noted that if concentration ratios are taken as an indicator of market power, there is an argument for defining the relevant market as national rather than regional. Many gas consuming areas receive gas from more than one producing area. This would limit the extent to which producers in any single area could control the price of gas even if they attempted to do so.

Since most gas supply contracts are for a long term, the market shares by firm do not vary much from year to year. However, the shares of annual volume under new sales contracts do change more rapidly from year to year. "In 1964 only one of the eight top sellers [new contracts] in Southern Louisiana was among the top eight in 1965, while in 1966 the top eight sellers comprised completely different companies from those in 1964 or 1968" [18]. This kind of turnover tends to make the higher concentration ratio observed in any year for new sales less significant than they would be if the same producers regularly dominated the new sales markets.

It is apparent that the national concentration of gas producers is less than in many manufacturing industries which, although more concentrated, have not been judged so concentrated as to warrant price regulation [19]. Yet there are some aspects of wellhead market structure that qualify the extent to which the market would be competitive without regulation. Producers often enter into joint ventures, particularly in the costly and risky operations offshore. The government leasing policies have made large financial resources a prerequisite to successful bidding for offshore leases. Small firms may have no choice other than a joint venture if they desire to enter into offshore production.

It is not clear how large a company has to be in order to make joint ventures unnecessary from a risk-sharing perspective. Neither is it clear at what size the advantages of risk sharing become outweighed by the prospects of collusion. To some extent this is no doubt a function of government leasing policy. The amount of monopoly power created by joint ventures is perhaps less important than is sometimes argued, primarily because offshore production represents only about 16 percent of the national interstate market [20].

On the buyer's side of wellhead markets are about thirty-three major interstate pipeline companies and seventy-four others [21]. Concentration ratios for four producing areas and for the national market are shown in Table 3–5. As one might expect, regional concentrations are generally higher than national concentration.

Table 3—5.   Natural Gas Purchases by Interstate Pipelines: Concentration Ratios for Selected Gas Areas

Number of Largest Firms Included	*Cumulative Percentage of Gas Purchases by Area*					
	Southern Louisiana (Onshore) 1972[a]	*Permian Basin 1972[a]*	*Texas Gulf Coast 1972[a]*	*Hugoton-Anadarko 1972[a]*	*National Market 1971[b]*	
1	24.1	45.1	18.6	21.2	11.2	
4	60.7	88.2	59.2	70.4	35.8	
8	88.0	Virtually 100	90.1	94.1	58.2	

Source: (a) *Sales by Producers of Natural Gas to Interstate Pipeline Companies, 1972* (FPC), extracted from Table D, p. XV, and Table 6, pp. 633–642.

(b) *Sales by Producers of Natural Gas to Interstate Pipeline Companies, 1971* (FPC), reported in the *Natural Gas Survey* (FPC, 1975) Volume I, p. 62.

As a historical note, it has sometimes been suggested that, absent regulation of wellhead prices, the pipelines might have some monopsony power in wellhead markets. The most well-known empirical work on monopsony is reported in studies by MacAvoy [22]. These studies differ from the relatively simplistic perspective offered by concentration ratios alone. MacAvoy constructed statistical tests to see if the variations observed in wellhead prices before these prices were regulated depended significantly on the number of pipelines in the market. He concluded that monopsony was not pervasive, although in a few cases there was some evidence of its existence. "As suggested by price formation in the 1950's, gas markets are diverse in structure and behavior, but are generally competitive or changing from monopsony toward competition" [23].

It would be difficult to repeat the MacAvoy tests for the present decade for two reasons. First, interstate wellhead prices are controlled by the FPC rather than market forces so that statistical tests of the sort performed by MacAvoy for the 1950s are not possible. Second, the remaining markets in which prices are unregulated are the ones for intrastate sales, and the data are not recorded in a centralized location (such as the FPC) or on a consistent reporting basis.

SOME CONSEQUENCES OF WELLHEAD PRICE REGULATION

The Shortage

During the 1970s the Federal Power Commission has found it increasingly difficult to maintain low prices in natural gas markets while at the same time ensuring adequate supplies of the resource. The United States has moved from a position of abundant and relatively inexpensive energy to one in which energy sources are scarce and expensive.

A summary of the national production and reserve data for natural gas appears in Table 3-6. It should be mentioned that these data are reported by the American Gas Association, and in the past there have been challenges to the accuracy of the data, particularly in the measurement of reserves. Because of the complex geological, geophysical, and engineering processes which are used as a basis for reserve estimates, it has been difficult to draw any firm conclusions about biases in the reporting. Rather than repeat much of the debate on this issue, we proceed to examine the data with this caveat in mind.

Until 1967 there was a trend of increasing reserves, to a peak of 292.9 trillion standard cubic feet, and additions to reserves in each year exceeded production. The fifth column of Table 3-6 shows

Table 3–6.   United States Natural Gas Production *(Volumes are in trillions of cubic feet at 14.73 psia and 60° F)*

Year	Production	Reserve Additions	Proved Reserves (1)	Total Reserves ÷ Production (2)	Reserve Additions ÷ Production (2)
1946	4.9	17.6	159.7	32.5	3.6
1947	5.6	10.9	165.0	29.5	1.9
1948	6.0	13.8	172.9	28.9	2.3
1949	6.2	12.6	179.4	28.9	2.0
1950	6.9	12.0	184.6	26.9	1.7
1951	7.9	16.0	192.8	24.3	2.0
1952	8.6	14.3	198.6	23.1	1.7
1953	9.2	20.3	210.3	22.9	2.2
1954	9.4	9.6	210.6	22.5	1.0
1955	10.1	21.9	222.5	22.1	2.2
1956	10.9	24.7	236.5	21.8	2.3
1957	11.4	20.0	245.2	21.4	1.7
1958	11.4	18.9	252.8	22.1	1.7
1959	12.4	20.6	261.2	21.1	1.7
1960	13.0	13.9	262.3	20.1	1.1
1961	13.5	17.2	266.3	19.9	1.3
1962	13.6	19.5	272.3	20.0	1.4
1963	14.5	18.2	276.2	19.0	1.3
1964	15.3	20.3	281.3	18.3	1.3
1965	16.3	21.3	286.5	17.6	1.3
1966	17.5	20.2	289.3	16.5	1.2
1967	18.4	21.8	292.9	15.9	1.2
1968	19.4	13.7	287.4	14.8	0.7
1969	20.7	8.4	275.1	13.3	0.4
1970	22.0	37.2 (3)	290.7	13.2	1.7
1971	22.1	9.8	278.8	12.6	0.4
1972	22.5	9.6	266.1	11.8	0.4
1973	22.6	6.8	250.1	11.1	0.3

Source: American Gas Association, as reported in the Natural Gas Survey (FPC, 1975), Vol. I, p. 221.

(1) Includes gas in underground storage.   (2) Computed prior to rounding.   (3) In 1970 26 Tcf of proved reserves in Prudhoe Bay (Alaska) were added to gas inventories.

that during the early 1960s, proved reserves were sufficient to supply gas for about twenty years at the then existing production rates. By 1967 this figure (total reserves divided by the annual production rate) had fallen to 15.9. This occurred even though reserves were growing since annual production increased at an even faster rate. After 1968 reserves fell for the first time since 1946. As Table 3–6 shows, the ratio of total reserves to production has continued to fall.

The gas shortage has had as its most obvious symptom the curtailments in service since 1970. Curtailment is defined as the difference between the gas actually delivered by pipelines to their customers (i.e., the amount actually supplied) and the contractual obligations of the pipelines (often called "firm requirements"). Data on curtailments are reported by the Federal Power Commission in two ways. Annual curtailments include the period from April 1 of one year to March 31 of the next. Heating season curtailments are measured for November 1 through March 31. Both sets of figures are shown in Table 3–7 for the years from 1970 through 1976. The rapidly increasing curtailment trend is apparent from these data.

It is important to note that curtailment figures probably greatly underestimate the amount of gas which consumers would like to purchase at existing prices, but cannot. Curtailment estimates focus on existing pipelines and their customers. Since the shortage has

Table 3–7. National Curtailment Trends

Year (April to March)	Annual Firm Curtailments (Tcf)	Heating Season (November to March) Curtailments (Tcf)
1970 to 1971 (1)	0.1	0.1
1971 to 1972 (1)	0.5	0.2
1972 to 1973 (1)	1.1	0.5
1973 to 1974 (1)	1.6	0.6
1974 to 1975 (1)	2.0	1.0
1975 to 1976	3.2 (3)	1.3 to 1.7 (2)

(1) Source: House of Representatives, Report No. 94–732 (94th Congress, 1st Session), p. 8.

(2) The 1.3 figure was the one anticipated for the winter period by Mr. Zarb, administrator, Federal Energy Administration, in the hearing before the Committee on Commerce, United States Senate, on the following bills: S. 2244, S. 2310, and S. 2330, serial number 94–34, September 15, 1975. The 1.7 number was suggested by Senator Hollings at the same hearings (see p. 18 of the transcript).

(3) The estimate of 3.2 appears in the FPC and FEA report on "The Economic and Environmental Impact of Natural Gas Curtailments During the Winter of 1975–76," which appears as Appendix V, House of Representatives, Report No. 94–732.

occurred, existing pipelines in many cases have not been able to provide service to potential new customers, even though these potential customers are willing to purchase gas. Curtailment data do not include this in their measurement. In addition, in some areas where potential customers are willing to purchase enough gas to justify the construction of a new pipeline, no such pipeline has been built. In order to receive permission to construct a new pipeline, the builder must show that it can obtain at least some minimum amount of gas from producers. Although the potential pipelines would have customers, they often cannot secure sufficient commitments of gas from producers to receive construction authority. Shortage of this type is also not included in curtailment data.

The effects of curtailments cannot be adequately summarized by a single national statistic. Some industries and regions of the country have been affected more seriously than others. While a detailed regional and industrial description is not presented here (it has been done elsewhere [24]), there are some facts worth noting. In advance of the 1975−76 winter, the Office of Technology Assessment estimated that a hard winter might lead to as many as 100,000 jobs lost nationally, over periods from twenty to ninety days, as a result of curtailments [25]. Some of the areas most vulnerable were the textile industry of the North Carolina and Virginia region, the brick industry in North Carolina, the steel industry in Ohio, Pennsylvania, and Maryland, the fertilizer industry in the East and Southeast, and the cement industry in some states [26]. While these effects might be less pronounced in the long term (over a period of several years, when some of these industries could convert from gas to other fuels), it would still remain important in some industries (such as the fertilizer industry) which require gas for specific purposes.

Although the nation was spared the worst of winters in the 1975−76 winter, the fears were realized with a vengeance in the winter of 1976−77. Estimates of temporary unemployment resulting from the shortage and the harsh winter soared, ranging from 600,000 to over two million job losses during January and February of 1977.

Income Redistribution

One convenient way of representing some of the effects of regulation is with the graph of Figure 3−1, as suggested by MacAvoy and Pindyck [27]. The supply schedule for producers is represented by S. The demand for gas can be considered in two parts. One set of consumers are the "fortunate" ones who are able to purchase gas at existing prices. Typically those consumers who have access to gas in one year will continue to have it in the next year. The demand sched-

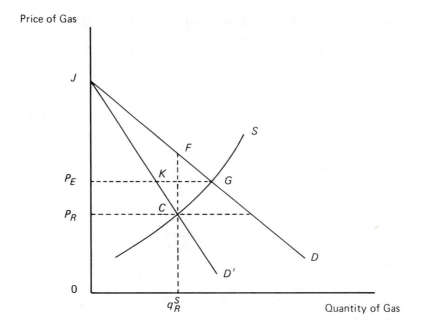

Figure 3—1. Effects of Regulation in Wellhead Markets

ule for this group of consumers can be represented by D' as in Figure 3—1.

As time has passed, other potential consumers have not been able to purchase gas because of the shortage, even though they are willing and able to pay for it. If the demand schedule for this "unfortunate" group were added to D', the total demand for gas could be represented by D. At a regulated wellhead price P_R, the quantity of gas which producers will provide is represented q_R^S, which also represents the quantity which the "fortunate" consumers are able to purchase.

If wellhead prices were not regulated, then the market would clear at a price such as P_E, at which the quantity desired by all customers equals the quantity which producers would be willing to supply. The existence of a shortage provides immediate evidence that P_E exceeds P_R. One approximation of the difference between P_E and P_R can be inferred by comparing the average wellhead price in interstate markets (in which wellhead price is regulated under FPC jurisdiction) and the average wellhead price in unregulated intrastate markets. The intrastate and interstate (jurisdictional) figures for selected dates between 1966 and 1975 are shown in Table 3—8 [28].

Table 3−8. Comparison of Intrastate and Jurisdictional Weighted Average
Prices *(prices in dollars per thousand standard cubic feet)*

Date of Contract	Intrastate	Jurisdictional
1966 (1)	$0.168	$0.185
1967 (1)	0.173	0.191
1968 (1)	0.175	0.192
1969 (1)	0.180	0.198
First half, 1970 (1)	0.207	0.202
July 1, 1970 to Sept. 14, 1971 (1)	0.241	0.284
Sept. 15, 1971 to Sept. 14, 1972 (1)	0.316	0.286
1975	0.60 (est.) (3)	0.40 (2)

Sources: (1) FPC data as presented in Report No. 94−732 (House of Representatives, 94th Congress, 1st session), p. 6.

(2) *FPC News* 8, 35 (August 29, 1975): pp. 1, 5.

(3) No hard data are available, but this figure was named as a consensus estimate by Chip Schroeder of the House Energy and Power
Subcommittee Staff. See "Cost of S. 3422's Pricing Provisions,"
by L. Kumins, Senate Report 94−907.

One can then identify two kinds of income redistribution that
have resulted from regulation. First, regulation has enabled consumers fortunate enough to get gas to purchase it at P_R rather than P_E.
Thus regulation has led to a redistribution of income from producers
to these consumers in an amount represented by the difference ($P_E -
P_R$) times the amount of gas purchased q_R^S. As Table 3−8 shows,
the difference between P_E and P_R was much less during the late
1960s than it was in 1975. (In fact, before 1970 the table shows that
interstate prices were even a bit higher than intrastate prices, which
suggests that regulation may not have held wellhead prices down at
all during this period.) Accordingly one would expect the extent of
the income redistribution for the fortunate consumers to have increased substantially since 1970.

MacAvoy has provided estimates of the magnitude of this redistribution for 1969 [29] and for 1975 [30]. His figures for 1969 place
the distribution in the range from $0 to $63 million, and for the
latter in excess of $1 billion. Braeutigam provides a simple indepen-
dent check on the 1975 figure [31]. In Table 3−8 the difference
($P_E - P_R$) is shown to be about $0.20 per Mcf (thousand cubic feet).
Since about two-thirds of the 24 Tcf (trillion cubic feet) or so produced nationally was sold in interstate commerce in 1975, the
amount of the redistribution could be approximated as the product

of $0.20 per Mcf and 16 Tcf. This amounts to $3.2 billion for the year, which is consistent with the MacAvoy estimate.

The second kind of income redistribution caused by regulation applies to those consumers who were not able to purchase gas (the "unfortunate" customers described earlier). Instead of purchasing gas at P_R, many of these customers were forced to increase their expenditures on energy by large amounts in purchasing alternative fuels. Helms [32] has suggested that the amount of this redistribution away from the unfortunate customers may well be of the same order of magnitude as redistribution benefit to the fortunate customers. Policymakers may have reasons for treating these two consumer groups separately. However, if they choose to consider the groups together, the increased expenditures of the second group will at least to some extent offset the benefits received by the first group.

Economic Efficiency

One could represent the loss in economic efficiency caused by regulation using the sum of consumer and producer surplus as a measure of welfare. The efficiency loss from regulation would be at least the familiar welfare "triangle" CFG (Figure 3—1) if new and old customers had equal access to wellhead gas [33]. However, if the "fortunate" customers referred to earlier are able to get gas while the unfortunate customers cannot, then the efficiency loss due to regulation would correspond to the area CJG.

MacAvoy and Pindyck [34] have attempted to estimate the amount of the inefficiency for the late 1970s, using a simulation model of the natural gas industry. They employed statistical techniques to characterize the nature of supply and demand schedules based on historical data, and then used this information to project the future under a variety of assumptions about regulatory policies and other variables. For example, the demand data serving as a basis for their work are for the years 1963 to 1969 for industrial users, and for 1963 to 1971 for residential and commercial customers. They excluded the 1970 and 1971 data for industrial users because there were curtailments during that period, meaning that the data on industrial purchases did not reflect the actual quantities desired by industrial users at regulated prices. The supply side was more easily identified (in the econometric sense) since no condition of excess supply existed over the period from which the data were drawn. With the simulation model MacAvoy and Pindyck estimate that the efficiency loss due to continued regulation at 1974 prices for the rest of the decade would amount to more than $2.5 billion annually in 1978 and more than $5.8 billion in 1980.

These estimates of efficiency losses are less reliable than the income redistribution estimates discussed earlier. Several reasons for this have been discussed in detail elsewhere [35]; however, two of the reasons are summarized here. They involve projections, with assumptions on many variables including the level of regulated prices. As shown earlier, wellhead prices have not remained at their 1974 levels, but have begun to rise quite rapidly. Also, MacAvoy and Pindyck have assumed that the demand schedules are linear. Their efficiency loss estimates require some assumption on the shape of the demand schedule over certain regions (particularly the upper part of the demand schedule) for which not much data were available. The amount of consumer surplus lost under regulation may be quite sensitive to the shape of the demand. It should be noted that the assumption of linearity could lead to either an overestimation or an underestimation of the actual loss.

Perhaps the most valuable insights than we can gain from the examination of economic efficiency are qualitative. There surely are efficiency losses caused by regulation. They may be quite large, perhaps in the billions of dollars annually as MacAvoy has suggested.

BEHAVIOR

In the first chapter we suggested several kinds of behavior that might be expected given the nature of the administrative process. In this section we will examine certain aspects of the activities of the Federal Power Commission and gas producers to see whether the behavior observed supports those expectations.

Equity in the Status Quo

In Chapter 1 we suggested that the judicial form of administrative law leads to a preference for fairness in substantive outcomes. The behavior which one would expect to observe on the part of the FPC is a tendency toward the selection of outcomes which appear to be distributionally fair. In the case of wellhead prices it becomes appropriate to ask what "prevailing norms" might have served as a benchmark for determining distributional fairness.

One could argue that the regulation of the natural gas industry in 1938 was closely patterned after the electricity generating industry which was regulated just three years earlier under the Federal Power Act of 1935. Alfred Kahn has succinctly linked the two types of regulation as follows:

> Effective regulation of local electricity rates has not been typically construed, for example, to require public utility regulation of the prices charged electricity generating companies by sellers of residual fuel oil or

coal, even though these constitute an important part of their service. The assumption has been that the industries supplying these important inputs have been sufficiently competitive to protect the consumer; and that as long as they remained financially independent, the regulated monopolies had no incentive to pay more than the competitive price. Whether the same is true of the field market for natural gas has been the subject of intense controversy [36].

Kahn's analogy is straightforward. If the regulation of electricity provided a "prevailing norm" for natural gas, the reluctance of the FPC to regulate wellhead prices could be understood as entirely consistent with that norm. The commission continued in its stance in this respect until the Supreme Court imposed a new primary norm in the *Phillips* decision in 1954, namely, the prevention of exploitation of consumers by producers. It is this mandate which has presumably served as a basis for the argument that a redistribution income from producers to consumers is "good," and the subsequent actions of the commission in holding wellhead prices for interstate sales below their market clearing levels.

One Equity Consideration Begets Another

The existence of a shortage provides ample evidence that economic forces remain at work despite regulatory fiats on wellhead prices. As mentioned earlier, the commission has sought to insure that adequate supplies of gas were available to consumers at the same time as it has attempted to keep gas prices at "reasonable" levels. Restated, it has tried to satisfy two policy objectives with one policy instrument, the level of wellhead prices. During the 1960s it was close to achieving these two goals; during the present decade it has not been so successful. The reason for this is clear from Table 3-8. During the 1960s the regulated wellhead prices were close to their market clearing levels. This was a fortunate circumstance for the FPC, dictated by the economic forces of supply and demand, rather than a consequence of shrewd regulatory behavior. The commission has been forced to supplement its price regulation with a second regulatory lever, curtailment priorities, which essentially ration gas in the face of the shortage. The nine curtailment priorities presently used by the commission are listed in Table 3-9.

To some extent the ranking makes sense. Categories with lower numbers have a higher priority for gas. Users with available alternatives for gas (those toward the bottom of the table) would probably not value gas as highly as they would if no alternative fuels were available. Also, users with interruptible clauses in their contracts could probably absorb some curtailment with only minimal effects.

Table 3-9. FPC Curtailment Priorities

1. Residential, small commercial (less than 50 Mcf on a peak day).

2. Large commercial requirements (50 Mcf or more on a peak day), firm industrial requirements for plant protection, feedstock and process needs, and pipeline customer storage injection requirements.

3. All industrial requirements not specified in (2), (4), (5), (6), (7), (8), or (9).

4. Firm industrial requirements for boiler fuel use at less than 3000 Mcf per day, but more than 1500 Mcf per day, where alternate fuel capabilities can meet such requirements.

5. Firm industrial requirements for large volume (3000 Mcf or more per day) boiler fuel use where alternate fuel capabilities can meet such requirements.

6. Interruptible requirements of more than 300 Mcf per day, but less than 1500 Mcf per day, where alternate fuel capabilities can meet such requirements.

7. Interruptible requirements of intermediate volumes (from 1500 Mcf per day through 3000 Mcf per day), where alternate fuel capabilities can meet such requirements.

8. Interruptible requirements of more than 3000 Mcf per day, but less than 10,000 Mcf per day, where alternate fuel capabilities can meet such requirements.

9. Interruptible requirements of more than 10,000 Mcf per day, where alternate fuel capabilities can meet such requirements.

Source: FPC Order No. 467-B, Docket No. R-469, March 2, 1973.

However, this approach also raises many problems. Are these categories really "correctly" defined and ordered? Is the gas rationed to uses where its value is greatest? Even if this is thought to be true at a coarse level, there are obvious problems at finer levels. For example, a residential user would have a top priority under this scheme to get additional gas to heat his home from $72°F$ to, say, $75°F$. But is the gas used in that way really more valuable than any use for gas in, for example, a plant classified in category nine? It would seem highly unlikely. Even the procedures of the FPC which allow parties to seek relief in special cases would not be adequate to make the many such adjustments which probably ought to be made. One can expect these problems to persist as long as allocations are made within the administrative process rather than by an "impersonal" market.

Strategic Use of Jurisdictional Boundaries

In Chapter 1 we indicated that firms often react to the jurisdictional boundaries of regulatory authorities in ways which ultimately allow them effectively to circumvent the intent of regulation. The case of natural gas provides as clear an example of this as any industry examined in this book.

Part of the story is told by Table 3—8. If a profit maximizing producer of gas has a choice as to whether to sell into interstate or intrastate commerce, it would choose to sell where the price is higher, in the intrastate market. The price disparity is even more pronounced than in Table 3—8. Remember that gas contracts are generally long term in nature, so the choice whether to commit reserves to interstate or intrastate commerce is often made for "new" gas. Before 1976 the "new" gas price in the interstate market was $0.52 per Mcf, a figure which was raised to $1.42 per Mcf in 1976. However new contracts for intrastate gas rose from about $0.18 per Mcf in 1968 to in excess of $1.32 per Mcf in 1975, and in some markets as high as $2.00 per Mcf. Between 1969 and 1975 new gas prices rose by 158 percent in interstate markets, compared with 650 percent in intrastate markets [37].

The jurisdictional strategy for commitments of new gas is sharply illustrated in Table 3—10. Between 1964 and 1969, when interstate prices were close to intrastate prices, about 33 percent of the net reserve additions were dedicated to intrastate commerce. Between 1969 and 1973 over 90 percent of the net reserve additions were committed to intrastate commerce. This shift from interstate to intrastate markets represents a major reason for the shortage in interstate markets and the resulting curtailments.

Incentives to "Hold Back" Production

Not all of the possible strategic uses of the administrative process can be demonstrated as graphically as the previous one. Producers are sometimes alleged to "hold back" or delay production until regulators raise prices in the future. The incentive to do this is not difficult to describe. It is based on the pattern of regulation that the FPC has established during the 1970s in which the commission reclassifies what is known as new gas at one time to old gas later on. At any

Table 3—10. Average Annual Net Reserve Additions to Interstate and Intrastate Pipelines

Time Period	Additions to Interstate Reserves, Trillion Cubic Feet	Additions to Intrastate Reserves, Trillion Cubic Feet
1964–1969	11.4	5.6
1970–1973	0.7	8.4

Source: House of Representatives, Report No. 94–732 (94th Congress, 1st Session), p. 56.

given time the price allowed for new gas will exceed the price allowed for old gas.

Producers have probably become accustomed to this pattern during the 1970s, and may have developed the expectation that it will continue. Suppose a producer is confronted with a decision as to when to initiate production from a newly discovered reservoir. The producer may initiate production now (call it time t_1) or may elect to wait until time t_2. If he begins production now, he starts to receive revenues immediately. However, the producer expects that when time t_2 arrives, the gas will be reclassified as old gas if he begins producing at t_1. If he waits until t_2 to begin production, he expects that the gas will be classified as new gas, and the producer will receive higher revenues for each Mcf produced after t_2 as a result of his decision to wait. The basic nature of the tradeoff is clear: Does he want higher revenues later, or lower revenues beginning immediately? Since the pattern has become established in the last few years, one could not attribute any of the shortage of the early 1970s to it. However, it is quite plausible that some producers may have delayed production more recently because of this incentive, although it is difficult to say by how much.

In summary, the natural gas industry provides support for both of the major themes emphasized in Chapter 1. First, during its existence the FPC acted to resist movements away from the status quo in two important ways. It refused to regulate wellhead prices before the *Phillips* case, and after the Supreme Court told it to regulate these prices in *Phillips*, it continued to hold prices down well below market-clearing levels. In so doing, it managed to attenuate the rate at which wellhead prices would have otherwise risen in response to rapidly increasing demand and production costs.

Second, as Chapter 1 argues, given a set of rules established through the administrative process, firms act to further their own interests much as they might in unregulated markets. The diversion of gas from interstate to intrastate markets and the recent concern over incentives to hold back production emphasize this point.

THE RECENT REASSESSMENT
OF PUBLIC POLICY

It took the Federal Power Commission twenty years to travel the tortuous path from the *Phillips* decision to nationwide rate making, a procedure which was at once deemed fair and expedient. Yet only four years later, the regulation of wellhead prices continues as a highly controversial topic. There are at least two reasons for this, both emphasizing that nationwide rate making did not really resolve the problems confronting the FPC.

First, it took a crisis to point out how the FPC is cornered in its attempts to regulate wellhead prices. While the Supreme Court ordered the commission to regulate those prices in 1954, it did not tell it how, with its existing powers, to face the economic facts of life which are posed by unregulated intrastate markets.

Second, as we discussed earlier, the equity arguments are not as simple in the 1970s as the Supreme Court made them out to be in 1954. The FPC apparently interpreted "the protection of consumers against exploitation at the hands of natural-gas companies" [38] to justify, among other things, a redistribution of income from producers to consumers. But the matter is more complicated than that. There is no representative consumer. If wellhead prices are used to redistribute income to consumers who are fortunate enough to secure gas, then it must be recognized that less fortunate consumers may have to increase their expenditures by purchasing from other sources of energy.

The recent call for deregulation of wellhead prices (and there have been at least five such measures introduced in Congress in the past five years) is probably motivated less by any consideration of the potential billions of dollars of economic inefficiency caused by regulation than by the fact that regulation is no longer perceived as unambiguously benefiting "the" consumer. Those deprived of gas by the shortage, while not necessarily consumers of gas now, are nonetheless consumers in the broader sense.

Some Alternative Measures

Although many alternatives and variations of alternatives have been suggested in addressing the shortage, they can be classified in four major categories:

1. Continue wellhead price regulation in the present manner (a status quo alternative)
2. Strengthen regulation of wellhead prices
3. Deregulate both old and new gas prices
4. Deregulate new gas prices, but maintain regulation of old gas prices.

The expected consequences of a continuation of the status quo have been discussed earlier in this chapter, so they will only be summarized here. The shortage in the interstate market will continue as long as wellhead prices are held below their market clearing levels.

Producers will continue to dedicate new reserves to intrastate markets, thereby exacerbating the shortage. Consumers fortunate enough to be able to purchase gas will effectively receive a redistribution of income, perhaps amounting to billions of dollars annually (this depends on the levels of prices chosen by the commission). Consumers unable to purchase gas even though they would like to do so will be forced to buy expensive alternative fuels, representing a redistribution of income away from them (perhaps also amounting to billions of dollars per year). Finally, overall economic welfare (as measured by the sum of consumer and producer surplus) will be held down; although quantitative estimates are difficult to make, as MacAvoy suggests, the inefficiency could amount to billions of dollars per year.

Strengthened Regulation

Two main kinds of strengthened regulation can be proposed for wellhead markets. One involves a continued regulation of wellhead prices in interstate markets, with an announced policy of only minimal price increases over time to adjust for rising costs of production. This could be accomplished with no new legislation under existing powers of the FERC. A second and more sweeping alternative would expand the power of the FERC to include control over wellhead prices in markets now beyond its jurisdiction, the intrastate gas markets. While this alternative may very well be unconstitutional, it is mentioned here because there is a real doubt that strengthened regulation of only interstate markets would be able to eliminate the shortage in those markets.

The probable consequences of the first alternative can be predicted as follows, based on earlier parts of this chapter. If the demand for gas continues to grow and intrastate markets remain unregulated, ever-increasing amounts of gas will be diverted from interstate markets to intrastate markets. Suppliers in gas producing states will continue to dedicate new reserves to intrastate markets whenever they can.

It is true that an announced hard line policy on price increases would remove the expectation that producers may have regarding future price increases, and this may in turn discourage speculative delays in production, as discussed above. However, this effect would most likely be very small relative to the major effect which channels reserves away from interstate markets. If reserves dedicated to interstate markets continue to dwindle, the issue of delayed production could become not only secondary, but moot.

Regarding the redistribution of income, the effects described under a continuation of the status quo would continue. The distinction between "fortunate" and "unfortunate" consumers would remain important. Interstate customers fortunate enough to get gas will effectively receive an income transfer from producers.

If the regulation of interstate prices continues, the difference between interstate and intrastate prices may increase, which may tend to make the transfer look larger. However, it is not clear that the quantity of gas sold in interstate markets will increase or even remain as large as it is if new gas reserves are not dedicated to interstate commerce. If the dedicated reserves decline over the long term, then the effective income redistribution may not increase at all, or it may even decrease.

The efficiency loss due to regulation follows the same general description explained above, under "Some Consequences of Wellhead Price Regulation." If increasing numbers of potential gas customers are excluded from the market because of a shortage, the efficiency loss in interstate markets (which may already be in the billions of dollars each year) can only be expected to increase in interstate markets.

Putting aside the question of constitutionality, it is of interest to ask what might happen if FPC jurisdiction were extended to intrastate wellhead markets. One of the major effects would be the ending of the special access conditions users in gas producing states presently have.

For the sake of argument, suppose that wellhead prices were equal everywhere under regulation, and that this were accomplished by bringing down intrastate prices from their present market clearing levels to the level of an interstate price. Producers would then have no price incentive to keep gas within any geographical region. If new reserves were discovered they would be as likely to be sold to one pipeline as to another.

The short-term picture for this alternative is not a clear one without further description of the plan's implementation. Perhaps a reasonable assumption is that existing intrastate contracts would be left in force until their expiration dates, after which renegotiated contracts would occur at a regulated price set by the FPC. Assume also that all new contracts occur at a regulated price, and, to make the picture as simple as possible, that there is no distinction between old and new gas.

If such a plan were implemented now, one would expect a shortage to develop over all wellhead markets in the long run. As lower prices take effect in previously intrastate markets, producers in those markets would experience reduced incentives to explore for and develop new fields. Gas production which was profitable at the higher prices would no longer remain so at the lower regulated price. It is only reasonable to expect some reduction in production. Yet at the lower prices, the quantity of gas demanded can be expected to increase.

If the interstate and intrastate markets were consolidated by extended regulation, then the wellhead market could be described as in Figure 3−1. The regulated price would presumably be below the market clearing price under this proposal, so it would not be surprising at all to see a gas shortage for the consolidated market, just as there is now in the interstate market.

The income redistribution and efficiency loss effects are similar to those just described for strengthened regulation of interstate prices, so they will not be repeated here. Some consumers will be able to get gas and will benefit from a redistribution of income, and other consumers may be hurt because they will be forced to use expensive alternatives. In short, an extension of regulation to intrastate markets, with price held below its market clearing level, cannot be expected to eliminate the shortage.

Deregulation of Old and New Gas Prices

Perhaps the strongest attraction of this alternative is that natural gas would be allocated efficiently in wellhead markets with total deregulation of wellhead prices. The wellhead price of gas would adjust so that the quantity of gas demanded just equals the quantity of gas supplied, i.e., there is no shortage of gas.

This old and basic story is one often told by economists to explain how the price system works admirably in allocating resources in so many markets. However, it is based on some basic assumptions which must be satisfied in order for the market to maximize net benefits. One of the important assumptions is that peoples' incomes are distributed in a reasonable way. If some people need gas very much, but have insufficient incomes to pay high prices for it, then the government may find it necessary to take action in order to get more purchasing power into their hands. There are several ways to do this. First, the government could provide transfer payments to supplement the income of persons deemed needy. The transfer payments could take the form of direct cash payment, or it might be in the form of a certificate good toward the purchase of an important commodity, in this case, natural gas. (Welfare economists point out that it is usually better to give the cash grant rather than a certificate of equivalent dollar value which must be used in the purchase of a specific commodity, but that is a secondary concern at this point.) The important point is that with transfer payments to redistribute purchasing power to those who are deemed needy, the market place can then be relied on to allocate resources efficiently while the needy consumers are treated "fairly."

Maintain Control Over Old Gas Prices

In the case of natural gas, there is concern that total deregulation would create billions of dollars of windfall profits on gas produced from reservoirs already in production. There are several parts to the argument that old gas should not be deregulated, even if new gas is deregulated.

First, it is contended that producers must be earning at least normal profits from their production of old gas, given their decisions to undertake production at regulated prices. If this gas were deregulated, its price would undoubtedly rise substantially when present contracts for old gas expire and new contracts are negotiated. To get a rough idea of the potential magnitude of windfall profits if old gas prices were deregulated, we note that almost all (over 90 percent) of the income redistribution estimated for interstate consumers as a result of regulation would be added to producer profits, and this was approximated at over $3 billion for 1975 (above, page 83). The amount could be higher if the average price of old gas rises by more than $1 per Mcf with deregulation.

In addition to eliminating enormous windfall profits for producers, we must ask what other consequences are likely to follow if regulation is continued for old gas. The definition of "new gas" will make a difference in at least two important ways. First, if new gas is deregulated it would appear desirable to set a date once and for all to define old and new gas. If the FPC continues to move the date along, reclassifying what was once new gas now as old gas subject to ceiling prices, it will create an incentive for producers to delay production from new reservoirs, just as it has done in its present practice (discussed above). If a permanent delineation date is announced, then prices received for old gas, even though they might be lower than new gas prices, should not have any significant effect on producer decisions to supply new gas.

Second, the definition of new gas should not permit producers to drill new wells in old gas reservoirs and then enable the gas from the new wells to be sold as new gas. This obvious loophole should be closed so that producers do not receive windfall profits on old gas.

If these two basic rules are followed, then it seems reasonable to expect producers to have the same incentives to explore for and develop new gas as they would if old gas prices were deregulated, and the windfall profits can be avoided. It may still be possible to allocate resources efficiently if old gas prices are regulated.

However, there remains an important consideration to be addressed if an efficient allocation of gas is to be achieved, namely, the price consumers actually pay for gas. One possibility would be to have consumers pay a weighted average price for gas, i.e., the price of old gas times the percentage of old gas in the stream (assuming only one vintage of old gas) plus the price of new gas times the percentage of new gas in the stream. Unfortunately, this will not lead to an efficient allocation of resources. Some consumers who would not be willing to pay as much as the true marginal cost of gas would nevertheless buy gas because the weighted average is less than the cost of the additional gas produced.

The efficiency loss under this arrangement would no doubt be less than the efficiency loss under the present system of regulation. This primarily results from the fact that with deregulated new gas prices, everyone willing to pay the marginal cost of gas will get it, and this is not true of the present system in which some people are deprived even though they may value gas much more than its marginal cost.

However, as shown above, some inefficiency would still exist. One way to eliminate the inefficiency is as follows. Place a tax on the consumption of gas, where the value of the tax per Mcf, plus the average weighted price of the gas stream equals the price of new gas determined in the market place. This would accomplish three things:

1. The price paid by the consumer would equal the marginal cost of gas, and thus the allocation of resources would be efficient. Wasteful uses of gas at lower prices would be discouraged.
2. Producer windfall profits from old gas would be averted.
3. The tax collected from consumption of old gas could be returned to consumers by a reduction in their social security tax (or some other tax). Thus consumers would receive the benefits of a lower price on old gas, but not by distorting the price paid for gas away from its marginal cost.

In closing, we should recognize that deregulation of wellhead prices might very well create an additional administrative problem for regulators in one of their other activities, the regulation of natural gas pipelines. There is concern over the fact that in many cases pipelines and producers are affiliated with one another, i.e., they are vertically integrated. Even if pipelines continue to be regulated as they presently are (except for wellhead price deregulation), and even if a producer delivering gas to an affiliated pipeline is surrounded by other competing producers, there is reason to be wary. If pipeline regulators are not observant, a producer could conceivably charge a higher than competitive wellhead price to its affiliated pipeline, thereby making excessive profits from its production activities. The pipeline might in turn try to pass the excessive prices it pays for gas through to its customers as a cost it has incurred. Note that even competitive wellhead markets would not eliminate the incentives for this strategic use of the administrative process.

One possible solution to this problem is to eliminate vertical integration of this sort. Perhaps pipelines could have producer affiliates, but not in the same wellhead markets in which the pipeline buys. Alternatively, vertical integration might be allowed if the pipeline regulator could recognize and disallow any excessively high prices charged by a producer affiliate, i.e., prices which exceed the competitive levels of nonaffiliated producers. The drawback here is evident. A regulator would have to be very watchful, and the task would not be easy since gas delivery contracts can be quite complicated. There is a lesson in this: Deregulation of one type of activity may create incentives for a strategic use of the administrative process elsewhere.

Chapter 4

Regulation of Service Industries: Real Estate Brokers and Title Insurers

INTRODUCTION

The economic analysis in this chapter is based on work that was directed to a rather obscure policy question: Should the California Department of Insurance allow real estate brokers to sell title insurance? [1] Examination of this narrow issue, however, leads to a fascinating story of regulation and competition at work in two quite different service industries. After we have told that story, we will try to draw from it some morals that are related to the ideas put forward in Chapter 1.

We will be dealing with three distinct but interrelated markets. The first is the market for residential real estate in a local area. The second is the market for the services of real estate brokers. The third is the market for various services that are required in order to complete a real estate transaction, especially title insurance. The first market is a traditional one, in the sense that the commodity (housing) is tangible, and there are many buyers and many sellers. The other two markets are essentially markets for information or transactional services.

The vast majority of residential real estate transactions in California involve the use of real estate brokers, title companies, and escrow companies. Unlike other states, attorneys are almost never involved in California residential real estate transactions. We shall loosely call brokerage, title insurance, and escrow "conveyancing services."

Information plays a crucial role in the market for real property and in the market for transactional services incidental to real property transfers. First, real estate brokers and title companies supply information about the housing market and about the quality of individual properties. The absence of such information might result in a much less efficient housing market, or even in the nonexistence of a housing market. Thus, the existence of these firms promotes efficiency in the quantitatively much more important market for housing. But, second, consumers are extremely unsophisticated buyers of conveyancing services. The average consumer buys a home only infrequently. Knowing that one wants to buy brokerage and title services is not the same as knowing which firms offer which combinations of price and quality. Moreover, the demand for some conveyancing services is dictated not by the buyer but by the lender.

Real estate brokerage services are demanded for the same reason that securities market brokerage services are demanded: in order to obtain access to the organized information structure of a market. Title services are also demanded because of the need to acquire information, in this case highly specialized information, about the "quality" of the product being purchased. The same comment applies to structural pest control inspections and the like. Buyers of asset commodities whose value is large relative to their portfolios are willing to pay something to reduce their uncertainty about the true value of the commodity. Of course, some risks will remain: risks which cannot be reduced because the required information costs more than the buyer's prior estimation of its expected value. An example might be the risk of natural hazards such as floods, earthquakes, and storms. Such risks can be and are insured against.

Home buyers and sellers who have a demand for conveyancing service must decide which firm to select to provide the services. They therefore will have a further demand for information about these services and their providers. In the context of a real estate transaction, the ready source of such information is the broker, who is the agent either of the buyer or the seller or both. The acquisition of information about conveyancing services from other sources is likely to be difficult, time consuming, and therefore potentially expensive since it threatens the likelihood of the principal bargain in question. Consumers will therefore tend to take their broker's advice on such questions, particularly since they may perceive him as a fiduciary, working in their interest. Thus, the common observation that brokers "control" the market for title insurance, escrow services, and related ancillary services. Brokers "control" the market because they are the cheapest source of information about the market, from the point of view of buyers. Thus, brokers can "direct" business to the title and escrow companies of their choice. Naturally, each such company tries to persuade brokers to direct business to it, and there is an incentive to "persuade" by offering kickbacks or other favors of economic value. The payment of kickbacks is the most effective way for title or escrow companies to compete with each other.

The California market for conveyancing services is highly developed compared to that in most other states. In some states virtually all such services are provided by a single agent—the broker, an attorney, or the bank [2]. By contrast, California has developed an industry in which individual firms specialize in particular services. There are separate brokers, title companies, escrow companies, and so on. Critics of the California system, such as the authors of the "HUD/VA Report" [3], argue that this high degree of specialization results in increased costs to consumers. Because there are more people involved in any given transaction, costs must be higher. The "HUD/VA Report" suggests costs are lower in, say, Denver, because there the broker routinely handles a number of transactions which in California are performed by firms specialized in escrow, title insurance, and other ancillary matters. But if this were the case, it would pay real estate brokers or others to offer such package services in California, thereby gaining a competitive edge in listings. Specialization can exist, in normal circumstances, only because it reduces costs. Thus, regional differentials in closing costs must be explained by other factors, or at least by some extraordinary pathology of the California market.

The prohibition of kickbacks and rebates by federal and state authorities [4] has resulted in a trend toward integration of function and, in particular, a trend toward real estate broker entry into the title insurance business. Those who regard specialization as the source of excessive closing costs should welcome this trend. But we shall argue below that the move away from specialization may actually reduce the efficiency of the conveyancing services market and raise prices to consumers.

Suppliers of conveyancing services find it difficult to compete (easy to collude) with each other in price because consumers are insensitive to and largely unaware of price differentials. Therefore, given a mechanism to control entry, such firms may be able to cartelize prices. But competition among these firms can take place in the form of rebates for brokers. We would expect such rebates, if legal, to reduce profits to normal levels in the supplying industry. Moreover, provided that brokers are competitive in prices, the full benefits of rebate competition will be passed on to consumers in the form of lower broker's fees. (The issue is more complicated if brokers do not compete in price, the actual case.) A legal prohibition on the payment of rebates will tend to induce integration of brokers with suppliers of other conveyancing services so that rebates can be paid as legal internal payments. This has the effect of eliminating the efficient division of labor in the market, with the result that costs to consumers will be increased.

TITLE INSURANCE

The legal conditions surrounding the ownership of land are unlike those affecting any other asset. The unique and often intricate legal factors involved in the possession and conveyancing of real property often make it difficult to determine whether an individual truly has a valid claim of ownership on any given parcel. The basic purpose of title insurance is to protect against the uncertainty inherent in land ownership. It does this in two ways. First, title insurance guarantees the accuracy of an abstract of title prepared (by the insurer or his agent) at the time of sale. Defects in title discovered at that time and disclosed in the abstract are usually *not* insured against. Second, title insurance protects against certain valid but unrecorded defects in the title, such as unrecorded mechanic's liens. The second function is relatively minor, but accounts for the bulk of the losses of insurers. Losses are generally less than 10 percent of revenues. Thus title insurers are mainly in the business of producing information, the "insurance" being a formal acknowledgment of strict liability for inaccuracies. Alternatively, a title insurance policy can be viewed as a service offered with an associated warranty: the title search is the service and the insurance policy warrants its accuracy.

Real property is extraordinarily valuable. Most individuals will own only one piece of real property at a time and that property will be the most significant investment of their lives—their home. Thus it is understandable that purchasers desire to protect their investment against any legal defects which might cause them to lose their most valuable investment. The need for such protection was recognized in England over four centuries ago. At the time there were difficulties with fraudulent land transactions in which unscrupulous persons would sell the same parcel of land to two or more buyers. In order to protect against such fraud in conveyancing, the Statute of Enrollments was passed in 1536. The statute instituted a public recording system which would keep track of all bargain and sale deeds so that prospective purchasers could determine whether the seller had previously transferred the same parcel. Thus, even in its earliest form the major aim of land recording was the protection of subsequent purchasers through the provision of information.

The practice of recordation has become widespread in the United States. Recordation has also expanded to cover a variety of interests in and claims against real property—not just bargain and sale deeds. Technology has also had an impact, and computerized land record systems can be found in many locations. But the practice and detail of land recordation is hardly uniform. Though all fifty states have recording statutes there are substantial differences in state laws.

California operates under a race-notice recording system. Under such a system the first bona fide purchaser of a property who is without notice of a prior conveyance or encumbrance gains a valid claim on the land. The rationale for such a procedure is twofold: (1) to provide a strong incentive for bona fide purchasers of property to immediately record their claims so as to place any potential future purchaser on notice of their claim; and (2) to provide a strong incentive for any purchaser to check land records to ensure that the seller has a valid interest in the land in question.

Each county in California has a recording office where property owners can record instruments affecting the title to real property. These instruments are generally kept in grantor-grantee indexes. When a transaction is completed the deed recording that transaction will be entered twice—once under the name of the grantee who acquires the property and once under the name of the grantor who sells the property. Thus, to trace the ownership of a parcel a prospective purchaser or his agent may check the grantee index until he finds the instrument by which the seller acquired title. The seller's previous grantor can then be traced through the grantee index and the process may be repeated as long as desired, or until the source of original title, a government patent, is reached. Furthermore, the name of each owner in the chain of title may be searched in the grantor index subsequent to the date of acquisition to determine whether there were any additional instruments affecting his interest in the property. Individuals who are not purchasing land but who are considering acquiring an interest in a parcel (e.g., a mortgage institution, or a purchaser of an easement) also check land records in order to safeguard their own interests.

Title Insurers

Though recordation is intricate and seems inclusive, it is not foolproof. There are times when it fails to place a prospective purchaser on actual notice of a claim against property. The failure may be a result of the structure of the records themselves, loopholes in recordation laws which allow certain interests against land to be valid and binding in spite of the fact that they are unrecorded, or an oversight in the tedious process of checking land records. Though prospective purchasers of land and their mortgage institutions often desire title information that can be obtained from land records, they are almost universally unequipped to gather the information themselves. A great number of records must be searched and interpreted and a certain amount of expertise is necessary to perform this function effectively. It is at this stage that title insurance companies enter the picture and provide two distinct services: (1) title information describing the results of their search through land record data (usually in the form of an abstract of title); and (2) title insurance designed to compensate the policyholder in the event he loses all or part of title to his property as a result of circumstances covered by the policy. Since title companies usually provide both search and insurance services to their customers it is easy to lose sight of the fact that title insurers perform these two distinct functions. The preparation of an abstract is an information function, and title insurers can be described as producers of information. The insurance function is partly true insurance and partly a guarantee or indemnity covering the accuracy of the information provided. To the extent that the purpose of the exercise is primarily the production of accurate information, title insurers are misnamed. They are not insurance companies in the standard sense, though they do write what amount to casualty policies for unrecorded defects, such as mechanic's liens.

There are a variety of methods of title search presently being used in the United States, but in California use of private title plants is predominant. These title plants contain the information found in the public recorder's office but indexed and stored in a manner which makes a title search easier to complete.

Title companies have four alternative ways to gain access to a private title plant. If a title company has been in operation in a certain county for a long period it will have accumulated a large set of title abstracts for its past customers. Firms which are relatively new in an area and attempting to enter a market may construct a title plant from scratch by examining and indexing information contained in the county recorder's office. Title firms with existing title plants will occasionally work out sharing arrangements with other title insurers. Under these arrangements the other title insurers pay the owner of the plant for shared use of the facility. Finally, a firm may acquire a title plant simply by purchasing a copy of a title plant already in existence.

One obvious problem with the title plant system is that it involves potentially inefficient duplication of records. If official records were integrated, properly indexed, and accessible, there would be no need for the private title plants which duplicate each other and the public records. Duplicate private plants may have been necessary in the days when manual record-keeping led to congestion problems if too many people tried to gain access to a single index at once. But computerized systems eliminate this problem. Table 4–1 shows, for selected California counties, the number of duplicate plants. Based on very rough cost data, it seems that elimination of private duplication might save the industry in California up to $14 million per year. If elimination of the county recorder function is added to this, an additional $11 million per year might be saved [5]. These numbers, however, are a very small fraction of total conveyancing costs.

Duplicate title plants grew up because of the unwillingness of incumbent and possibly monopoly firms, in any county, to allow entrants to share the plant. To do so would be to increase competition, and, prior to electronic technology, to increase plant congestion problems. Plant sharing is now on the increase in California, probably because there are now so many plants in some counties that the incumbent firms are competing for new partners to share the overhead costs of the plants.

The title search function is not completed simply by collecting and abstracting all relevant documents. These documents must then be examined and considered in light of California law in order to determine their implications. This "opinion" aspect of title search is critical: it affects the willingness of the insurer to insure against certain potential defects and may well influence a potential purchaser not to acquire a parcel because of associated title problems.

Economic Structure of Title Insurance Industry

There are two types of title insurance company in California: underwriters and underwritten agencies. The former provide the full range of title insurance services, operate statewide or nationally, and are subject to more or less standard insurance company regulations. Underwritten title companies may be no more than agents for underwriters, receiving a commission for each sale. However, some underwritten companies own title plants and provide abstracting services themselves. Underwritten companies are typically but not universally limited to a single county. Capital and licensing requirements for underwritten companies are much less strict than those applying to underwriters. Until recently underwriters doing business directly with the public wrote the vast majority of title insurance in California. But there has been recent rapid growth in the market share of

Table 4–1. Title Companies and Plants, Selected California Counties

County	No. of Companies	No. of Plants	No. of Companies Owning Plants*	No. of Companies Leasing Plant Services	No. of Companies Searching Ct'y Records
Alameda	8	4	6	1	1
Contra Costa	9	4	8	1	0
Fresno	7	2	2	5	0
Kern	7	2	2	3	2
L.A.	13	4	8	5	0
Marin	7	7	7	0	0
Orange	15	8	8	7	0
Placer	5	4	4	1	0
Riverside	10	5	5	5	0
Sacramento	7	6	6	1	0
San Bernadino	8	4	4	2	2
San Diego	12	5	5	6	1
San Francisco	10	7	7	0	3
San Mateo	9	3	8	0	1
Santa Clara	13	3	12	0	1
Solano	7	7	7	0	0
Sonoma	8	5	5	1	2
Yolo	4	4	4	0	0

Source: B.M. Owen and J. Grundfest, "Licensing Brokers as Underwritten Title Agents," Stanford Economics Dept., 1976, Table 8, p. 47.
*Including partial or joint ownership.

underwritten companies, particularly those owned by real estate brokers.

The California title insurance industry is best characterized as an oligopoly. A few large firms have most of the market (see Table 4—2). There exist barriers to entry in the form of licensing requirements (including capital costs) and in the form of relatively high costs of initiating a title plant, if a sharing arrangement can not be obtained.

Every oligopoly has an incentive to try to achieve some sort of collusive solution to the problem of competition, but each firm in a cartel also has an incentive to "cheat" on the agreement if it can do so without excessive risk of retaliation. Depending on the nature of the industry, these forces will balance each other in varying degrees.

In the case of title insurance, the opportunity for collusion or competition is present along several dimensions. The first is price. The second is quality of service. The third is what we shall loosely characterize as "marketing practices." Successful collusion is most likely to take place in dimensions where information about other firms' activities is easily obtained [6]. It is less likely to be successful in dimensions not highly visible to other firms. In the title industry, prices are public by law, and deviations from published rate schedules are illegal. Moreover, price cuts would be unlikely to increase market share significantly because consumers do not appear to be vigorous price shoppers. It is therefore not surprising to find that the prices charged for this service are highly uniform among companies, and that "price wars" and similar price competition are virtually unknown.

The industry may reasonably be assumed to have achieved a stable cartel arrangement as to prices in spite of the highly cyclical nature

Table 4—2. Market Shares of Largest California Title Insurers, 1969—74
(Estimated Percentage Share of California Revenues)

Year	TI*	Safeco	First American	Trans America	Total Top 4
1969	36	15	5	8	64
1970	33	17	6	9	65
1971	33	18	7	9	67
1972	31	16	7	7	61
1973	30	17	7	8	62
1974	30	25	10	8	73

Source: Annual Reports of the California Commissioner of Insurance.
*Title Insurance and Trust.

of demand generated by fluctuations in the housing market. The strength of this arrangement is underscored by the successful maintenance of what is apparently price discrimination in the rate structure.[a]

It is more difficult to characterize quality of service. Presumably this would include the promptness of the firms in responding to orders. But the most important dimension of service quality—the accuracy of reports and the solvency of the insurance operation—is not readily evaluated by consumers, and indeed the first is insured and the second regulated for this reason. Significant opportunities for competition in this dimension are therefore likely to be absent, even though collusion is more difficult.

Competition in "marketing practices" for market share has, until recently, taken the form of competition for referrals by real estate brokers and lending institutions. This competition took the form of various devices amounting to commissions paid for such referrals [7]. Such payments are difficult for the industry to police, and information about payments by one firm (partly because they are illegal) is inaccessible to its competitors. As a result, one would expect vigorous competition in this dimension, competition perhaps sufficiently vigorous to reduce title industry profits to competitive levels despite price collusion.

Any cartel faced with such a problem has only one option—to seek government intervention making this form of competition illegal, and subject to penalties [8]. For this reason and others, such payments are now in fact illegal, under the terms of RESPA, state law, and the regulations of the California Department of Insurance. One would expect such legal prohibitions to increase industry profits by ending the most likely avenue of competitive activity.

At present, the major source of market discipline in the title insurance industry is the prospect of new entrants' obtaining significant shares of the market. However, the share and identities of the top underwriters have remained highly stable over the past ten years (see Table 4–2). One reason for this is the relatively high capital cost of entry on a significant scale, occasioned by regulatory requirements and the requisite title plant in each county. There has, however, been an increase in the market share of "foreign" (out-of-state) title insurers, operating through underwritten title companies. Stewart, TI of Minnesota, and Chicago have obtained fairly significant market shares by underwriting or even helping to organize broker-controlled title companies. Some "domestic" (California-based) underwriters have followed.

---

[a]Rates are roughly proportional to insured value; costs are not.

Broker-controlled title companies have been in existence for many years. However, in recent years there have been two developments which have brought the problem of controlled business to a head. First, the market share of broker-controlled firms has been rapidly increasing. Second, individual brokerage houses, sometimes with statewide operations, have been applying for licenses to begin underwritten companies. Previously, such firms were owned by groups of broker-stockholders, each of whom might have a relatively small stake in the operation. This new entry is presumably partly the result of the antirebate reforms.

Thus, the incentive to form broker-controlled underwritten title companies comes both from brokers seeking to escape the antirebate regulations and from title underwriters who are seeking to increase their market shares. The result is a rather dramatic increase in the proportion of business done by broker-controlled underwritten title companies. This proportion grew from 10.2 percent in 1970 to 18.3 percent in 1975, in the eleven largest California counties. Applications to form such companies were backlogged at the Department of Insurance in 1975 and 1976, including one by a large statewide realty company, Coldwell-Banker. The applications were opposed by the California Land Title Association.

One key to the success of collusive arrangements in the title industry is the means of information and coordination provided by regulation and the cooperation of county recorders. County recorders supply title companies with compilations of the number of documents filed by company—a kind of daily cartel score sheet. Regulation, of course, provides a nexus of coordination in price setting by requiring public filing of rates and by making deviations from the published schedule illegal. A customer who attempts to bargain over title prices will be told that it is illegal for the company to offer him a lower price.

The Structure of Rates

A glance at the data on title insurance rates (Tables 4–3 and 4–4) reveals a number of interesting phenomena. First, prices in this industry are and for the last ten years have been highly uniform across companies. Second, rates have been highly stable; 1975 rates are only 14 percent higher than 1965 prices. Third, rates vary with the liability of the policy (the purchase price of the property), even though there is little relationship between cost and liability.

The uniformity of rates is one piece of evidence suggesting that the industry sets prices collusively, or possibly by a system of price leadership. The stability of prices is not surprising because the rate schedule has built-in inflation protection. As the cost of living rises,

Table 4–3. California Title Insurance Prices, 1975*

Coverage	American	Lawyers	Trans-America	Safeco	TI**	Chicago	F.A.
10,000	104.75	104.75	104.75	104.25	117.50	117.50	104.75
20,000	147.25	147.25	147.25	147.25	152.50	152.50	147.25
30,000	189.75	189.75	189.75	189.75	195.00	195.00	189.75
40,000	222.25	222.25	222.25	222.25	227.50	227.50	222.25
60,000	287.25	287.25	287.25	287.25	292.50	292.50	287.25
80,000	347.25	347.25	347.25	347.25	352.50	352.50	347.25
100,000	407.25	407.25	407.25	407.25	432.50	432.50	407.25

Source: Rate schedules on file with the California Department of Insurance.
*Basic Title Insurance Rate A—without escrow service.
**Title Insurance and Trust.

Table 4-4. **Rate for $25,000 Liability Standard Coverage Homeowner's Policy in Southern California**

Year	*Rate in Effect for Most of Year (Deviations Noted)*				
	Trans-America	*Safeco*	*First American*[g]	*TI*[h]	*Western*[g]
1965	147.00	157.75[c]	147.00	147.00[i]	147.00
1966	147.00	157.75[d]	147.00	147.00	154.75
1967	147.00	157.75[d]	147.00	157.75[j]	157.75
1968	157.75[a]	157.75	157.75	157.75	157.75
1969	157.75	157.75	157.75	157.75	157.75
1970	157.75	157.75	157.75	157.75	157.75
1971	168.50[b]	168.50[e]	168.50	168.75[k]	167.75
1972	168.50	168.50	168.50	168.75	167.75
1973	168.50	168.50	168.50	168.75	167.75
1974	168.50	168.50[f]	168.50	168.75	167.75
1975	168.50	168.50	168.50	168.75[l]	167.75

Source: Data supplied by firms.
a. Effective 1/23/68.
b. Effective 3/1/71.
c. Effective 2/1/65.
d. Price increased to 220.00 from 9/28/66 to 1/18/67.
e. Effective 6/1/71.
f. Price increased to 187.05 from 5/1/74 to 7/26/74.
g. Effective dates not supplied; presumably year-end rates.
h. Los Angeles and Orange counties.
i. Effective 2/1/65.
j. Effective 1/15/67.
k. Effective 5/10/71.
l. Raised to 173.75 effective 8/11/75.

property values increase and so does premium revenue. Indeed, the fact that there has been a 14 percent rate *schedule* increase means that title insurance for a given piece of property may have risen in price by as much or more than the cost of living. For instance, title *rates* have increased by about 14 percent between 1965 and 1975, while the average residential home price in Los Angeles increased 38 percent over the same period. Thus average title *prices* have increased by 52 percent. Finally, it appears that the rate schedule embodies price discrimination, a practice which would be very difficult to maintain on an industrywide level if there were price competition. Firms that were competing in price would tend to bid down the price of the highly profitable larger policies, and would be reluctant to offer the low face-value policies that are relatively unprofitable at present prices.

Title Insurance and Antitrust Law

Prior to 1944 it was held by the Supreme Court that the business of insurance did not fall within the realm of interstate commerce that could be validly regulated by the federal government, and thus insurers were immune from federal antitrust laws. Then in 1944 the Supreme Court, noting the widespread nature of the insurance business, reversed itself and found that insurance could in many instances be considered interstate commerce within the scope of federal jurisdiction and thus fully subject to federal antitrust regulation [9].

The insurance industry then prevailed upon Congress to pass the McCarran-Ferguson Act [10] which effectively allowed state regulation to supersede federal regulation of the insurance industry. In California it was recently decided that title insurance is insurance within the meaning of the McCarran-Ferguson Act and that sufficient state regulation exists to exempt the title insurance industry from the Sherman Act [11]. Thus, basic antitrust regulation of the insurance industry must originate from the state, not the federal, level. As "insurance" companies, title insurers are immune from federal antitrust law.

Regulation of title insurers in California takes the form of capitalization and reserve requirements. The insurance commissioner has the power to set minimum and maximum rates, but does not do so. However, all rates must be publicly filed with the commissioner, changes must be on thirty-day notice, and deviations from published rates are illegal.

The California supreme court has considered the question of whether insurance companies charged with antitrust violations are to be judged under the standards of the Cartwright Act, California's general antitrust law, or under the more specific standards of the Insurance Code. The court decided that the Cartwright Act is "expressly superseded and contravened by the *specific provision* of the Insurance Code" [12]. [Emphasis added.]

However, insurance companies are not wholly immune from antitrust attack under the Cartwright Act. Only insofar as the alleged antitrust violations "clearly concern the regulation of rates charged by title insurers and title companies, and rate regulation has traditionally commanded administrative expertise applied to controlled industries" [13] will the allegations be weighed under the provisions of the Insurance Code and not under the Cartwright Act. But it is not clear what sort of antitrust action should be brought against title companies, if any. There is little doubt that title companies do not compete in price. Given the nature of consumer behavior, there is also little reason to suppose that title companies need to work very hard at maintaining an implicitly collusive price structure. Collusion is aided by the use of a price structure, which is a rate schedule, rather than negotiated prices, and by the legal prohibition on departures from published rates. The industry's main concern in the price dimension must be to avoid setting prices so high as to attract entry. It cannot be said that they have been successful in this regard. Efforts by these firms to eliminate rebate competition have presumably been successful. However, given the anxiousness of brokers to form underwritten title companies, it would be difficult or impossible to force them to compete in the price dimension, particularly if present regulatory policies remain intact. Structural relief is not relevant to the problem. Of course, price competition could have a beneficial effect on those consumers who *are* inclined to shop, and it is possible that the number of such consumers might eventually be significantly large. But this benefit may not be sufficiently large to justify the effort of an antitrust action. On the other hand, the antitrust immunity afforded by the McCarren Act has little social benefit in the case of title insurance. Even though the threat of antitrust action may not be a very effective spur to price competition, it can hardly hurt.

Conclusions

The title insurance industry has taken good advantage of its antitrust exemption, its natural immunity to price competition (resulting from consumer insensitivity to prices for this service), and of the benefits of regulation. Vigilant enforcement of the rebate law by the Department of Insurance ensures that the most likely nonprice mechanism of competition is suppressed. The public filing of rates and the illegality of deviation from published rates is sufficient in this industry to eliminate price competition. The title companies continue to compete in quality dimensions and in sales effort. Entry is not terribly difficult, especially for established out of state firms. Indeed it is unlikely that title insurance companies earn excessive profits, although the official data do not permit this issue to be addressed. Whether or not profits are high, the structure of the industry is consistent with the existence of excess capacity and therefore excessive costs, leading to economic inefficiency. The rebate prohibitions give title insurers an incentive to assist brokers in forming underwritten title companies so that rebates can be paid legally, in the form of commissions.

BROKERS

Real estate brokers are primarily in the business of providing information about the housing market and of "making the market" for such property. The seller of a home lists it with a broker because prospective buyers are apt to contact brokers. Brokers know what homes are for sale, and have expert knowledge of the market. Brokers themselves pool their housing market information by forming "multiple listing service" (MLS) organizations. Each broker-member of an MLS knows what properties are for sale through each other member, and is free to try to sell those properties and share in the commission at a rate offered by the listing broker. Prospective sellers and buyers both must go to a member broker in order to gain access to the organized information structure of the market. Real estate brokers are, in this respect, performing the same function as stockbrokers with stock exchange seats.

Consumers are likely to regard the real estate broker as a professional or "expert" with specialized knowledge of the housing market and of the conveyancing process. Reliance on brokers may be especially important in the California market where lawyers are rarely involved in the transaction. Moreover, since the broker is the agent of the seller or the buyer or both, and has certain fiduciary duties to each, consumers are likely to listen to their broker's advice on technical matters incidental to the transaction. Among these matters is the selection of a title insurance company, an escrow company, a termite inspector, and possibly even a lending institution. The natural tendency of consumers to listen to their broker on such matters is no doubt reinforced by the pace and timing of real estate transactions, where one or both parties may often feel under considerable pressure of time. The "purchase agreement," which both parties sign when an offer is accepted, typically sets forth the names of particular firms which will perform the above-mentioned services. Brokers generally supply standard-form purchase agreements for their clients; sometimes these are preprinted with the names of particular title companies, escrow companies, and so on.

In California, brokers are licensed by the State Department of Real Estate, after satisfying certain educational requirements and passing an examination. As is true of occupational licensure generally, this tends to restrict supply [14]. Nevertheless there are thousands of brokers in major California cities (many of them part-time or inactive), and with access to an MLS, each can supply consumers with relevant information about the local market.[b] Such an industry is monopolistically competitive. One would expect such firms to

---

[b]In 1976 California had about 72,000 licensed brokers and about 171,000 licensed salespersons, not all active. In San Francisco, there were 186 licensees per square mile!

compete in prices and in quality of service. One would not expect to find uniform prices since competition should result in lower fees for houses that were relatively easy to sell, and higher fees charged by brokers with relatively greater skill in selling.

It is therefore surprising to find that brokerage fees are highly uniform. A random sample of 622 residential real estate closing statements from twelve different institutions in California in 1976 revealed that 75 percent of all transactions involved 6 percent brokers' commissions. Eighty-four percent of the new residential listings in San Francisco for the week of May 31, 1976, were at 6 percent, and the balance were either at 7 percent or on a scale which gave 6 percent on the first $50,000, 5 percent on the second $50,000, and 2½ percent commission on the balance of the purchase price over $100,000. Of nearly 22,000 residential listings sampled from the multiple listing books of the San Diego Board of Realtors over the period January 1974 to March 1977, more than 92 percent were at exactly 6 percent.

As with title insurers, the uniformity of brokers' commission rates is a symptom of collusion and price fixing.[c] But in the case of brokers, the allegation of price fixing has less prima facie plausibility. After all, there are nearly 178,000 active brokers in California. Moreover, consumers are likely to be a good deal more sensitive to brokers' price differentials than to title company price differentials. On a $40,000 home, the title work may cost as little as $225, while the brokers' fee will be $2,400. The pressure on brokers to cut prices in order to increase their business must be very great. Yet there is little evidence that they do so.

One possible explanation of the absence of price competition is the coordination mechanism provided by the MLS organizations. Just as the New York Stock Exchange for many years used membership in the exchange as a device to fix stock brokerage commission rates, so local real estate firms may use membership in the MLS to enforce uniform real estate brokerage fees. A member broker who departs from the fixed rate may be threatened with expulsion from

---

[c]There is nothing mysterious about this. Until the early 1960s it was widely believed that price fixing by professional associations was legal, and local realty associations simply set fee schedules, which were typically at 6 percent for residential property. When the Justice Department began attacking such fee schedules, numerous realty associations signed consent decrees abolishing the fee schedules, but they remained in tacit effect since housing prices increased at least as rapidly as the cost of living and there was no need to adjust the cartel price. Recently, some efforts have been made to increase the fee to 7 percent, a move that requires outright conspiracies. The U.S. Antitrust Division has been able to bring at least two criminal indictments in this area and one conviction.

the MLS. Without access to the MLS, a broker will have a difficult job staying in business. Furthermore, the MLS structure has a built-in mechanism to detect secret price cutting, since commissions are split between the listing and selling offices. The cooperative aspect of MLS organizations also allows sanctions less drastic than expulsion to be enforced; for instance, members thought to be cheating on the cartel fee level may find other members less anxious to sell their listings, even though the commission offered to the selling broker is the same. Other punitive measures are also available.

When prices are above their competitive level, we expect entry to take place. The resulting increase in supply tends to drive prices down to a competitive level, at which firms earn only "normal" profits. But if prices are fixed at supra-competitive levels, entry has the effect of creating excess capacity. Real estate broker cartels can control entry only imperfectly (by persuading state authorities to increase the severity of the licensing requirements and by trying to restrict access to the MLS). We would therefore expect to find that there are "too many" brokers, each insufficiently busy on the average when compared to the competitive situation. "Insufficiently busy" needs a word of explanation. The high, uniform price of brokers' services tends to attract too many brokers into the market. Brokers may work as hard as or harder than they would if prices were competitive, but on average each will sell fewer houses.[d] Competition takes place in the dimension of selling effort, rather than price. This increased selling effort is not without benefits for consumers. Nevertheless, many consumers may prefer less selling effort and lower commission rates.

Apparently the market discipline provided by the potential of individual sellers "going it alone" by not using a broker is not very important. Only about 10 percent of urban sellers fail to use brokers. The brokers, in addition to offering sales services and convenience, have an important asset (the MLS information market) which is evidently very valuable to sellers and to buyers.

Thus, it is apparent that real estate brokers are able to set prices collusively even though they are relatively unconcentrated. (In urban markets, it is rare to find the largest brokerage firm with more than 8–10 percent of the market.) The logic of the situation suggests that MLS organizations are responsible for this. Nevertheless, entry is not fully controlled, with the result that brokers are too numerous, and

---

[d]In Los Angeles county in 1974 the average "active" licensee sold three homes, earning about $8,500 in commission. Of course, many legally "active" licensees are not really in the business or are part timers.

may earn only "normal" returns, on average. Since the California residential housing market had a volume in 1974 of roughly $26 billion dollars, the resource misallocation involved may be fairly serious. Brokerage commissions in that year totaled about $1.4 billion for the state. Of course, there is no way to measure the fraction of this figure that represents wasted resources due to price fixing.

Fixed commission rates prevent the benefits of competition among title companies and other ancillary conveyancing firms from being fully passed on to the public. Competition among the ancillary firms simply increases revenues in the brokerage industry and attracts still more brokers to the market.

Although the government has obtained a number of consent decrees, there do not appear to be any antitrust judgments against brokers who engage in price fixing activities in which the government is the plaintiff.[e] There are a few private suits which have been brought to judgment, mainly by brokers excluded from or harmed by the cartel when they offered lower rates.

The law on price fixing by professional associations presently draws on the *Goldfarb* [15] decision. However, there are serious problems involved in enforcing the antitrust laws in this area. First, it is clear that structural remedies are irrelevant to the circumstances. Clearly one does not want to outlaw multiple listing services. Second, it is not possible to rely on private actions by individual customers harmed by such practices because each will have too small a stake in the matter (even with treble damages) to overcome the litigation costs. Occasional suits by individual brokers who are harmed by the local cartels are of limited utility since the potential costs to the cartel are probably small compared to the gains from continued collusion. State and federal prosecutors might bring criminal actions against price fixers, but judges are traditionally reluctant to impose jail sentences or severe fines in such cases.

Kickbacks

We have already seen that title insurance companies have an incentive to pay real estate brokers for client referrals. This is no different from the problem of kickbacks by medical specialists to general practitioner MDs, which are sometimes alleged to take place. Escrow companies and termite inspectors face similar incentives. The broker who is asked for advice by his client in the selection of a title company must consider three factors. The first is the speed of service. Brokers who expect a $2,600 commission on a $40,000 transaction

---

[e]But see footnote *c supra*.

are not likely to steer business to a slow or sloppy title company (and thus endanger the entire commission) in return for any conceivable kickback from the $225 title insurance premium. Second, in selecting among the title companies which offer fast, efficient service, the broker will consider the amount of the kickback offered. He may even be willing to select a slightly slower or slightly more inefficient title company in return for a slightly larger kickback. (It must be remembered that the individual salesperson does not get the entire 6 percent commission in typical cases, the listing office gets half, and the salesperson's employer will get part of the remaining half.) Finally, the broker must consider whether he is willing to subject his license to whatever risk results from his receipt of secret profits in violation of his fiduciary duty. As an economic expectation, the last item is no doubt of little significance, but individual brokers may put a high moral value on honesty in such matters. Nevertheless, on the margin, title companies that offer higher kickbacks, other things equal, can expect to get more business. The effect of this is to keep title company profits down to "normal" levels, and to transfer income from title companies to the brokerage industry.

Now, if brokers were competitive in prices, the effect of their receipt of kickbacks would simply be to reduce brokers' commissions. Brokers who were in competitive equilibrium before the payment of kickbacks would, after such payments were made, be in disequilibrium with excess economic profits. Price competition would drive commissions down to a new equilibrium level as the rebates are passed on to consumers. This could make consumers worse off only if brokers were led to refer clients to potentially insolvent title companies. (As we shall see, the role of lenders makes this unlikely.)

However, brokerage commissions are fixed and not competitively determined. What is the effect of kickbacks in such an environment? First, they continue to have the effect of increasing the income of brokers and reducing the profits of title companies. But with fixed rates brokers' commissions do not fall as a result of the increased revenues from kickbacks. Instead, there is a further signal to potential entrants into the brokerage industry, and the number of brokers increases even more than it does as a result of high fixed commission rates alone. Selling effort increases still more. And brokers' incomes are forced down to "normal" levels.

Now consider the effect of a strictly-enforced legal prohibition on rebates, such as that undertaken by the California Department of Insurance. The equilibrium number of brokers is now smaller than that which existed prior to the prohibition. Unless something is done, some brokers will have to exit the industry, and meanwhile they earn, on average, below normal profits. Thus, there is an incentive to circumvent the prohibition. One way around the prohibition is to become a licensed title insurance agent and earn the now illegal kickbacks in the form of arguably legal commissions. And this is just what we observe happening in the California real estate industry.

The effect on consumers of this tendency toward broker-title company integration is not straightforward. If the agencies are nonexclusive (that is, if brokers form agencies which write the policies of more than one underwriter) then the effect is simply to undo the rebate prohibition. But if the agencies are exclusive, the effect may be to reduce the quality of service, since title companies will no longer be competing for broker's referrals. In either case, however, the integration results in losses of economies of specialization which the previous market structure revealed to exist. Thus, costs to consumers probably rise as a result of the rebate prohibition.

Mortgage Lenders

Mortgage lenders are, perhaps to a lesser extent than brokers and escrow companies, business influencers with respect to the placement of title orders. Title companies have responded to this by keeping demand deposits, which do not bear interest, spread over a wide variety of banks. One title company was recently fined for this practice, the Department of Insurance viewing it as a form of illegal rebate. Title companies also keep balances at and own stock in savings and loan associations.

The primary role of lending institutions in this market, however, lies in their insistence on a policy of title insurance in the first place. Such a policy is necessary in order to protect the security upon which the loan is based, and in order to rediscount the mortgage to the national secondary market. Thus, lending institutions have an incentive to make sure that the title-assuring firm is solvent and reliable. This source of expert intervention in the market works to the buyer's advantage, and makes it much less troublesome that buyers may be unable to interpret the significance of "clouds" on title excepted from the insurance coverage. It also makes state regulation of insurer solvency arguably unnecessary.

Any tendency of brokers to recommend title companies that offer high rebates and poor service is countered by the presence of the lending institution in the transaction. Lenders are unlikely to approve the selection of a title company which is in prospect of insolvency or which does sloppy abstracting. On the other hand, lenders are unlikely to be concerned with the price of title service so long as all competing lenders insist on it.

THE ROLE OF REGULATION

Before the legal prohibitions on rebates and kickbacks were enforced, the business of brokerage and the business of title insurance were largely separate. It is reasonably clear that enforcement of the prohibitions has resulted in a trend toward integration of these two businesses, at least in the sense that brokers are becoming title insurance agents. The integration is not costless. Brokers cannot simply "sign up" as agents to sell title insurance. They must form underwritten title companies, meet capital and other licensing requirements, purchase liability insurance, and undertake substantial recordkeeping requirements. This is a more expensive structure for the industry than the specialization that preceded it. Given this state of affairs, there were four policy choices facing the state. It could either prohibit (or enforce existing prohibitions on) rebates and kickbacks or permit these kickbacks to take place. In either case it could allow or prohibit the broker formation of underwritten title companies. Faced with these four choices, the California Department of Insurance picked what seems at first a middle ground. The prohibitions on rebates are to be enforced, and brokers will be licensed as underwritten title agents under certain conditions. The conditions are that the broker make full disclosure of the potential conflict to his clients, and that the broker-owned title company seriously solicit outside title business rather than relying solely on its "captive" market. The test criterion is that 50 percent of the title business comes from outside sources. (Firms which do not meet this test have a burden of proof to demonstrate that they are making serious efforts to solicit outside business.) If title referrals are largely controlled by brokers, no broker-owned title company will be able to solicit outside business because competing brokers will not make referrals to a rival broker. Thus, the effect of the policy is to place a probably insuperable entry barrier in the path of broker entry.

This decision, which was taken after a period during which broker applications for licenses were held up, will no doubt be appealed to the courts. Meanwhile, title insurers have a breathing space of some years in which to find other solutions to their problems, a delay consistent with the hypothesis of Chapter 1.

It must be acknowledged that the title insurance industry has made good use of the administrative process. First, it has succeeded in becoming "regulated" by the simple expedient of calling itself an insurance industry. Title companies are no more in the insurance business than any firm that offers a guarantee with its product.[f] The benefits of regulation for this industry are manifest: federal antitrust immunity, public filing of rates, prohibitions on departures from published rates, public enforcement of private cartel rules against secret rebates, and (in California at least) protection from broker entry. The title industry does not even face most of the usual costs of regulation. Insurance commissioners are preoccupied with issues in life and health insurance, medical malpractice, and the like; even to them, title insurers are a negligible factor, and rate hearings are rare indeed.

The original purpose and major benefit of insurance regulation was to protect consumers from firms with insufficient reserves, or to reduce the likelihood that a valid claim would be presented to an insolvent company. But would an unregulated title insurance industry really have a substantially higher insolvency rate? The answer depends on the extent to which the present highly sophisticated national mortgage markets exert discipline on the selection of insurers by lending institutions. It seems very likely that this discipline would be substantial, and that the institutional market would be able to make the appropriate tradeoff between price and risk. There is, after all, no guarantee that regulated firms provide just the right level of risk versus cost. Some insureds may wish they could buy insurance at even lower risk levels from firms with even higher reserves, at a higher premium. More likely, there are people who would be quite happy with lower premiums and a somewhat greater risk of loss. In other fields of commerce, firms can coexist with differential product qualities and prices. The necessity of regulation must therefore be found in institutional conditions making it very likely that consumers will be systematically misled. In this market, the presence of highly sophisticated institutional buyers (the mortgage market) makes it fairly unlikely that consumers will be misled.

By contrast with title insurers, real estate brokers have not been successful users of the administrative process. In California, state regulation of brokers is limited to licensing and enforcement of behavior standards. The commissioner of real estate must by law be a real estate broker with an active license. The educational requirements for licensees have occasionally been raised in efforts to limit entry, but the result can hardly be viewed as satisfactory to the industry, given the very large number of licensees.

Occupational licensing generally is thought to have an anticompetitive effect, and indeed is often initiated by the licensed professions

---

f This is a slight overstatement. Coverage against unrecorded defects in title, such as mechanic's liens, is true casualty insurance. Title insurers have "loss ratios" (claims paid divided by premiums received) on the order of 10 percent.

in order to control entry, especially entry by "fly by night" operators who may charge low prices for low quality service. It is a controversial point whether, even in medical professions, the benefits of such licensing to the public are worth the costs. In the case of brokers, the restraint on entry caused by the licensing requirements may actually have a salutory effect, given the existence of uniform commission rates. The uniform rates attract unwarranted entry, at least some of which is presumably cut off by the licensing process. Thus, the resource misallocation which results from the price fixing is less than it would otherwise be.

It is probably the case that the licensing standards were once more nearly geared to the maintenance of excess profits in the presence of price fixing of commission rates. But the sudden acceleration of housing prices in California in the past five or ten years, combined with the flat percentage fee for commissions, has made the licensing standards an ineffective barrier to entry. It would not be surprising to see renewed efforts by brokers and by the Department of Real Estate to further increase the licensing standards.

There is much in this case study to support the traditional models of pathological regulation, just as there is much to illustrate the principles set out in the first section of Chapter 1. There are also instances of protective delay. When broker-owned underwritten title companies began to enjoy significant market shares, the California insurance commissioner stepped in, froze pending license applications, and set the whole matter for extended study and hearings. In the end, broker applications were effectively denied. Lengthy appeals to the reviewing courts will ensue. There can be no question that the regulatory agency acted to preserve the status quo in the face of a sudden and fairly drastic threat to the financial viability of the title industry in California.

Chapter 5

Regulation of a New Technology: Cable Television

INTRODUCTION [1]

Between 1955 and 1975 the number of cable television subscribers grew at an average annual percentage rate of 23 percent. The cable phenomenon has resulted in the creation of a major controversy, in which the broadcast industry and its allies see cable as a destructive force threatening both their own and the public interest in free over-the-air broadcasting, while cable television companies and their allies see a vast increase in consumer choice and freedom, as well as potentially great profits.

Television is a major, perhaps the major, entertainment industry in America. The A.C. Nielsen Company estimates that the average American family watches more than six hours of television per day. Television advertising revenues in 1976 were $5.1 billion, with profits of $1.3 billion. There are approximately 70 million homes with TV in the United States (98 percent of all homes), and 112 million TV sets in use. Advertising prices range from $5 for thirty-second commercials in small towns to $225,000 for a minute of network time during the superbowl [2]. The average network prime time program costs about $250,000 per hour to produce. Table 5–1 provides an overview of the growth of TV and cable TV households. Existing television service is worth billions of dollars per year to viewers, and viewers place substantial value on additional TV options.[a]

---

[a] Estimating the economic value of television to viewers is difficult because consumers do not pay directly. However, estimates of viewers' willingness to pay for cable TV service suggest that, nationwide, viewers would be willing to pay as much as $30 billion per year rather than do without the existing level of service.

Table 5–1. Television Households and Cable Subscribers, 1955–1975

| Year | Number of TV Households (millions) | Percent of All Households Having TV (%) | Cable Television | | Percent of TV Households with Cable (%) |
			Number of Systems	Number of Subscribers (thousands)	
1955	31	65	400	150	0.5
1960	46	87	640	650	1.4
1965	53	93	1,325	1,275	2.4
1970	60	96	2,490	4,500	7.5
1975	70	98	3,366	9,800	14.0

Source: *TV Factbook*, Services Vol., No. 44 (1974–75): 65a; *TV Digest* 15, 48 (Dec. 1, 1975): 2.

Cable television, despite its rapid rate of growth, is still very small compared to broadcasting. There are now about ten million cable subscribers who pay about six dollars per month for service—giving the cable industry annual revenues of about $700 million.

Figure 5—1 shows the physical design of a cable system. The typical system has twelve channels, mainly devoted to rebroadcasting local TV signals in order to improve the quality of reception. Some systems carry a local origination channel, mostly programmed with time and weather forecasts. Most systems also carry, to the extent permitted by FCC rules, TV signals from distant cities which cannot be received in the area with rooftop antennas. A growing number carry one or more special channels with new movies, for which a separate charge is made. These are "pay-TV" channels, whose operation is also closely regulated by the FCC [3]. An estimated 1.6 million households will subscribe to such pay-TV channels by the end of 1977. The largest cable system in the country is in San Diego, with about 100,000 subscribers. The top fifty cable companies (multiple system operators) have more than 70 percent of all cable subscribers. The largest such company is TelePrompter Corporation, with over one million subscribers.

Cable systems tend to have the characteristics of natural monopolies in their local areas. Costs decline as the number of subscribers increases within a given area. The higher the ratio of subscribers to homes "passed" by the cable, the lower the cost per subscriber. This does not preclude the existence of two or more cable systems in a city, provided that they serve different areas. The financial viability of a cable system depends on population density, income levels, quality of over-the-air reception, number of over-the-air signals, and the like, all of which may vary considerably within a television market. Hence, cable may be viable in some parts of a market and not in other parts.

The TV rating services list over 200 TV "markets" in the United States, defined roughly by the coverage areas of TV stations assigned to a city or adjacent cities. Table 5—2 lists the top 100 of these markets and Table 5—3 shows the FCC broadcast financial data for stations in these markets. Most TV revenues and profits go to VHF network affiliates in the top 100 markets. This is not surprising, given the distribution of population: one-third of all TV households are in the top ten markets, 68 percent in the top fifty, and 87 percent in the top 100. TV stations are in the business of selling audiences to advertisers. The larger the audience, the more advertisers are willing to pay, other things equal. Therefore TV revenues are greater in larger cities than in smaller ones.

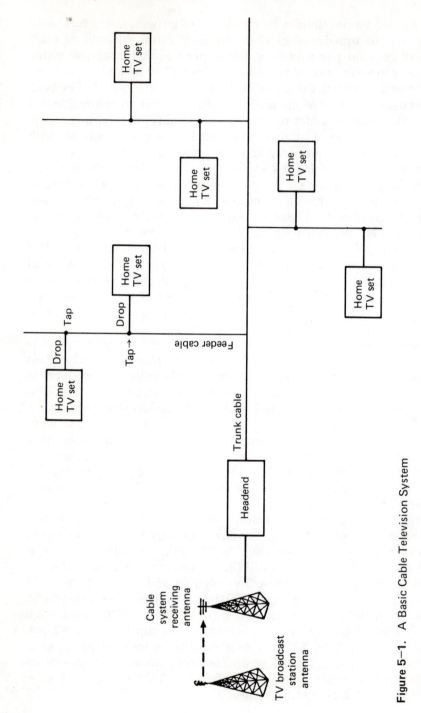

Figure 5–1.   A Basic Cable Television System

Source: Carl Pilnick and Walter S. Baer, *Cable Television: A Guide to the Technology*, The Rand Corporation, R–1141-NSF, June 1973, p. 4.

The FCC cable television rules are also organized by market, with different treatment accorded to cable systems in larger than in smaller markets. These differences are discussed below. Although the FCC's rules and much of the research on cable and its effects involves distinctions among these television markets by size (e.g., "top 50," or "largest 100 markets") it must be emphasized that there are important distinctions not captured by these classifications. Thus, while "top 50 markets" is a shorthand way of referring to large metropolitan areas with generally abundant over-the-air TV service, there are some markets in the top fifty with special characteristics which make them more or less conducive to cable growth. Thus, Table 5-4 lists nineteen of the largest 100 "standard metropolitan statistical areas" as defined by the Department of Commerce, in which there is no *local* commercial VHF station, as defined by the FCC and the broadcast industry. Many of these SMSAs have UHF service, and others are served by VHF stations in nearby cities. Statements about the impact of or prospects for cable in the "top 50" or any other such market grouping must be regarded as broad generalizations with important exceptions.

HISTORICAL BACKGROUND

The historical development of federal regulation of cable television can only be understood in the broader context of radio and television regulation [4]. The Congress in 1927 nationalized the radio spectrum and in 1934 granted regulatory authority over wire and radio communications to the Federal Communications Commission [5]. As demand for television programs grew in the postwar years, the FCC was faced with the problem of allocating spectrum to this new service.

The commission at first seriously underestimated demand, and allocated only eleven VHF channels to the new service. Moreover, it continued its policy of "localism" in allocating these channels, attempting to maximize the number of localities with a station, rather than attempting to maximize the number of signals available to the population [6]. Assigning a frequency to a city meant that that frequency could not be assigned to nearby cities without causing interference. The effect was to create an excess demand for licenses, which began to change hands at prices far in excess of the value of tangible property involved.

The undersupply of spectrum to television service had a number of effects, aside from the production of excess profits for VHF licensees.

Table 5–2.   The Top 100 TV Markets

The table shows the largest 100 TV markets as defined by the FCC in its 1972 rules. Most markets cover a dozen or more counties, and sometimes several states. The number of commercial TV stations in each market is from *Broadcasting Yearbook* (1975), pp. B–1 ff. The percentage of TV households subscribing to cable is from a November 1973 survey appearing in *TV Factbook* (1974/75), pp. 95–a ff.

No.	Market	Network VHF	Network UHF	Independent VHF	Independent UHF	Cable Penetration %
1	New York, N.Y.-Linden-Paterson, N.J.	3	0	3	3	5
2	Los Angeles-San Bernardino-Corona-Fontana, Calif.	3	0	4	4	8
3	Chicago, Ill.	3	0	1	3	2
4	Philadelphia, Pa-Burlington, N.J.	3	0	0	3	15
5	Detroit, Mich.	3	0	1	2	1
6	Boston-Cambridge-Worcester, Mass.	3	0	0	2	7
7	San Francisco-Oakland-San Jose, Calif.	3	0	1	3	20
8	Cleveland-Lorain-Akron, Ohio	3	0	0	2	10
9	Washington, D.C.	3	0	1	1	7
10	Pittsburgh, Pa.	3	0	0	1	23
11	St. Louis, Mo.	3	1	0	1	2
12	Dallas-Fort Worth, Tex.	3	0	1	1	6
13	Minneapolis-St. Paul, Minn.	3	0	1	0	3
14	Baltimore, Md.	3	0	0	1	1
15	Houston, Tex.	3	0	0	2	3
16	Indianapolis-Bloomington, Ind.	3	0	1	1	12
17	Cincinnati, Ohio-Newport, Ky.	3	0	0	1	2
18	Atlanta, Ga.	3	0	0	2	9
19	Hartford-New Haven Britain-Waterbury, Conn.	2	2	0	1	n.a.
20	Seattle-Tacoma, Wash.	3	0	2	0	20
21	Miami, Fla.	3	0	1	1	2

No.	Market					
22	Kansas City, Mo.	3	0	0	1	5
23	Milwaukee, Wis.	3	0	0	1	2
24	Buffalo, N.Y.	3	0	0	1	12
25	Sacramento-Stockton-Modesto, Calif.	3	0	0	0	18
26	Memphis, Tenn.	3	0	0	0	7
27	Columbus, Ohio	3	0	0	1	9
28	Tampa-St. Petersburg, Fla.	3	0	1	0	10
29	Portland, Oreg.	3	0	0	0	12
30	Nashville, Tenn.	3	0	0	1	6
31	New Orleans, La.	3	0	1	0	2
32	Denver, Colo.	3	0	0	0	4
33	Providence, R.I.-New Bedford, Mass.	3	1	0	0	0
34	Albany-Schenectady-Troy, N.Y.	3	0	0	0	13
35	Syracuse, N.Y.	3	0	0	0	14
36	Charleston-Huntington, W. Va.	3	0	0	0	29
37	Kalamazoo-Grand Rapids-Muskegon-Battle Creek, Mich.	3	0	0	0	8
38	Louisville, Ky.	2	1	0	1	6
39	Oklahoma City, Okla.	3	0	0	0	9
40	Birmingham, Ala.	2	1	0	0	7
41	Dayton-Kettering, Ohio	2	1	0	0	9
42	Charlotte, N.C.	2	1	0	1	8
43	Phoenix-Mesa, Ariz.	3	0	1	1	5
44	Norfolk-Newport News-Portsmouth-Hampton, Va.	3	0	0	1	1
45	San Antonio, Tex.	3	0	0	1	7
46	Greenville-Spartanburg-Anderson, S.C.-Asheville, N.C.	3	1	0	1	6
47	Greensboro-High Point-Winston Salem, N.C.	3	0	0	0	6
48	Salt Lake City, Utah	3	0	0	0	6
49	Wilkes Barre-Scranton, Pa.	0	3	0	0	45
50	Little Rock, Ark.	3	0	0	0	5
51	San Diego, Calif.	2	1	1	0	27
52	Toledo, Ohio	2	1	0	0	17

(Table 5-2. continued overleaf)

Table 5-2. continued

No.	Market	Number of Commercial TV Stations				Cable Penetration %
		Network VHF	Network UHF	Independent VHF	Independent UHF	
53	Omaha, Nebr.	3	0	0	0	2
54	Tulsa, Okla.	3	0	0	0	6
55	Orlando-Daytona Beach, Fla.	3	0	0	1	21
56	Rochester, N.Y.	3	0	0	0	14
57	Harrisburg-Lancaster-York, Pa.	1	4	0	0	39
58	Texarkana, Tex.-Shreveport, La.	3	0	0	0	6
59	Mobile, Ala.-Pensacola, Fla.	3	0	0	0	12
60	Davenport, Iowa-Rock Island-Moline, Ill.	3	1	0	0	9
61	Flint-Bay City-Saginaw, Mich.	2	0	0	0	12
62	Green Bay, Wis.	3	0	0	0	7
63	Richmond-Petersburg, Va.	3	0	0	0	11
64	Springfield-Decatur-Champaign-Jackson-ville, Ill.	1	2	0	0	19
65	Cedar Rapids-Waterloo, Iowa	3	0	0	0	7
66	Des Moines-Ames, Iowa	3	0	0	0	4
67	Wichita-Hutchinson, Kans.	3	0	0	0	13
68	Jacksonville, Fla.	2	1	0	0	11
69	Cape Girardeau, Mo.-Paducah, Ky-Harrisburg, Ill.	3	0	0	1	10
70	Roanoke-Lynchburg, Va.	3	0	0	0	11
71	Knoxville, Tenn.	2	1	0	0	10
72	Fresno, Calif.	0	3	0	2	8
73	Raleigh-Durham, N.C.	2	1	0	0	11
74	Johnstown-Altonna, Pa.	2	1	0	0	55
75	Portland-Poland Spring, Maine	3	1	0	0	15
76	Spokane, Wash.	3	0	0	0	20
77	Jackson, Miss.	2	1	0	0	29

No.	City					
78	Chattanooga, Tenn.	3	0	0	1	7
79	Youngstown, Ohio	0	3	0	0	3
80	South Bend-Elkhart, Ind.	0	3	0	1	4
81	Albuquerque, N. Mex.	3	0	0	0	9
82	Fort Wayne-Roanoke, Ind.	0	3	0	0	3
83	Peoria, Ill.	3	3	0	0	5
84	Greenville-Washington-New Bern, N.C.	3	0	0	0	4
85	Sioux Falls-Mitchell, S. Dak.	1	2	0	0	7
86	Evansville, Ind.	2	1	0	0	7
87	Baton Rouge, La.	3	0	0	0	3
88	Beaumont-Port Arthur, Tex.	3	0	0	0	3
89	Duluth, Minn.-Superior, Wis.	2	0	0	0	14
90	Wheeling, W. Va.-Steubenville, Ohio	3	0	0	0	40
91	Lincoln-Hastings-Kearney, Nebr.	2	2	0	0	12
92	Lansing-Onondaga, Mich.	1	1	0	0	11
93	Madison, Wis.	2	0	0	0	2
94	Columbus, Ga.	3	4	0	0	18
95	Amarillo, Tex.	0	2	0	0	35
96	Huntsville-Decatur, Ala.	1	0	0	0	42
97	Rockford-Freeport, Ill.	3	0	0	0	14
98	Fargo-Valley City, N. Dak.	2	2	0	0	10
99	Monroe, La.-El Dorado, Ark.	1	0	0	0	16
100	Columbia, S.C.	1	2	0	0	3

Table 5–3. Profitability of Television Stations, 1974

Commercial TV Stations	Number of Stations	Income Before Federal Tax (thousands) (1)	Original Cost of Tangible Property Less Depreciation (thousands) (2)	Percent (1) of (2) (3)
Small market (below 100):				
Network:				
UHF	59	(–$900)	$26,584	(1)
VHF	219	33,460	127,954	26.2
Independent:				
UHF	8	(–1,927)	1,847	(1)
VHF	11	(–3,330)	8,503	(1)
Total, small market	297	27,303	164,888	16.6
Large market (top 100):				
Network:				
UHF	58	7,200	45,595	15.8
VHF	244	474,951	379,676	125.1
Independent:				
UHF	52	(–10,345)	42,655	(1)
VHF	20	11,677	46,165	25.3
Total, large market	374	483,483	514,091	94.0
All stations:				
Network:				
UHF	117	6,300	72,179	8.7
VHF	463	508,411	507,630	100.2

Independent:				
UHF	60	(-12,272)	44,502	(1)
VHF	31	8,347	54,668	15.3
Total, all stations	671	510,786	678,979	75.2

Source: FCC
(1) Loss.

Table 5–4. Cities Among Largest 100 SMSAs With No Local VHF Commercial TV Stations

SMSA	1970 Population Census (thousands)
Nassau-Suffolk, New York	2553
Newark, New Jersey	1857
Anaheim, California	1420
Paterson, New Jersey	1359
San Bernadino, California	1143
Akron, Ohio	679
Gary, Indiana	633
Fort Lauderdale, Florida	620
Jersey City, New Jersey	609
Youngstown, Ohio	536
Springfield, Massachusetts	530
Fresno, California	413
Bridgeport, Connecticut	389
Canton, Ohio	372
Wilkes-Barre-Scranton, Pennsylvania	347
Worcester, Massachusetts	344
Peoria, Illinois	342
Bakerfield, California	329
Trenton, New Jersey	304

First, the market responded with supplementary technologies: boosters, satellite stations, translators, and cable television systems, all means of improving reception in rural areas. Second, the FCC responded by allocating a relatively large number of new channels to television service. Unfortunately, these channels were allocated in the UHF band, and stations on that band were at a technical disadvantage vis-à-vis VHF stations. Not only did most sets manufactured in the fifties and early sixties lack UHF tuners, but UHF signals do not travel as far or as clearly as equally powerful VHF signals. This "UHF handicap" has persisted (though it is diminishing) despite the FCC's efforts to eliminate it. (The efforts included a requirement that all TV sets have UHF tuners, and later, that they have "click-stop" tuning dials.) It is generally agreed that the FCC made a serious error in its UHF decisions; if the commission had shifted all TV broadcasting to the UHF band, or if it had not mixed UHF and VHF stations in the same markets, the resulting abundance of channels might have reduced the need for cable television. This would have eliminated the handicap of UHF stations in competing with VHFs. However, by the time the implications of the FCC's error were apparent in the late 1950s, the VHF broadcasters were politically too powerful to dislodge [7] .

The supplementary technologies which grew up in the fifties were designed to bring TV signals to rural fringe areas where the primary signals were weak or plagued with interference. Boosters, satellites, and translators all receive these weak signals and rebroadcast them with greater power. Cable television systems do the same, but use wires rather than rebroadcasting the signals. Cable television systems have the disadvantage of being much more expensive than satellites and translators for small numbers of channels, but they have two overwhelming advantages: because they use wire, they can at relatively little expense charge consumers for the service they provide, and because of the technical characteristics of coaxial cable, they can carry a relatively large number of channels. Cable systems typically have twelve channels, many more than the number of over-the-air stations available to most viewers. There is no technical limit to the number of cable channels; some systems are being built with twenty or more channels.

The selling point of cable systems during the fifties was simply the provision of clear signals; this service was uncontroversial, and even welcomed by broadcasters, because it increased their audiences. In 1959 the FCC refused to accept regulatory jurisdiction over cable, asserting that it was neither a broadcast facility nor a wire common carrier [8] .

Between 1959 and 1966 the situation changed radically. Cable operators discovered that they could increase the demand for their service by "importing" distant TV signals using microwave relay systems. Subscribers were willing to pay to receive these additional nonlocal signals, and there was plenty of capacity on the coaxial cable. Distant signal importation aroused the ire of broadcasters; it had the effect of increasing the choices available, and thus of "fragmenting" the audience of local broadcasters. This reduced advertising revenues. The new audiences gained by the distant station were of little value to the imported station's own local advertising clients. (In 1974, local advertising accounted for 31 percent of the revenue of independent VHF stations, and 53 percent of the revenue of independent UHF stations.) Also, cable for the first time began to grow in the big cities, where the most profitable stations are found.

In opposing cable, broadcasters employed two strategies. The first was to press the FCC for restrictions on cable television, and the second was to challenge cable in the courts, on the grounds that distant signal importation infringed the copyright of program producers. The FCC first asserted jurisdiction over the microwave relay system used to import distant signals (1962), then in 1965–66 asserted full regulatory jurisdiction over cable television and "froze" all such systems in the largest 100 television markets, forbidding importation of additional signals [9]. These actions were upheld in the courts [10]. The copyright challenge did not go so well for the broadcasters. In 1968 the Supreme Court held that cable systems had no copyright liability for retransmitted local signals and in 1974 held similarly with respect to distant signals [11]. Not until 1976 did Congress pass legislation making cable operators liable for copyright payments on distant signals, under a compulsory license.

The years following the freeze were ones of intense pressure for the industry and for the commission. Despite the freeze, cable systems grew rapidly in numbers of subscribers. The political strength of the cable industry grew as well, in part because the more spectacular potential services which cable might offer caught the imaginations of a number of writers, who produced a growing flood of academic and semipopular literature and interest in cable [12]. These "blue sky" services included free public soapbox channels, channels for education, the arts, and government, electronic voting, shopping, meter reading, and access to electronic program libraries with limitless possibilities. A major criticism of broadcast TV has been the difficulty of access and the scarcity of channels; cable was called the "medium of abundance."

In 1971 intense negotiations among the trade groups under the auspices of FCC chairman Dean Burch and Office of Telecommunications Policy director Clay T. Whitehead resulted in a "compromise" solution to the conflict [13]. This compromise involved a formula for payment of royalties for distant signals, and a specified limit to the number of such signals that could be imported, which varied with market size and other factors. The compromise was intended to be embodied in a massive set of FCC rules, promulgated in 1972 [14]. The 1972 rules, in addition to regulating the number and type of distant signals which might be imported, imposed a number of requirements on cable systems. Among these were the provision of free channels for various uses, local origination, and technical and capacity rules designed to ensure the more rapid development of the "blue sky" services. By 1977 many of these requirements had been relaxed or abandoned entirely.

The details of the 1972 rules will be explored below. They were truly a compromise in the sense that the FCC convinced itself and the cable industry that they were the minimum conditions necessary to get cable moving, while not irreparably harming the broadcasters. The free channels and other requirements imposed on cable systems were designed to ensure that cable lived up to its promise of "abundance," rather than simply existing on the retransmission of broadcast signals. These requirements were on the whole technically and financially unrealistic, and have been relaxed as their effective dates approached. In an important sense, the public service and capacity requirements were necessary to get the vote of "liberal" commissioners, particularly Nicholas Johnson.

After 1972, the major issues in cable regulation were pay television, copyright, pole rentals, and the question of federal versus state and local jurisdiction over cable. There has been a gradual relaxation of the FCC rules against pay television on cable systems (as well as over-the-air), but the rules were still quite restrictive until 1977, when the D.C. Court of Appeals held them to be illegal. A major change came in 1975, when the FCC allowed cable pay-TV systems to use movies less than four years old [15]. The previous rule was three years. The pay-TV rules are discussed in detail below. The Congress in 1976 passed an omnibus copyright act which included compulsory licenses for distant signals allowed by the FCC, with royalties paid to a central pool for distribution to copyright owners.

Relations between the cable industry and the telephone company have been strained over the issue of prices charged by telephone companies for the use of poles and conduits. This issue is related to the question of jurisdiction, which is still not settled; both issues are discussed below. In 1974, the Cabinet Committee on Cable Communications issued a report which put forward a new regulatory framework for cable, based on the separation of transmission and content functions. Cable would be a common carrier under the committee's proposal, and there would be no federal regulation of content on such systems. The rationale for this is that local cable transmission is a natural monopoly, which for competitive and First Amendment reasons ought not to be translated into a monopoly of control over content. If all cable channels were competitively programmed, there would be no scarcity and less need for federal regulations, such as the fairness doctrine, which impinge on freedom of expression [16].

FORCES AND ISSUES

The history of cable regulation can be viewed politically as a struggle among interest groups, with resulting regulatory decisions rationalized by public interest rhetoric. It can also be viewed less cynically as a process by which the FCC has gradually acquired, as a result of adversary processes, the information it requires to properly interpret the public interest in cable regulation. The evidence seems to suggest that the former view is the more correct one.

The major interest groups are easily identified:

Broadcasters, represented by the National Association of Broadcasters (NAB) and the Association of Maximum Service Telecasters (AMST), have opposed the development of cable for the obvious reason that cable growth implies increased competition in the major TV markets. The increased competition takes place because of distant signal importation, and because of additional channels supported by subscriber payments for programs (pay-TV), and perhaps new cable networks.

Cable operators, represented by the National Cable Television Association (NCTA), naturally are in favor of cable growth. They have successfully pressed for favorable copyright legislation and for federal preemption of jurisdiction over cable. Originally weak and ineffectual, NCTA has grown in strength over the years.

Copyright owners, mainly Hollywood studios represented by the Motion Picture Association, are generally in favor of cable growth and relaxation of the rules barring pay-TV, but supported broadcasters' efforts to impose copyright liability on cable systems.

Negotiations among these three groups led to the 1971 compromise on distant signals and copyright liability described below. At the FCC, the broadcasters were predominant until about 1972, but are now more evenly matched by the cable industry, largely as a result of the creation of a separate cable television bureau to promote cable industry interests within the FCC. Other, less central, interest groups include:

1. *AT&T*, which has seen cable as a potential long-term threat to its local service monopoly, and has been accused of using the pole rental issue to obstruct cable growth.[b] Cable systems are most cheaply constructed by using telephone poles and ducts for which they pay rent. Cable operators allege that present rental rates are excessive. It is still a question whether the FCC or the less sympathetic (to cable) state utility commissions have jurisdiction over these rates; federal legislation in this area is pending.

2. *State and local* regulatory jurisdictions, which are interested in maximizing the scope of their authority over cable.

The interaction of these groups has set the stage for the various regulatory, judicial, and congressional actions affecting cable television. A less cohesive, but not inconsiderable influence has been brought to bear by academic and semipopular writers, who have generally been favorably disposed toward cable, particularly during the years preceding the 1972 rules.

The crucial issue to each of the interest groups is the effect of regulation on the future position of their members. However, the issues are seldom stated so baldly. Each group is required by the nature of the administrative process to express its position in terms of the public interest objectives of regulation. The public's interest in cable and in broadcasting is clearly a matter of the number and quality of television signals available, and the price charged for them. Thus, the debate about cable is carried on in terms of its effects on viewers [17].

The effect of cable on viewers' welfare is not entirely obvious. Subscribers are clearly better off as a result of cable, because they have the choice of subscribing or not, and choose to do so. Nonsubscribers are not worse off unless cable somehow affects the quantity or quality of over-the-air signals available to them. This could happen if increased competition from cable drove TV stations off the air, or

[b]In the very long run, cable technology may develop to the point that it can offer services which compete with those of the telephone system. Also, the telephone company has been developing a technology, called fiber optics, which may allow it to provide cable service quite cheaply.

if such competition resulted in lower quality programs being broadcast. This would be most serious for viewers who, because of their location, did not have access to a cable system. This is the fundamental economic issue of cable regulation. Nearly all of the current regulatory framework is nominally designed to prevent harm to non-subscribing viewers resulting from a deterioration in over-the-air broadcasting. This objective is, of course, coincident with the broadcasters' objective of maintaining their current profit levels.

There is a second (and in the debate much less important) issue: freedom of expression and regulation of mass media content [18]. Libertarians have seen cable as a means to reduce or eliminate the present rather extensive government regulation of television content, aimed at the private concentration of control created by other government policies. The Cabinet committee's common carrier recommendation was derived from this goal. If there were no concentration of control of program content, there would be no need for government intervention or licensing of programmers. The FCC has chosen to exert the same potential content jurisdiction over cable that it enjoys over broadcasters.[c]

These two issues—harm to viewers and regulation of content—underlie most of the political and economic debate about cable regulation. In an important sense, the government itself created these issues in its early decisions on spectrum allocation. Much of the cable phenomenon can be simply and accurately viewed as an attempt by the market to work around artificial restrictions imposed by government actions. However, these actions have created what are, in effect if not in law, property rights in the existing industry structure and output for producers and consumers both.

The market forces that manifest themselves in the growth of the cable television industry threaten the profits of existing broadcasters, or at the least subject those profits to future risk. Since the ultimate effect of unrestrained cable growth on viewers is not perfectly predictable, and since *some* viewers may be temporarily or permanently disadvantaged, they too are subject to risks. The effect of regulation has been to delay the realization of a new equilibrium, and this effect has been achieved by means that are quite specifically justified by the desire to protect stations and their viewers. The policy debate on these issues reveals an overwhelming emphasis on preventing harm to those who would lose as a result of the unleashing of market-technological forces. Thus, we find that broadcasters make

[c]The first explicit FCC assertion of jurisdiction over persons who lease channels from cable operators came in 1975, and was apparently regarded as necessary to the enforcement of the pay-TV rules.

strategic use of the administrative process precisely by bringing into the debate exaggerated "estimates" of the risks faced by viewers; the regulators find this emphasis on risk appropriate. The cable example illustrates both of the themes of Chapter 1.

A major policy goal of the FCC has been the promotion of "localism" in licensee control and program content. In theory, local stations have absolute control of and responsibility for program content. Unfortunately this goal (which has perfectly respectable political credentials) is inconsistent with the pattern of demand for TV programs and the economies of spreading program costs over large audiences. Most popular programming is selected not by local stations but by networks. In this respect TV is rather different from the newspaper industry, which was the model the FCC probably had in mind in its original allocation policies. FCC protection of broadcasters from the growth of cable was predicated in large part on the harm cable was thought to bring to the viability of local programming. Of course, with the exception of local news, there is no significantly viewed local programming; it is too unprofitable to produce such programs. What there is, is done to the extent necessary to get licenses renewed. In 1973, less than 15 percent of the schedules of commercial TV stations was devoted to locally produced programming, including news [19]. Ironically, cable and especially pay cable may be the means of finally achieving significant levels of locally produced programs. This is so because cable systems reach an audience sufficiently local to attract local advertisers, and because they may be able to charge small groups of viewers with intense interests in local events enough to cover the costs of production. Perhaps most important, the large number of channels on cable will allow a degree of specialization which is not possible with over-the-air broadcasting. As the degree of specialization increases, the cable programming industry may come to resemble the periodical industry, in which small-circulation, specialized publications can be profitable, and which have relatively low production costs. In the short run, however, cable will do what the FCC expects: depend on local signals and imported stations, especially large-city independents, and pay channels with movies and sports, all of which are mass-audience offerings.

THE CURRENT REGULATORY SCHEME

The FCC now regulates cable as a service "ancillary" to broadcasting. It has preempted the field, although certain regulatory activities, such as franchising, have been delegated to state and local authorities. Its authority to regulate cable is derived from the Communications Act of 1934, which does not mention cable specifically. This assumption of power has been upheld by the Supreme Court, in *Southwestern Cable* [20] and *Midwest Video* [21], on the grounds that it is necessary to preserve the FCC's scheme of broadcast regulation, but with the recognition that an explicit congressional mandate would be preferable.[d]

The essential ingredients of FCC cable regulation are those relating to distant signal importation, technical standards, pay television, and programs produced by cable operators. The goal of these regulations is to prevent cable growth from causing serious economic harm to broadcasters and to promote public interest objectives with respect to the services offered by cable systems themselves. The regulations have been in flux for ten years: The commission's approach has been evolutionary [22]. In general, since 1972, the regulations have become gradually less restrictive of cable growth, most significantly by allowing slightly older movies onto pay-TV channels, and by removing or delaying some of the expensive technical requirements, such as twenty channel minimum capacity and two-way communications capability. Each relaxation has been justified by the argument that there is insufficient proof of harm to broadcasters, and that the commission has the power to remedy any serious effects which might result from the relaxation. It is important to note, however, that there is a difference between this approach and one in which cable is "deregulated." The FCC strenuously resists efforts to remove any of its regulatory power over cable. This is necessary if the commission is to assure broadcasters that untoward effects will be remedied. Two excerpts from the FCC's comments on the Office of Telecommunications Policy's draft cable bill illustrate the point:

> ... Thus, it is clear that any proposed regulatory scheme must rest on two principles:
>
> 1) Regulation of the industry must be sufficiently flexible to admit of change; and,
> 2) Cable should not be regulated without regard to other communications media.
>
> In our judgment the legislation proposed by OTP would ignore both of these cardinal principles and create a jurisdictional structure for the regulation of cable which would severely limit this agency's ability to deal with the emerging cable industry. It would remove significant jurisdictional authority from this Commission and substitute statutory regulation by

---

[d]The *Home Box Office* decision, in striking down the FCC's pay-cable rules, may begin to define the limits of such extensions.

Congress. We believe that by having Congress create a detailed body of regulation for cable television, such as is proposed by this bill, an inflexible system would result. The philosophical foundation upon which this, and other regulatory agencies is based is that on-going regulation of emerging and/or mature but evolutionary industries requires constant review, modification, and above all, flexibility. The proposed bill is directly contrary to that philosophy. . . .

Section 709 of the bill would prevent the Commission (or any other governmental authority) from imposing fairness, equal time, origination, and designated access channel obligations on cable systems. Thus the Commission would be precluded from weighing matters involving the public interest and imposing requirements to serve that interest. We have, for instance, often stated our posture with respect to fairness and equal time obligations. The Congressionally mandated policy embodied in Section 315 of the Communications Act was adopted to insure diversity in a medium of scarcity. Cable origination channels are also a scarce resource, controlled by a single entity. We continue to believe that these concepts are, for now, appropriately applicable to cable television originations . . . [23].

Outline of FCC Cable Rules

The commission's rules affecting cable are extensive, and their complexity defies brief summary [24]. The following outline provides a very broad view; the actual rules are much more complicated.

1. *Certificate of Compliance:* Cable systems that retransmit broadcast signals cannot operate legally without what is in effect a license from the commission.

2. *Franchising Standards:* Licenses are not granted unless the cable system has a franchise meeting certain standards; requirements are imposed both on cable systems and franchising authorities. Franchises must be limited to a maximum of fifteen years; construction must begin within one year; the local authority must regulate rates; due process is required in franchise awards; franchise fees are limited; and local authorities are preempted on most other matters.

3. *Signals:* Cable systems must carry local signals and over-the-air signals which, although nonlocal, are "significantly viewed" in the market (i.e., have a specified minimum share of the local audience). In addition, systems may import at least two signals, and as many more as are necessary so that:

Systems in markets 1–50 have 3 independents plus 3 networks
Systems in markets 51–100 have 2 independents plus 3 networks
Systems in markets 101+ have 1 independent plus 3 networks
Systems outside TV markets have no restrictions.

These rules can be illustrated: Suppose a cable system is in one of the largest fifty markets. First, it must carry all the local stations. Second, it must carry any nearby station that manages to obtain 5 percent or more of the local over-the-air audience. It may then, in addition, import from distant cities two stations and enough more so that it carries at least three network stations and three independent stations. However, the imported signals are subject to two further limitations.

First, there is the "leapfrogging" rule, which generally requires cable systems to import the *nearest* qualified distant signals. The leapfrogging rule is apparently meant to encourage localism, since the natural tendency of a cable system would be to import the stations which have the best programming, and these are likely to be independent VHF stations in the very largest cities. If these stations were widely imported, they might begin to form the basis for regional TV networks, capable of tapping regional advertising markets. This already takes place to a certain degree; an example is Oakland's KTVU, which is extensively imported to the intermountain west. The leapfrogging rules discourage this, by often forcing cable systems to pickup nearby underfinanced independent UHF stations. This benefits the imported station and the local broadcasters, and hurts viewers and the cable system.

Second, local stations' "exclusivity" rights must be protected, by blacking out on any imported signal program material for which a local station has broadcast rights. Park has provided preliminary estimates of the effect of the exclusivity provision; a typical system in the top fifty markets would probably have to black out programming on imported nonnetwork signals about 40 percent of the time [25]. Both the leapfrogging and exclusivity rules vary by size of market, and in the case of exclusivity, by type of programming.

4. *Origination:* The 1972 rules required cable systems to originate their own programming on at least one channel, and to make available free channels for, respectively, public free access, local government, and the local school system. Channels not devoted to retransmission of TV stations are subject to the FCC broadcast content regulations, including the fairness doctrine, equal time provisions, pay-TV rules, and obscenity rules.

5. *Capacity:* The 1972 rules imposed a minimum channel capacity constraint (twenty channels) and a two-way communications requirement. These have since been relaxed [26]. The 1972 regulations also contain the so-called $n + 1$ rule:

Whenever all of the channels described in sub-paragraphs (4) through (7) of this paragraph are in use during 80 percent of the weekdays ... for 80 percent of the time during any consecutive 3-hour period for 6 consecutive weeks, such system shall have 6 months in which to make a new channel available ... [27].

This rule, apparently designed to ensure adequate capacity without regulating prices, is very difficult to interpret.

6. *Leased Channel Programming:* Systems may lease channels to others; if they do so, they may not control program content on the leased channels. The FCC asserts jurisdiction to regulate the content and operations of such channel leasees.

7. *Ownership:* Cable systems may not be owned by telephone companies, TV stations in the same market, or networks.

8. *Pay TV:* [Prior to the *HBO* decision.] Cable systems that carry per-program or per-channel pay-TV must meet the following requirements on the pay channels:

   a. No advertising.
   b. Maximum of 90 percent combined sports and movies.
   c. No sports programs if the event has been broadcast in the market within five years; new events cannot be shown for five years after their first occurrence.
   d. No movies between four and ten years old.

The purpose of these rules was to prevent pay-TV channels from bidding away programs which would otherwise have been shown on "free" over-the-air television. Since they were meant to prevent such siphoning of programs to pay-TV, they were called "anti-siphoning" rules. For instance, most movies shown on television now are between four and ten years old; pay-TV systems could not bid on such movies, though they could show newer ones, competing with theatrical exhibitors. The effects of the pay-TV rules are discussed more extensively below.

In addition, there are regulations affecting cable television at the state and local level. Various state governments have created special cable regulatory commissions or awarded such jurisdiction to their public utility commissions. Vermont, Massachusetts, New York, and Connecticut, in particular, are active in this area. The line between federal and state jurisdiction has not yet been clearly drawn. To the extent that cable systems resemble communication common carriers, state governments may have complete authority over intrastate operations. To the extent cable systems resemble broadcasters, FCC authority is supreme. The telephone company and the local jurisdictions seek to limit federal preemption of cable regulation; the cable industry, broadcasters, and the FCC favor it. The FCC has initiated a study to deal with the jurisdiction issue [28]. For a survey of cable's status in the states, see Table 5–5. The FCC has been widely criticized for preempting too much of the responsibility which ought to be exercised at the state and local level with respect to cable; this has worked to the advantage of the cable industry.

Finally, it is worth recounting an incident which may illustrate the divergence between FCC nominal and "real" goals. The cable "freeze" was justified largely in terms of its beneficial effect on UHF TV stations. The argument was that cable systems would have the greatest impact on the financially weak, small UHF stations, and that this was contrary to the commission's long-standing policy to promote UHF development. But economic analysis demonstrated that cable actually *helped* UHF stations, by putting their signals on a technical par with VHF signals [29]. Moreover, the FCC's "freeze" was limited to the top 100 markets, not to the small markets where cable was likely to have the greatest impact, and the only places where broadcasters might go off the air. It is noteworthy that the top 100 markets account for most of the revenues and profits of broadcast stations. And it is in the largest markets that cable is least likely to grow on the basis of distant signals, because of the availability of good over the air local signals. Whatever its goals, the FCC's pre-1972 freeze on distant signals in the top 100 markets had the effect of protecting the profits of big city VHF network-affiliated television stations at the expense of cable television operators, UHF and independent stations, and the viewing public. The post-1972 rules have roughly the same effect, but are less draconian, since they allow some distant signals to be imported. In both cases, the FCC has placed enormous emphasis on gradualism in the face of relatively small risks.

THE IMPACT OF CABLE REGULATION

There have been a number of studies of the effect of various proposed FCC rules on the growth of cable systems, the profitability of TV stations, and the welfare of viewers. These studies focus on the impact of varying the number and type of distant signals allowed under some assumptions about copyright liability.

Table 5–5. FCC Survey of Franchising and Other State Law and Regulation Pertaining to Cable Television—Coded Summary

State	State Regulation	Franchising Authority			A.G. Opinion	Nonfranchise Statutes
		State	County	Municipality		
Alabama	N	N	AP	S(S)[1]	N	N
Alaska	PU	S(S)	N	N	N	N
Arizona	N[2]	N	S(S)	S(S)	N	N
Arkansas	N	N	C(B)	C(B), S(B)	N	Y
California	N[2]	N	S(B)	S(B)	N	Y
Colorado	N	N	CJ, AP	S(B)	N	N
Connecticut	PU	S(S)	N	N	N	Y
Delaware	PU[2]	P, S(S)	N	S(S)	N	Y
Florida	N	N	C(B), S(B)	C(B), S(B)	U	Y
Georgia	N	N	AP	S(B)	N	N
Hawaii	PU	S(S)	N	N	N	Y
Idaho	N	N	AP	S(B)[3]	N	N
Illinois	N	N	S(S)	S(S)[3]	O	N
Indiana	N	N	CJ, Q, AP	S(S)	N	Y
Iowa	N	N	N	S(S)	N	N
Kansas	N	N	C(B)	S(S)	N	N
Kentucky	N	N	C(B)	C(B)	N	N
Louisiana	N[2]	N	S(B)[4]	S(B)	N	Y
Maine	N[2]	N[2]	N[5]	S(S)	N	Y
Maryland	CC	N	S(B), AP	S(B)	O	N
Massachusetts	CC	N	N	S(S)	N	Y
Michigan	N	N	C(B) S(B)[5]	C(B), S(B)	O	Y
Minnesota	CC	N	S(S)	S(S)	N	Y
Mississippi	N[2]	N	N	S(B)	U	Y
Missouri	N	N	C(B)[6], AP	S(B)[7] CL	N	N
Montana	N	N	N	S(B), AP	N	Y
Nebraska	N	N	S(S)	S(S)	N	N

State						
Nevada	PU	S(S)	N	N	N	N
New Hampshire	N	N	Q	S(S)	N	N
New Jersey	PU²	S(S)	N	S(S)	N	Y
New Mexico	N²	N	AP	C(B)	O	N
New York	CC	N	S(S)	S(S)	N	Y
North Carolina	N²	N	S(S)	S(S)	N	Y
North Dakota	N	N	N	S(B)	O	N
Ohio	N	N	C(B), S(B)	C(B), S(B)	N	N
Oklahoma	N	N	N	S(B)	N	N
Oregon	N	N	C(B), AP	C(B)	N	N
Pennsylvania	N	N	N	CL, AP	U	N
Rhode Island	PU²	S(S)	N	N	N	N
South Carolina	N	N	AP	C(B), S(B)	U	Y
South Dakota	N	N	N	S(S)	N	N
Tennessee	N	N	S(B), CJ	S(B)	U	N
Texas	N²	N	AP	S(B)	N	Y
Utah	PU	S(S)	S(B), CJ	S(B), CJ	N	Y
Vermont	P	N	N	N	N	N
Virginia	N	N	S(S)	S(S)	N	Y
Washington	N	N	AP	S(B)	U	N
West Virginia	N	N	S(S), AP	S(S)	O	Y
Wisconsin	N	N	N⁵	C(B), CJ	N	N
Wyoming	N	N	N	S(B)	N	N

1. Specific local bills must be adopted.
2. Cable television is defined not as a public utility by AG opinion, State case or statute.
3. Except townships.
4. Parishes are the equivalent of counties.
5. County has no unincorporated areas or little area outside of incorporated municipalities.
6. Only home rule counties; all others governed by statute.
7. Only charter cities; all others governed by statute.

(Table 5-5.   continued overleaf)

Table 5–5.   Notes continued

Basis of Franchising Authority

AP — alternative proposal accepted by the FCC.
C(B) — broad constitutional authorization.
CJ — claim of jurisdiction unchallenged: no specific statute.
CL — case law; jurisdictional issue taken to court and upheld.
N   — no franchising authority for cable television.
P   — partial regulation of cable television.
Q   — authority questionable intrastate.
S(B) — broad statutory authority for franchising; statute not specifically directed toward cable television.
S(S) — specific statutory authority for franchising of cable television systems.

Attorney General Opinion

O   — official published opinion by the state Attorney General.
N   — none.
U   — unofficial comment or letter from a state Attorney General's office.

State Regulatory Authority

CC — independent cable commission.
PU — public utility-type regulation (PUC, PSC, PSB).
N   — none.

Non-Franchise Statutes

N   — no statute adopted on cable television areas other than franchising, if any.
Y   — statute(s) other than or in addition to franchising adopted on cable television.

Source: Sharon A. Briley, *Cable TV—State Regulation: A Survey of Franchising and Other State Law and Regulation on Cable Television*, Federal Communications Commission, Cable Television Bureau, May 5, 1975, revised, December 17, 1975.

Distant signals in big cities are probably necessary for cable to be economically viable. They increase demand for the system's services at relatively low cost, and this may allow the operator to achieve sufficient penetration of the market to make other services profitable, notably pay-TV channels containing movies. More exotic and specialized services, such as alarm systems, meter reading, and electronic shopping, are much talked about. It is argued that these exotic services cannot be offered until cable systems have a high penetration, and that distant signals are a necessary preliminary step. The evidence in some studies suggests that distant signals *may be* just enough to make cable systems marginally profitable in large cities with good over-the-air signals [30]. The amount of copyright payment and the costs of services required by regulators may make the difference. Thus, while none of the parties deny the necessity for copyright liability, it took many years to settle on the particular formula contained in the 1976 Copyright Act, which fixes payments at a small percentage of gross cable revenues, to be paid into a central pool.

Because of the evolutionary approach taken by the FCC to cable regulation, it is difficult to measure the effects of that regulation quantitatively.[e] Clearly FCC regulation has harmed consumers who would otherwise have been able to subscribe to cable service, and has harmed subscribers by limiting their range of choice. Clearly FCC regulation has maintained the profits of broadcasters and networks at levels higher than they would otherwise have been. Possibly FCC regulation has prevented or delayed some consumers from being subjected to a diminution in the quantity or quality of available over-the-air signals.

Economic Effects

The following summarizes what is known about the economics of distant signals and pay-TV; most of the studies deal with the question, what would happen if there were unlimited distant signal importation?

Impact on Cable. All of the econometric studies agree on one point: imported distant signals increase cable penetration [31]. They disagree on the *magnitude* of the effect, but these disagreements do not appear to be statistically significant. Moreover, such disagreement as does exist centers on predictions of regulatory policy.[f] Un-

---

[e]The rules are changed often enough to make the experimental data limited due to adjustment lags.

[f]That is, it appears that after differences in assumptions about future regulatory policy are taken account of, the various econometric predictions are probably about the same.

limited distant signal importation will make cable initially viable in some markets where it is not now viable. For instance, cable appears to be viable in cities as large as San Diego, which has a large and profitable "grandfathered" cable system, and which ranks about fiftieth in size. The studies do not permit very accurate predictions because the existing data are conditioned by the FCC's present and past restrictive rules, discussed above.[g] Unlimited importation is likely to bring cable to many, perhaps a majority of the top 100 markets. But in the very largest markets, cable growth probably depends on pay programming as well as more free signals because they already have three clear network signals and several independent stations. Of course, the situation in individual markets will vary according to local conditions, such as terrain, the number of local signals, and whether many local stations are UHF.

It is important to point out that we are dealing with a threshold effect. In many of the top 100 markets, distant signals will provide the initial incentive to investment and construction of systems which will later be able to add riskier penetration-increasing services, such as pay-TV. Full deregulation of distant signals is probably a necessary but not sufficient condition for the creation of a truly national cable television service over the next decade.

The econometric studies (which generally attempt to relate existing cable penetration to the number and type of signals available) vary in their methodology and assumptions. Generally, they predict that unlimited distant signal importation would increase the number of cable subscribers by between four and eleven million in the top 100 markets, compared to present policies. Table 5—6 shows the range of estimated increases in subscribing households predicted by two of the studies under various assumptions. A middle estimate would be 7 million. There are presently 5.8 million subscribers in the top 100 markets, so this would be a significant increase. Curiously, the studies show that imported *duplicate* network signals have as much impact as imported independent stations. This may be due to the value of nonnetwork syndicated programming (outside prime time) on network stations.

Most of the proposals for deregulation of distant signals assume that all local stations will be carried, and that all local stations would be protected from simultaneous duplication of their programming by blacking out identical programming on imported signals. This does viewers little or no harm, and protects the local stations' audiences.

---

[g]Cable systems with a given number of imported signals now are not necessarily importing the most profitable signals, because of the leapfrogging roles.

Table 5–6. Increase in Cable Households in Top 100 Markets Due to Two More Independent Imported Signals Plus 0, 1, 2, and 3 Duplicate Network Signals *(Based on 57.1 Million Television Households in Top 100 Markets)*

	2 More Ind* + 0 Dup Nets	2 More Ind + 1 Dup Net	2 More Ind + 2 Dup Nets	2 More Ind + 3 Dup Nets
Park Estimate (Low)	994,000	2,835,000	3,907,000	4,672,000
Park Estimate (High)	1,554,000	4,427,000	6,106,000	7,300,000
CRA Estimate Linear Model	2,490,000	4,781,000	7,072,000	9,362,000
CRA Estimate Nonlinear Model	1,565,000	6,632,000	9,584,000	11,698,000

Source: Unpublished compilations by V. Sardella from studies by Park (1972) and Charles River Associates (1973).
*In addition to local signals.

Impact on Broadcasters.   Measurement of cable impact on broadcast station profits is hampered by the absence of accurate data. The "official" FCC reports of station financial data simply are not credible. For instance, these data show drastic changes from year to year and from (similarly situated) station to station in individual line items. Moreover, the accounts purport to show the continued existence over twenty years of stations which make consistent accounting losses, and which nevertheless change hands at positive prices. There is no uniform system of accounts, and conglomerate ownership makes accounting artifice a distinct possibility.

Nevertheless, the studies would seem to support the following statements [32]. Cable penetration in the top 100 markets (serving 87 percent of the population of the country) will not cause stations to go off the air. It will necessarily, however, reduce the revenues of VHF network affiliates.

Generally, since independent UHF stations are helped by cable, and since both UHF and VHF network affiliates are quite profitable to begin with, the only stations likely to face any danger of going off the air as a result of cable growth are small-market independent VHFs. There are only eleven such stations below the top hundred markets. If the "danger list" is extended to the next most vulnerable group, network UHF stations in markets 101–200, only fifty-nine additional stations are involved. Thus the total number of "endangered" stations is much less than 10 percent of all TV stations, and the affected viewing population is probably less than 1 percent of the total population. The reduction in revenues to stations due to increased competition will reduce the stations' ability to pay high prices to talent for local programming. Except for news, such programming is already *de minimus*, and in any event is apparently not of much value to consumers (audiences are very small). These effects will take place because (and only if) viewers in fact *prefer* the alternative programming provided by cable.

In the smaller markets, it is possible that a very few stations may be driven off the air by cable. Again, this will happen *because* (and *only if*) viewers prefer to watch the imported material. To the extent that significant numbers of consumers do not have access to cable, it will pay the broadcasters to stay on the air, because the cost of doing so will be small, and lower than the advertising revenues to be gained. If not, rural areas may well be profitably served by community- or cable-owned broadcast repeaters. However, it should be pointed out that until 1972 these smaller markets were not protected by the FCC from cable, and that the number of TV stations on the air in these markets has actually *increased*.

Unfortunately, the only adequate study of the impact of cable on broadcasting is one done in 1970 by R.E. Park. Table 5−7 summarizes the Park predictions. The numbers in Table 5−7 are percentage revenue losses compared to the situation with no cable. The predictions may be overstated (that is, the impact on broadcasters may be less than that indicated) for the following reasons: (1) The predictions were based on higher levels of cable penetration than seem to have taken place, in part because (2) Park assumed that the FCC would allow more distant signals than it in fact did allow. Also, (3) the impact predictions do not take account of the effect of increased advertising revenues to stations being imported. (This explains the negative revenue effect shown in Table 5−7 for VHF independents in the top fifty markets.)

Clearly, the biggest impact of cable is in the markets below the top 100, comprising 96 percent of the nation's land area, but only 14 percent of the population. It is in these markets that cable penetration is already greatest, because of the scarcity of over-the-air signals.

Table 5−7. Estimated Percentage Change in Revenue Due to Cable During the 1970s[a]

	Market Rank				
Type of Station	*1–50*	*51–100*	*101–150*	*151–200*	*1–200*
Network VHF	−17	−24	−31	−55	−20
Network UHF	+12	−18	−15	(b)	−14
Independent VHF	−11	(b)	(b)	(b)	−11
Independent UHF	+20	+20	(b)	(b)	+19
All	−15	−23	−30	−56	−18

Source: R.E. Park, *Potential Impact of Cable Growth on Television Broadcasting*, R–587–FF, The Rand Corporation, 1970, p. 5.

Notes:

[a] All figures reflect the effect on local audience only. The advertising value of distant audiences increases station revenues in some cases.

[b] Classifications with fewer than five stations are not reported in detail, but are included in the totals.

[c] The following table shows the number of stations by type as of 1974, along with their reported profits:

	Markets 1–100		Markets 101–200	
	No.	*Profits*	*No.*	*Profits*
Network VHF	244	474,951	219	33,460
Network UHF	58	7,200	59	−900
Independent VHF	20	11,677	11	−3,300
Independent UHF	52	−10,345	8	−1,927

(Profits or losses in thousands of dollars.)

If stations in these small markets are, despite the historical evidence to the contrary, forced off the air, there exist means to cope with the problem. The staff of the House Subcommittee on Communications has proposed that a program like REA be established, to ensure that combinations of cable systems, broadcast translators, and repeaters are available for this purpose.

The Park estimates of revenue impact from cable cannot be directly translated into predictions of profit losses for broadcast stations. This is so because stations faced with increased competition will not react passively. They will adjust their programming patterns and thus their expenses. It is very difficult to model this behavior or to make profitability predictions, but it is clear that it cannot be assumed that expenses will continue to grow at the old rate while revenues grow at a slower rate.

The most relevant and striking piece of evidence on the question of harm to broadcasters comes from history. In the decade prior to 1972 the FCC did not protect TV stations from cable if those stations were in small markets—below the top-100. All the economic studies agree that the adverse impact of cable on broadcasters is greatest in these small, one and two station markets. And by 1973, cable penetration in below the top-100 markets averaged 32 percent, which is about the penetration level predicted for top-100 markets with unlimited distant signal importation in several studies. Therefore, one might expect to find that the number of viable broadcast stations in small markets declined over the decade before 1972. But nothing could be further from the truth; the number of stations on the air in these markets actually *increased* from 295 to 340.

The broadcast industry's contention that viewers will suffer a widespread diminution of over-the-air broadcast service as a result of cable television's ability to give viewers more choice is therefore not very plausible. Some stations will actually be benefited. Others will have lower revenues, expenses, and profits than they otherwise would. In any event, there will be little or no impact unless cable achieves relatively high penetration rates, which it can do only by offering consumers a service which is worth subscribing to, and therefore better than the service now available.

Impact on Consumers. [33]   As was pointed out above, increased cable penetration will happen if and only if most consumers are better off as a result. Consumers who subscribe do so because they value the greater range of choice provided by cable. Consumers who choose not to subscribe in the large markets where most of the population is found are very unlikely to be worse off. This is because the worst that can happen is a diminution in the quantity and quality of local programs, which are already unpopular and unprofitable, except for local news, which is probably so profitable that it is in no danger. (The profitability of local news is attested to by the extreme reluctance of local stations to accede to network plans to increase the length of the network news shows.) That small proportion of the population which resides in small towns in the hinterland already has access to cable (penetration rates in Montana are 34 percent, Wyoming 44 percent, and West Virginia 34 percent). Isolated farmhouses and villages too small to wire are already and will continue to be served to some degree by low cost repeaters and translators, perhaps eventually operated by cable systems themselves. Increased competition in the broadcast market will not significantly reduce present levels of service to viewers; indeed, it is almost a contradiction in terms. The alleged "harmful" effects of cable occur only if cable offers increased service to the public.

Pay Television

The effect of pay television depends on two supply elasticities: the extent to which increased prices will call forth additional programs and channels. Cable provides (and over-the-air broadcasting does not provide) a very elastic supply of channels. There is broad agreement that the supply of series-type entertainment programming is similarly elastic. Movies and sports will be dealt with below.

The Hollywood program production industry is composed of many small firms. Indeed, most series-type programs are produced by a group of people who come together for that purpose alone, then break up to form new groups around other programs. The cost of producing series-type programs is not inherently high. But very successful programs that are sufficiently popular to attract the twenty million or more viewers needed for network viability can command high prices. "All in the Family," an incredibly successful program, started out costing only about $25,000 per episode. Of course, when it became successful, the competition for it in effect drove up the price, and the price that could be charged for other Lear (the producer) programs. Thus, it is competition on the demand side, backed by the very large profits from network advertising, that leads to high prices for programs, not basic production costs [34]. (The high prices paid for successful shows go to producers and actors in the form of "economic rents." These are payments in excess of what is needed to get them on the air. Lower revenues would result in lower payments but not discontinuation of the programs.) The supply of programming is very elastic, and the increased demand created by allowing people to pay for programming will result in more programs, not just higher rents to existing factors of production. It is noteworthy, in this connection, that the Hollywood actors' unions claim to have an 85 percent unemployment rate [35].

Besides calling forth an increased supply of programs, pay-TV has an additional advantage. Consumers can express the intensity of their preferences by, as it were, "voting with dollars." Consumers are now allowed to do this with respect to virtually all commodities except television. Removing the restrictions on pay-TV will allow relatively small groups of consumers with intense demands to support specialized programming which cannot profitably be supplied by advertiser-supported broadcasters [36]. (Pay-TV also allows consumers to pay for the right to be free of commercials if they wish.) Just as the present thousands of small-circulation periodicals and newspapers could not exist on advertising revenue alone, thousands of potential TV programs are barred from the market by the exclusive dependence on advertising fostered by present regulations.

Pay-TV does not make consumers better off if program supply is not increased by increased prices. This is certainly true of a handful of unique and popular events, such as the Super Bowl and the World Series. Other, less unique, sporting events are in relatively elastic supply. For example, there has been an increase in college bowl games as a result of increased TV revenues over the past decade. Allowing the unique events in sporting onto pay-TV will not make consumers better off. But allowing other sporting events onto pay-TV will make consumers better off, by increasing the number of such events available to them.

We now turn to motion pictures. Broadcasters argue that motion pictures will be "siphoned" from broadcast TV to pay-cable. This ignores the fact that such films are already marketed through time on a variety of media. Theatrical motion pictures typically are exhibited in one or two "exclusive run" theaters in a city, then in several "first run" theaters in suburban areas, then in the neighborhood or "second run" theaters, then on network television, and finally on syndicated television. The timing of this sequence varies from film to film, and some films skip one or more steps. Pay-cable exhibition *at worst* may *delay* slightly the television exhibition of such films. (At best, it may actually bring the films to "free" television more quickly, as cable displaces second-run theatrical distribution.) Even if cable penetration were very much greater than it is likely to be for the foreseeable future, such films would still be released to television after their pay-cable run, in order to capture the advertising revenues of those audiences who were unwilling to pay to see the movie earlier. This is exactly what happens at present with the sequence from theatrical exhibition to television exhibition.

Broadcasters have argued with enormous success over the years that pay-TV rules will result in people having to "pay for what is now free." And there is a grain of truth in the slogan. Many popular entertainment events will be available on pay-TV before they are broadcast on free TV. But until cable and pay-TV penetration rates are very much higher than they are likely to be for the next decade, even with deregulation, this is not going to pose a noticeable problem for consumers. In any event, paying for what is now "free" will be a small matter when compared to the increased supply of entertainment and information which will result from giving consumers the freedom to purchase what they want, rather than what the advertisers want them to have. The resistance of public officials to the notion of free markets in programs is convincing evidence of their reluctance to seem to deprive the public of its equity rights in the status quo.

POLICY STUDIES

There have been four major policy studies of cable television in the 1970s: The Sloan Commission Report (1971), the Cabinet Committee Report (1974), the Committee for Economic Development Report (1975), and the House Subcommittee on Communications Staff Report (1976) [37]. While there are differences in emphasis among these studies, their conclusions are remarkably similar. Each recommends that the rules against pay television be relaxed, with the exception of "major" sports events. Except for the Sloan Commission, each recommends that cable channels be open to nondiscriminatory paid access, without control of content by the operator or by the government. Each recommends a greater role for state and local government in regulating cable, and a more limited role for the FCC. Each recommends that the FCC cease to protect broadcasters from cable competition, while endorsing some form of copyright liability for distant signals.

Considering the prestige and resources of the groups who labored over these policy studies, it seems worthwhile to review their recommendations.

The Sloan Commission was established by the Alfred P. Sloan Foundation to study cable communication policy issues. Its sixteen commissioners, headed by Professor Edward S. Mason, included two former mayors, several university presidents, and a number of other distinguished citizens. The commission's staff sponsored a number of studies of cable by academic experts in economics, engineering, the arts, education, and public broadcasting. The principal thrust of the Sloan report is that cable represents an opportunity to achieve a wide range of social and cultural goals, and is therefore worthy of promotion by the government. At the same time, the Sloan Commission emphasized the use of cable for what has been called "social engineering," and therefore favored rather close government control. This was probably the main reason for their rejection of a common carrier role for cable. Just as each of the other reports does, the Sloan report acknowledges the problem of broadcast-cable competition, and deals with it by suggesting that cable have full copyright liability for distant signals, so that the competition is "fair," but then proposes no limit on the number of imported signals.

The Cabinet Committee was established in 1971, and included the secretaries of Commerce, HEW, and HUD, along with two White House aides, under the chairmanship of the director of the office of telecommunications policy, Clay T. Whitehead. The Cabinet Committee's report, issued in early 1974 after a number of delays, put great emphasis on a reduction in the degree of federal regulation of cable, along with the separation of cable programming from cable transmission services. One of the objections of the cable industry to this separation policy is that it will result in rate of return regulation of cable operators as common carriers. The Cabinet Committee recommended that such regulation be prohibited, on the grounds that for the foreseeable future cable systems would continue to have significant local competition from broadcast and print media. The Cabinet Committee rejected all of the FCC's public service requirements for cable, on the grounds that this would slow the growth of cable. The committee emphasized a general laissez-faire federal policy toward cable, but with broad freedom for state and local governments to make policies not inconsistent with the separations principle. Finally, the Cabinet Committee, like the Sloan Commission, recommended an end to the anti-pay-TV rules, except for major sports events.

The CED report, issued in 1975 by a committee of the CED which included several dissenting broadcasters, did not go quite so far as the Cabinet Committee. The CED recommended nondiscriminatory access to cable, but with cable-operator control of a "limited" number of channels. The CED suggests gradual relaxation of the rules against pay-TV, except for major sports events, and copyright liability for distant signals. As in the other reports since the Sloan Commission, the CED suggested that more power be given to state cable commissions, and less to the FCC.

The study by the staff of the House Subcommittee on Communications, issued in early 1976, is in many ways the most comprehensive and best argued of all the policy studies of cable. The staff report deals with the "harm to broadcasters" issue by strongly suggesting an end to FCC protectionist policies, imposing copyright liability for distant signals, and establishing a program to provide services to rural viewers who might be affected by cable's impact on over-the-air service. As did all the previous reports, the staff study recommends an end to the rules restricting pay-TV, except for major sports events. Finally, the staff study goes even beyond the Cabinet Committee in endorsing application of the separations principle.

The list of public officials and private citizens who have been responsible for these studies and reports is long and impressive, and their recommendations are remarkably consistent. None has taken very seriously the broadcasters' argument that the public will be damaged by the growth of cable and of pay television. On the contrary, each has seen cable as a dramatic opportunity to increase the range and diversity of entertainment and other communications services to the American public, each has seen the FCC as an overly conservative and protectionist agency, and each has called for federal legislation to set things right. In view of these studies it is remarkable that the Domestic Council Task Force on Deregulation in 1976 chose to conclude that there had been insufficient research on the question of cable's impact on broadcasters to support an administration effort to "deregulate" cable television [38].

CONCLUSION

The surrender of the Ford Administration cable deregulation effort was a surrender to the political power of the broadcasting industry. In this respect, broadcasting is almost unique among regulated industries, since many politicians believe, rightly or wrongly, that television has an important effect on political fortunes, and that TV news coverage of their own activities may be affected by their stand on policy issues touching the broadcasters' pocketbook. In the face of this it is remarkable that cable has made as much progress as it has.

The crucial element in the story was the willingness of the FCC to assert, and the willingness of the courts to uphold, regulatory jurisdiction over cable growth. Given that jurisdiction, the development of the industry could be controlled in an "orderly" way, both because the administrative process inherently favored slow resolution of issues and because the FCC itself wished to minimize the risks faced by those few broadcasters and those very few viewers that might be harmed by cable growth.

Chapter 6

Surface Freight Transportation: The Regulation of Intermodal Competition

INTRODUCTION

The regulation of freight transportation in this country has become increasingly complex over the past few decades.

At the heart of the dilemma one finds the development of extensive rivalry among alternative transport modes, commonly referred to as intermodal competition. Almost all kinds of freight can be carried either by railroad, over waterways, or via motor carriers over the highway. Liquid or gaseous products often go by pipeline, and a small part of the freight transported in this country is shipped by air.

Freight transportation presents a radical departure from the textbook case for regulation that is usually developed for a single product firm, with a monopoly in its market, operating with economies of scale. First, intermodal competition means that shippers may have a choice in purchasing transportation service instead of having to deal with a single supplier. In addition, transportation firms will usually supply many kinds of service, and must be regarded as multiproduct firms rather than as single product firms. Finally, some of the competing modes may operate with economies of scale, while others do not.

In light of the increased intermodal competition of the past few decades (see Table 6-1), many questions regarding the appropriate stance of regulation have been raised. Should all modes be regulated if some of the modes are not characterized by economies of scale? Should any of the modes be regulated? If some or all of the modes

Table 6–1.   Intercity Freight Traffic in the United States, by Mode of Transport and by Percentage Federally Regulated *(in billions of ton miles)*

Year	Airways	Railroads	Inland Waterways		Motor Carriers		Oil Pipelines	
			Total	Percentage Regulated	Total	Percentage Regulated	Total	Percentage Regulated
1940	0.014	379.2	118.1	n.a.*	62.0	33.4	59.3	n.a.
1950	0.318	596.9	163.3	6.0	172.9	37.9	129.2	79.0
1960	0.778	579.1	220.3	n.a.	285.5	n.a.	228.6	n.a.
1967	2.592	731.2	274.0	n.a.	388.5	n.a.	361.0	n.a.
1976	4.0	796.0	352.0	n.a.	490.0	46.0	525.0	n.a.

Sources: A.F. Friedlaender, *The Dilemma of Freight Transport Regulation*, (Brookings Institution, 1969), Table C.1.
D.V. Harper, *Transportation in America*, (Prentice-Hall, 1978), Table 10–2.
P. Roberts, "Some Aspects of Regulatory Reform of the U.S. Trucking Industry," forthcoming in the conference volume for the Workshop on Motor Carrier Economic Regulation, National Academy of Sciences.

*n.a. means not available.

are to be regulated, what kind of pricing, entry, or other controls are needed in order to efficiently use transportation resources? What do economic principles tell us about the relationships between tariffs, the allocation of shared costs (i.e., costs which are incurred in the provision of two or more services), and the extent to which inter-modal competition may be desirable?

We begin by reviewing briefly some of the technological and legal developments surrounding the regulation of intermodal competition in freight transport. This will be followed by a discussion of some of the ways in which the administrative process has been used to resolve the inevitable conflicts that arise with intermodal competition. We then discuss some recent economic research which shows how pricing and entry decisions should be related to one another in order to efficiently use transportation resources, particularly when one of the modes operates with economies of scale. We will conclude by comparing these principles with those which have evolved from administrative law, the courts, and regulatory practice.

LEGISLATION AND INTERMODAL COMPETITION: A BRIEF BACKGROUND

Although there were earlier attempts to control rates and profits under the charters of some railroads, the first widespread regulation of freight transport occurred with the Granger movement in the 1870s. The railroads became a focus for agrarian discontent following the Civil War. Historical accounts cite several reasons for the dissatisfaction. Postwar rail rates continued to be higher than farmers had generally expected. There was extensive price discrimination on the part of the railroads, which often charged very high prices to shippers who had no available alternatives to rail transport. The need for large amounts of capital in the construction of railways attracted much foreign investment in the industry, and foreign ownership was resented by many. In addition there was a great deal of financial instability among railroads. When a new firm entered, or an existing one attempted to expand its market, it would often cut rates in order to divert traffic to itself. Rate wars were common, and railroads often gave secret rebates to large shippers (such as the Standard Oil Company) in order to attract their business.

As a result, during the 1870s Minnesota, Iowa, Wisconsin, and Illinois enacted laws designed to control the activities of railroads in their respective states. While these laws (often called Granger laws) were not identical, their basic provisions were quite similar. They specified maximum tariffs on various types of commodities, prohibited higher charges for a given commodity hauled over shorter distances, and established state commissions to administer the law.

The regulation stemming from the Granger laws was not notably effective. The rate provisions were not very flexible, and legislators and administrators had very little experience to guide them through conditions of economic fluctuation, such as the panic of 1873. In fact, in Minnesota, Iowa, and Wisconsin, the laws were ultimately repealed. But they helped to set the stage for regulation at the federal level.

The Interstate Commerce Act

The basic conditions which led to the Granger laws continued into the 1880s. While the Granger laws had some control over intrastate commerce, the courts held that states could impose no direct restrictions on interstate commerce [1]. The Interstate Commerce Act in 1887 established the Interstate Commerce Commission to regulate the interstate activities of the railroads.

There are two major views about the primary forces that led to the passage of the Interstate Commerce Act, and much has been written about each. Alfred Kahn calls the first the traditional view, and summarizes it as follows:

> The traditional view has been that the entire corpus of railroad legislation, beginning with the state Granger laws of the 1870's, was the response above all else to public outrage at the monopolistic exploitations of the railroads; that the roads themselves bitterly opposed this legislation and exerted themselves continuously and with almost complete success during the first twenty years of the Commission's life to hamstringing its regulatory efforts; and it was the combined pressures by shippers, the public at large, and the ICC that finally produced the Hepburn Act of 1906 and Mann-Elkins Act of 1910, which gave the Commission the authority it needed to protect the public" [2].

The second viewpoint, as presented by Gabriel Kolko, is that the single most important advocates of regulation were the railroads, not the farmers and small shippers [3]. According to this view, the primary reason for this advocacy was that the railroads had not succeeded in their attempts to cartelize the industry throughout the 1870s and 1880s. Efforts to stabilize prices and market shares failed to prevent recurrent price wars and cutthroat competition [4]. As a result, Kolko argues that the railroads turned to a political solution to bring about stability—government intervention through regulation.

The resolution of this debate is not the central issue here. The main point for our purposes is that the Interstate Commerce Act dealt primarily with the railroads, and only tangentially with the intermodal competition between the railroads and the only other major mode of the time, the water carriers. The act imposed regulation on water carriers only where a carrier provided a transport service with a route partly by rail and partly by water. It did not give the ICC jurisdiction over firms which engaged only in the provision of water transportation.

Two of the provisions of the act which might have had some effect on intermodal competition were held by the courts to be quite weak. First, although the commission could rule that a rate was unreasonable, the courts held that the act did not empower the commission to prescribe either maximum or minimum rates [5]. It could only accept or reject existing rates. The commission could not prescribe maximum rates until the Hepburn Act was passed in 1906, and it could not set minimum rates (the ones most likely to concern intermodal competition directly) until the passage of the Transportation Act of 1920 (see Table 6-2).

A second provision of the Interstate Commerce Act which might have affected intermodal competition was the long-and-short-haul clause. Consider travel over a single line in a given direction, through (in order) points A, B, and C. The route from B to C forms a part of the route from A to C. The long-and-short-haul clause stated that the rate for a given commodity should not be higher for the B to C route than for the A to C route, where the transportation services were provided "under substantially similar circumstances and conditions" [6].

The strength of the clause was tested in *Interstate Commerce Commission* v. *Alabama Midland Railway Company* in 1897 [7]. The commission argued before the Supreme Court that the presence of other rail carriers between two more distant points (such as A and C) and the absence of such competition between two nearer points (such as B and C) did not create circumstances which were dissimilar enough to render the long-and-short-haul clause inapplicable. In other words, the commission felt that the clause should apply in such a case. The Court disagreed.

It was not until the Mann-Elkins Act of 1910 that the commission received the power the Court had denied it in the Alabama Midland case. The Mann-Elkins Act removed the phrase "under substantially similar circumstances and conditions," and made the long-and-short-haul clause applicable in all cases, unless an exception was allowed

Table 6–2.   Effect of Selected Legislation on Intermodal Competition

Date	Legislation	Major Bearing on Intermodal Competition
1887	Interstate Commerce Act	Established entry and rate regulation for rail by the ICC
1906	Hepburn Act	ICC regulation of oil pipelines ICC prescribes maximum rail rates
1910	Mann-Elkins Act	Strengthened rail long- and-short-haul clause Limitation on rail rate changes in response to water competition
1912	Panama Canal Act	Separation of rail and water interests where intermodal competition is reduced
1920	Transportation Act of 1920	ICC prescribes minimum rail rates
1935	Motor Carrier Act of 1935	ICC regulates rates and entry for large portion of the motor carrier industry
1940	Transportation Act of 1940	ICC regulates rates and entry for small portion of inland water carrier industry Congressional expression for preservation of the inherent advantages for each mode
1958	Transportation Act of 1958	Congressional expression against umbrella rate-making
1976	Railroad Revitalization and Regulatory Reform Act of 1976	Rail rates are freed to fluctuate within certain limits

Source: See text.

by the commission. The Mann-Elkins Act took a further step with respect to intermodal competition. If a rival carrier reduced its rates along a route in order to meet competition from water carriage, it could not increase these rates at a later time, unless the commission recognized that increased rates were warranted by changing conditions other than the elimination of competition from water carriers.

The congressional concern for intermodal competition was further evidenced by the Panama Canal Act of 1912. This legislation was intended to separate the ownership and operation of rail and water transport activities where competition between the two was possible. The separation of interests was to be without exception in the case of the Panama Canal. Where existing firms provided both rail and water service, a continuation would be allowed as long as water competition was not reduced as a result. The act also gave the ICC the power to order a railroad to interconnect with the dock of a water carrier. This prohibited railroads from refusing interconnection in order to force shippers to use only rail transport to a destination when water carriage was possible over part of the route.

Thus, by the time motor carriers became a viable mode in the 1930s, the regulation of intermodal competition had become quite complex. The ICC had jurisdiction over all interstate railroad and oil pipeline transport (the latter having been established with the Hepburn Act of 1906), but only limited control over interstate water carriage. In historical perspective, one could argue that a pattern had begun to emerge. The two modes which required large amounts of capital for entry, and which were most likely to have economies of scale were placed under the jurisdiction of the ICC.[a] The remaining mode was left largely outside the jurisdiction of the ICC. With the arrival of the motor carriers, this pattern was no longer to hold.

Motor Carriers and Intermodal Competition

With the federal funding of highways and improvements in the internal combustion engine, the motor carrier share of intercity freight began increasing during the 1930s.

In 1930, the railroads carried approximately 74 percent of the total of domestic intercity freight traffic, while motor carriers carried less than 4 percent of the total, oil pipelines about 5 percent, and inland waterways 15 percent. In 1969, the railroads hauled only 41.09 percent of the intercity freight traffic. In the same year the motor carriers had increased their share to 21.78 percent [8].

[a] The issue of economies of scale in rail transport has been investigated many times by economists, and still awaits conclusive resolution. This will be discussed more extensively below, under "Optimal Pricing."

There were several factors which led to the passage of the Motor Carrier Act of 1935. Increased competition from motor carriers created many problems for the railroads and their regulators. First, railroads were already experiencing reduced freight transport demands and lower revenues because of the depression. Excess rail capacity increased at the same time. Motor carriers compounded the financial problems of the railroads by diverting still further traffic to the highways.

Competition from motor carriers also made it difficult to protect traditional discriminatory pricing policies, which included high prices for high-value services (manufactured goods) and low tariffs for bulk commodities, such as agricultural produce. Before motor carrier competition became severe, regulators could satisfy agrarian interests for low bulk commodity rates and rail interests for adequate profits with the traditional pricing scheme. However, unregulated motor carriers naturally viewed the high-value (manufactured goods) market as having the more profitable potential. Their entry into those markets made it difficult (if not impossible) for bulk commodity rates to remain low while railroad profits continued at their preentry levels. Those familiar with regulation will recognize this as an example of creamskimming. Given a rate structure for extant firms which makes one market appear profitable and another not, a rational entrant will choose to enter the former if he is allowed to do so.

Some large motor carriers, with well-established markets, also favored regulation in order to insulate themselves from the price and market share fluctuations that might occur without regulation. According to Friedlaender, "The support of the Motor Carrier Act from the large truckers, who desired some modification in the extent of the price competition, and the shippers who favored rate stabilization, was based on a desire to limit the excesses of competition" [9].

All three of these forces (the protection of the railroads' financial position, the protection of the traditional pricing scheme, and the desire for stability by some interest groups) do appear to have influenced the decision to pass the Motor Carrier Act. In addition, there is a fourth explanation based on the inertia that regulatory systems often seem to possess. This position is stated succinctly by Pegrum:

> The alternatives, as seen by the Coordinator [of Transportation] at the time, were to abandon the regulation of transportation to the antitrust laws and to subject all of the agencies to the same type that had been developed for the railroads. *No analysis was made of the fundamentally different economic characteristics of the various agencies [modes], nor was any consideration given to a program of regulation that might be in accordance with these differences.* Instead, legislation was recommended that

would regulate common carriers by motor essentially in the same way that railroads were controlled and force the other motor carriers as much as possible into the same mold. This became the basis of the Motor Carriers Act of 1935, which has survived with minor modifications to the present time [10]. (Emphasis added.)

While the act extended regulation to large parts of the motor carrier industry, it did not include all interstate motor carriage. Two kinds of carriers were placed under both rate and entry regulation, common carriers and contract carriers. Common carriers, those which serve the general public, were required to obtain a certificate of public convenience and necessity indicating the route or area to be served, in order to provide service. Their rates now must be approved by the ICC, and are published for the public record.

Contract carriers provide special kinds of service under individual agreements with shippers. The commission generally allows contract carriers to provide their special services as long as they do not interfere substantially with the business of common carriers. Contract carriers must obtain permits to provide service, and are presently required to file their rates with the commission.

Other kinds of motor carrier activities defined by the act are not subject to entry and rate regulations. If a firm not engaging in transportation as its primary enterprise (such as a manufacturer) desires to transport its own commodities rather than hire a common or contract carrier, it may do so. Such transportation is referred to as private carriage. A private carrier may not offer its services for hire to other firms.[b]

Among other activities which are not regulated, perhaps the most significant is the carriage of agricultural commodities. Congress has not felt it necessary to prescribe common carrier obligations for motor carriage in order to guarantee adequate service for agricultural shippers. This exemption represents probably the most important difference in motor and rail transport regulation; there are no such exemptions for the railroads.

According to his most recent estimates, Professor Paul Roberts indicates that approximately 46 percent of the ton-miles of motor carrier intercity freight falls within the jurisdiction of the ICC [11].

---

[b]The distinction between private carriage and carriage which may be subject to regulation is not always a clear one. For example, suppose a private carrier transports its own commodity from A to B, and wants to avoid empty backhauls from B to A. If it buys another commodity at B, transports it to A and sells it, then there is a question as to whether this B to A link should be considered private carriage. Administrative hearings, or if appealed, the courts must determine whether the backhaul activity is closely enough related to the primary enterprise of the firm to qualify as private haulage.

An additional 12 percent is regulated by either state or local authorities. Of the remaining 42 percent, exempt agricultural commodities account for 11 and private carriers for the other 31 percentage points.

The Extension of Regulation to Water Carriers

The regulation of intermodal competition spread still further with the Transportation Act of 1940. Until this time the inland water carrier industry remained largely outside the domain of direct regulation. Under the Transportation Act of 1940, the ICC was directed to regulate certain types of water carriers, including common carriers and contract carriers. Certain exemptions on bulk commodities and liquid cargoes in tank vessels were made. Common and contract carriers subjected to the same kinds of entry and rate controls as their motor carrier counterparts, and private water carriers remained unregulated.

Although in form the legislation much resembles the Motor Carrier Act of 1935, regulation affects only a small portion of the water carrier industry. As Table 6—1 shows, only about 6 percent of the industry was federally regulated in 1950. Pegrum estimates that the figure for 1968 was about 7.3 percent [12].

The Congressional Directives
to the Administrative Process

By 1940, the ICC was responsible for regulation which included four modes—rail, water, oil pipeline, and motor. It did not include control over the interstate transmission of natural gas (which fell within the jurisdiction of the Federal Power Commission beginning in 1938) and interstate civil aviation (which was regulated by the Civil Aeronautics Board after 1934).

Congress attempted to state some guidelines for the regulation of intermodal competition in the Transportation Act of 1940. It declared that its national transportation policy included all of the following objectives:

> . . . to provide for fair and impartial regulation of all modes of transport subject to the provisions of this Act, so administered as to recognize and preserve the inherent advantages of each; to promote safe, adequate, economical and efficient service and foster sound economic conditions in transportation and among the several carriers; to encourage the establishment and maintenance of reasonable charges for transportation services, without unjust discriminations, undue preferences or advantages, or unfair or destructive competitive practices; to cooperate with the several States and the duly authorized officials thereof; and to encourage fair wages and equitable working conditions;—all to the end of developing, coordinating

and presenting a national transportation system by water, highway, and rail, as well as other means, adequate to meet the Commerce of the United States, of the Postal Service, and of the national defense [13].

Congress did not state in detail how these objectives were to be met. It was not clear exactly what constituted "sound economic conditions," "unjust discriminations," "undue preferences or advantages," or "unfair or destructive competitive practices." The resolution of these issues awaited further definition by administrative law, court decisions, and additional legislation.

An issue that became increasingly thorny was that of pricing. Should the rates for one mode (e.g., railroads) be set at levels which preserve competition from other modes, even if lower rail rates would cover marginal costs? The preservation of all modes might not be consistent with the provision of transport services at the lowest possible rates. The practice of setting rates in order to preserve intermodal competition is known as umbrella rate-making, since it provides a protective umbrella for modes which might otherwise be eliminated. Congress addressed this practice in the Transportation Act of 1958, which stated that umbrella rate-making should not be the primary objective of rate making:

> Rates of a carrier shall not be held up to a particular level to protect the traffic of any other mode of transportation, giving due consideration to the objectives of the national transportation policy declared in this Act [14].

While this legislation attempted to state one way in which rates should *not* be set, it failed to resolve the hard pricing and entry control issues left open by the 1940 statute. The Interstate Commerce Commission has found itself confronted with a most difficult task, the need to set forth an operational rate-making scheme which achieves the generally defined and sometimes seemingly inconsistent congressional directives.

The prescription of minimum rates is particularly complicated by the fact that transportation firms typically carry a number of products over several routes. The commission has generally attempted to require that the minimum rate which a carrier may charge for transporting a given commodity over a specified route should generate revenues which cover a "fair" share of the total costs incurred by the carrier. Over the past two decades a number of administrative law and court cases have focused on the development of an acceptable cost basis for calculating minimum rates and on an appropriate concept of a fair share of costs [15]. Many of the difficulties with this approach were demonstrated in the famous *Ingot Molds* case. The important role of the regulatory process in administering the law is apparent from this case.

THE ROLE OF THE ADMINISTRATIVE PROCESS

The Ingot Molds Case: Background
Between 1953 and 1963 almost all of the shipments of ingot molds from Neville Island and Pittsburgh, Pennsylvania, to Steelton, Kentucky, were made by combination barge-truck service. The rate for this joint service after 1960 had been $5.11 per ton. Rail transportation between the same points was provided by a joint service of the Pennsylvania Railroad and the Louisville and Nashville Railroad. In 1963, these railroads lowered their tariff for ingot molds from $11.86 to $5.11 per ton. The suppliers of the barge-truck service complained to the ICC that the lowered rail rate would destroy the "inherent advantage" of the barge-truck service, and was therefore inconsistent with the national transportation policy.

Out-of-Pocket Costs and Fully Distributed Costs
The ICC often refers to two kinds of costs in its proceedings—long-term, out-of-pocket costs and fully distributed costs. "Out-of-pocket costs have been regarded generally in these cases as equivalent to what economists refer to as 'incremental' or 'marginal' costs . . . [and] are defined generally as the costs specifically incurred by the addition of each new unit of output and do not include any allocation to that unit of pre-existing overhead expenses" [16].

The notion of fully distributed cost arises because a firm might not break even if tariffs were set equal to out-of-pocket costs for all services. For example, suppose a firm produces two services, where x_1 and x_2 represent the number of ton-miles of each. Assume that the marginal (or out-of-pocket) costs for the two services are c_1 and c_2, which are both constant, and that there is a fixed cost F which is incurred, regardless of the levels of x_1 and x_2.[c]

Then the total costs for the firm can be written as C, where

$$C = F + c_1 x_1 + c_2 x_2 \ . \tag{6.1}$$

[c]In the example, assume that F, c_1, and c_2 include an allowance for a normal economic profit for the activities of the firm, so that if all costs are just covered by total revenues from the two services, the firm is left with a normal profit after all of its expenditures are made.

If the tariffs for the services, p_1 and p_2 respectively, are set equal to the out-of-pocket costs, c_1 and c_2, then the firm incurs a deficit equal to F.[d]

If a deficit is to be avoided, the tariffs in one or both markets will have to deviate from out-of-pocket costs in order to generate revenues sufficient to cover F. Suppose a regulator assigns shares of F to each service as follows: f_1 is the fraction of F which the revenues from service 1 must cover in addition to the out-of-pocket costs for that service, and f_2 is the similarly defined fraction for service 2. If total revenues must equal total costs so that no deficit occurs, then

$$f_1 + f_2 = 1 \tag{6.2}$$

and $$p_1 = c_1 + f_1 F/x_1 \tag{6.3}$$

$$p_2 = c_2 + f_2 F/x_2 . \tag{6.4}$$

Equations (6.3) and (6.4) indicate what the appropriate tariffs, p_1 and p_2 will be when F is "fully distributed" over the services.[e] For a given level of output x_1, the fully distributed costs of service 1 will be $c_1 + f_1 F/x_1$. An analogous statement can be made for service 2. Thus, fully distributed costs include out-of-pocket costs plus a share of the fixed cost F.

This example helps to explain what the ICC means when it defines fully distributed costs as the

out-of-pocket costs plus a revenue-ton and revenue ton-mile distribution of the constant cost, including deficits, [that] indicate the revenue necessary to a fair return on traffic, disregarding ability to pay [17].

It should be apparent that in principle the fractions f_1 and f_2 in the example are arbitrary, as long as they sum to unity. This means that there are an infinite number of ways to allocate the shared cost, F. For example, one could allocate F in proportion to the observed ton-miles of traffic for each service in a recent period, or according to the fraction of gross revenues generated by each service, or according to other criteria. At this point we will not critique the practice of fully distributed costs further, other than to say that this type of

[d]In this case, total revenue, R, will be $p_1 x_1 + p_2 x_2$ or $c_1 x_1 + c_2 x_2$ since $p_1 = c_1$ and $p_2 = c_2$. But $R - C = -F$.

[e]Note that the revenues from market 1 are $p_1 x_1 = c_1 x_1 + f_1 F$ and from market 2 are $p_2 x_2 = c_2 x_2 + f_2 F$. Thus $R - C = 0$.

pricing bears no direct relationship to economically efficient pricing since it attempts to set prices based on costs alone, with no considerations for the demand schedules for the service. The concept of economic efficiency in pricing with intermodal competition is discussed in much detail in this chapter, under "Optimal Pricing."

In the *Ingot Molds* case, the ICC found the cost relationships in Table 6—3 for the two modes contesting the lower rail rate. It is interesting that the fully distributed costs and out-of-pocket costs for the combination barge-truck service were equal. This reflects the lack of large fixed costs for barge and truck operations, so that if prices were set equal to out-of-pocket costs (or marginal costs), the modes would not be incurring any deficit. (Note the contrasting situation for the railroads.)

Table 6—3. Modal Cost Findings of the ICC in Ingot Molds

Mode	Rate Prior to 1963 ($/ton)	Rate After 1963 ($/ton)	Fully Distributed Costs ($/ton)	Out-of-Pocket Costs ($/ton)
Rail	$11.86	$5.11	$7.59	$4.69
Combination Barge-Truck	$ 5.11	$5.11	$5.19	$5.19

Source: See text

The Arguments of the Suppliers

The arguments of the groups providing the transport services, as presented to the ICC, can be summarized as follows [18]:

1. The railroads contended that they should be allowed to maintain the $5.11 per ton rate since it exceeded out-of-pocket costs, and therefore enabled them to make some profit on the service.

2. The railroads also argued that the fact that the $5.11 per ton rate was less than fully distributed costs was irrelevant, since they would still be making some profit on the service.

3. The barge-truck combination argued that fully distributed costs constituted the appropriate criterion on which the inherent advantage of the two modes ought to be determined. If the railroads were allowed to charge the lower rate, they would be diverting a substantial portion of traffic away from the mode with the inherent advantage.

4. The barge-truck combination contended that "the fact that the railroads' rate would be profitable was merely the minimum requirement under the statute" [19]. (Note the apparent problem that this

argument suggests for the barge-truck combination, since the $5.11 per ton rate they charged was less than their own out-of-pocket costs! This was not a major concern in the case since the actual rate was "close" to the out-of-pocket costs.)

5. Finally, the railroads argued that "inherent advantage" should be determined by a comparison of out-of-pocket costs rather than fully distributed costs, and they produced several economists to testify that, from the standpoint of economic theory, the comparison of out-of-pocket, or incremental, costs was the only rational way of regulating competitive rates" [20]. (We will show that this argument does not make economic sense, below, under "Optimal Pricing" and "Conclusion.")

The ICC Decision

The ICC rejected railroad arguments that out-of-pocket costs were the appropriate basis for a determination of "inherent advantage," and reasserted that fully distributed costs constituted the appropriate basis for comparison. It then concluded that if the lower rail rate were allowed, the barge-truck combination (the mode with the inherent advantage) would lose much of its traffic unless the barge-truck rates were readjusted to a level well below out-of-pocket costs.

The decision was appealed to the courts. At the district court level the decision of the ICC was reversed. The court held that the law intended that the relevant basis for a determination of "inherent advantage" should be out-of-pocket costs. The court considered any rate which was at least as high as out-of-pocket costs to be "compensatory," and ruled that railroads ought to be allowed to charge any rate which was compensatory.

The Supreme Court Decision

The case was ultimately appealed to the Supreme Court in *American Commercial Lines, Inc., et al.* v. *Louisville and National Railroad Co., et al.* [21]. The Court overturned the lower court decision and affirmed the position of the ICC. It ruled that the intent of the law regarding the determination of inherent advantage involved more than the compensatory notion as interpreted by the district court. If Congress had intended so simple a meaning for inherent advantage, it could have used much more direct language designed specifically to prevent wholly noncompensatory pricing by regulated carriers; yet the Transportation Act of 1940 amended the Interstate Commerce Act in a manner that moved away from the simpler compensatory basis. The Court noted that "at least one version of such clear language was proposed by the railroads and rejected by the Congress"

[22]. The Court went on to differentiate between the role of a court of general law and the administrative law process:

> The courts are ill-qualified indeed to make the kind of basic judgments about economic policy sought by the railroads here. And it would be particularly inappropriate for a court to award a carrier, on economic grounds, relief denied it by a legislature. Yet this is precisely what the District Court has done in this case.
>
> We do not mean to suggest by the foregoing discussion that the Commission is similarly barred from making legislative judgments about matters of economic policy. It is precisely to permit such judgments that the task of regulating transportation rates has been entrusted to a specialized administrative agency rather than to courts of general jurisdiction. Of course, the Commission must operate within the limits set by Congress in enacting the legislation it administers. But nothing we say here should be taken as expressing any view as to the extent that Section 15a(3) constitutes a categorical command to the ICC to use fully distributed costs as the only measure of inherent advantage in intermodal rate controversies . . . it "may be" that after due consideration another method of costing will prove to be preferable in such situations as the present one. All we hold here is that the initial determination of that question is for the Commission [23].

In summary, the Supreme Court ruled that as long as the laws were not clearly violated by the ICC, the determination of an operational rate-making rule should be left to the commission, with its expertise in such matters [24]. The Court did not endorse fully distributed cost pricing per se; rather, it supported the authority of the ICC to select an appropriate rate-making rule within the guidelines of the law.

ICC Docket No. 34013

During the 1960s the ICC considered Docket No. 34013, entitled, "Rules to Govern the Assembling and Presenting of Cost Evidence." This docket addressed the relationship between rates and costs at a much broader level than in the specific context of the *Ingot Molds* case. At the conclusion of the proceedings in 1970, the ICC announced the following findings [25]:

1. The commission found that "the adoption of specific cost formulas, with a view toward giving prima facie validity to formula based costs, are not shown to be necessary or desirable."

2. The term "out-of-pocket costs" was changed to "variable costs," and the term "fully distributed costs" was changed to "fully allocated costs."

3. "The allocation of constant costs to particular services, for rate-making purposes, should result in the assignment of an equitable portion of such expenses to the particular services, and no single method can be considered as universally applicable to all transportation services."

4. There is no universally acceptable method of apportioning joint or common costs, and any method of apportionment utilized for rate-making purposes should be designed to reasonably reflect the specific circumstances attending the transportation performed.

5. "In appropriate circumstances, (a) 'fully allocated costs' are representative of the full expense level assignable to particular services; (b) relevant 'variable costs' are indicative of the minimum level of expenses which must normally be recovered by a carrier in providing particular services; and (c) 'incremental' or 'marginal' costs, in appropriate shortrun situations, may be utilized as indicative of a minimum expense level for rate-making purposes."

The commission has encouraged the search for better methods of measuring costs, allocating costs which are shared in the provision of two or more services, and defining appropriate relationships among costs, rates, and the structure of intermodal competition. Many of the unanswered questions which arose with the Transportation Act of 1940 remain so, as the conclusions in ICC Docket No. 34013 indicate.

In 1976 Congress passed further legislation which deals with the nature of intermodal competition. This legislation, entitled the Railroad Revitalization and Regulatory Reform Act of 1976 (sometimes called the Quad-R Act), provided for the establishment of minimum and maximum limits within which rail rates would be free to fluctuate, where the limits would be relaxed over time. It is still early to assess the effects of the law. On the one hand, it can be argued that it is tantamount to a partial deregulation of rail rates, where the extent of the deregulation depends on the exact way in which the restrictions are relaxed. On the other, some feel that the legislation will not seriously affect the present practices of the ICC with respect to intermodal competition. Professor Roger Noll has commented on the legislation as follows:

The problem is two-fold. The 1976 Act, in the long-standing tradition of regulatory legislation is vague and self-contradictory, and the courts, in keeping with *Nebbia* vs. *New York* are unlikely to overturn any ruling by a regulatory agency as long as some subsection of the law contains a mandate consistent with it, and the administrative procedures surrounding the ruling were consistent with established practices of law [26].

The administrative process will undoubtedly play an important role in the implementation of the 1976 legislation, just as it did with the national transportation policy as outlined in the Transportation Acts of 1940 and 1958. It will require some time to see whether the 1976 legislation has a significant impact on intermodal competition.

The "Theory of Rate-making"

Several observations can be made regarding the alternatives for rate-making which ICC proceedings have addressed. There has been an emphasis on the fairness of rates rather than on whether the rates lead to an economically efficient allocation of resources. The conclusions of ICC Docket No. 34013 confirm this tendency. The commission understands the law to mean that rates should at least cover marginal costs (this does bear some relationship to efficiency), and that rates should normally cover the relevant variable costs. It also concludes that the allocation of shared costs (those incurred simultaneously in the provision of two or more services) to individual services, "for rate-making purposes, should result in the assignment of an equitable portion of such expenses to the particular services" [27].

There are many notions of fairness which could be used in rate-making. For example, Faulhaber has proposed an interesting alternative [28]. Suppose that a firm is producing n services in quantities $x_1, x_2, \ldots, x_n$, and that the total cost of production is denoted by $C(x_1, x_2, \ldots, x_n)$. Then Faulhaber suggests that a fair price of the ith service, p_i, might be defined as any price which generates revenues from the ith service which are at least as large as the difference in costs caused by the production of that service. In symbols, the price of the ith service would be fair as long as

$$p_i x_i \geq C(x_1, x_2, \ldots, x_{i-1}, x_i, x_{i+1}, \ldots, x_n) - C(x_1, x_2, \ldots,$$

$$x_{i-1}, 0, x_{i+1}, \ldots, x_n) \quad .$$

This definition approximately corresponds to the requirement that revenues from the ith service cover incremental costs, where the increment of significance is the entire level of output for the ith service. Faulhaber and Zajac also discuss other possible notions of equity in pricing for multiproduct firms [29].

The emphasis on equity rather than economic efficiency has occurred because of two things. First, congressional directives have repeatedly charged the administrative process with the obligation to be fair. The administrative process is an adversary one. When cases involving intermodal competition are heard, the various modes will seek to protect their positions in transport markets wherever possible. Other interest groups which might be affected by a ruling, such as shippers and organized labor, will also strive for gains and, at the minimum, argue against their own losses. This strong relationship between equity and the status quo, which we have observed for transport regulation in this chapter, follows the same characteristic of the administrative process which was suggested in Chapter 1.

Second, economic theory has only recently made significant progress in addressing the problems of economically efficient pricing for multiproduct firms engaged in intermodal competition. The existence of economies of scale, common or joint production costs, and multiple modes have contributed to the difficulties in describing the relationships between efficient prices and the structure of transport markets. The next section discusses those relationships.

OPTIMAL PRICING WITH INTERMODAL COMPETITION

The Multiproduct Monopoly: The Case Without Intermodal Competition

We begin the discussion of efficient pricing by examining the case of a multiproduct firm with a monopoly in each of its markets. Suppose a firm produces n services in quantities $x_1, x_2, \ldots, x_n$. Assume that the cost function for the production of these commodities can be represented by $C(x_1, x_2, \ldots, x_n)$. Then basic economic principles indicate that the most efficient allocation of resources is achieved when the price equals marginal cost in each market, where the marginal cost can be written as $\partial C/\partial x_i$ for the ith service. Since this is the most efficient pricing scheme, economists sometimes refer to it as "first best." The first best pricing rule can therefore be written as:

$$p_i - \frac{\partial C}{\partial x_i} = 0, \; i = 1, 2, \ldots, n \; . \tag{6.5}$$

Unfortunately, for many regulated firms, the pricing rule suggested by Equation (6.5) would lead to a deficit.[f] Policymakers have essentially three alternatives in this case. First, they can subsidize the firm by an amount at least large enough to cover the deficit so that the

[f]Consider the cost function in Equation (6.1). If the firm sets price equal to marginal cost in each market ($p_i = c_i$), then the firm will incur a deficit equal to F.

firm will remain in business. Second, they could allow the firm to engage in some form of price discrimination in some of its markets. It may be difficult to identify those consumers who are willing and able to pay more for a service. It may also be difficult to prevent arbitrage (creamskimming) in the market, in which case the firm would quite likely observe most or all of its sales being made to customers who can purchase it at the lowest tariff, and then resell it to other customers.

With both the subsidy approach and price discrimination it may be possible for the firm to continue to reach a first best operating point without incurring a deficit, as long as consumers who are just willing and able to pay a price as large as the marginal cost of the service would be able to purchase it. However, if policymakers reject these two approaches, they will have to charge prices which are different from marginal costs if the firm is to avoid a deficit. This has led to the definition of the so-called second best problem, which refers to the determination of the prices which lead to the greatest economic efficiency possible while avoiding (1) a deficit for the firm, (2) direct subsidization of the firm, and (3) price discrimination.

A set of second best pricing rules was first suggested by Frank Ramsey in 1927, and then more explicitly formulated by Baumol and Bradford in a classic article in 1970 [30]. The pricing rules derived are those which maximize economic efficiency (as measured by the sum of consumer and producer surplus) subject to a constraint which allows the firm to avoid a deficit [31]. For simplicity, assume that the demands for each of the services of the monopoly firm are independent of one another, i.e., a change in the price of one service will not affect the quantity of another service which consumers wish to purchase. Then the second best prices are those which satisfy Equations (6.6) and (6.7):

$$R \triangleq \left[\frac{p_i - \frac{\partial C}{\partial x_i}}{p_i} \right] \epsilon_{p_i} = \left[\frac{p_j - \frac{\partial C}{\partial x_j}}{p_j} \right] \epsilon_{p_j} \qquad (6.6)$$

for all i, j

and,

$$\sum_{i=1}^{n} p_i x_i - C = 0 \qquad (6.7)$$

where,

$$\epsilon_{p_i} = \left(\frac{p_i}{x_i} \right) \left(\frac{\partial x_i}{\partial p_i} \right),$$ the price elasticity of demand in

the ith market, and the terms equal to R, as defined in Equation
(6.6), are sometimes called Ramsey numbers, based on early work on
the theory of second best by Frank Ramsey.

Equation (6.7) represents a condition in which the firm is breaking
even (total revenues equal total cost). Equation (6.6) represents the
well-known rule that in each market the amount by which price deviates from marginal cost is inversely related to the price elasticity of
demand. The theory can be extended to cover the case in which the
demands are interdependent, resulting in a slightly more complicated
form for the Ramsey numbers. The basic idea remains unchanged in
characterizing second best, namely, the Ramsey numbers are equal in
all markets, and the firm is earning no monopoly profits.

There is an essential difference between the approaches to pricing
taken by regulators and by Ramsey. Regulators tend to allocate
shared costs first, and then judge the fairness of prices based on that
allocation. In the work of Ramsey, efficient prices are determined
directly, based on a combination of cost and demand information.
No prior allocation of shared costs is undertaken, and second best
prices may be quite near or quite far from the prices regulators determine from fully distributed costs. It is possible to determine how
shared costs should be allocated in order to reach second best once
the efficient prices have been found, but such an allocation would be
performed *after* prices are determined, *not* before.

The Nature of the Problem
with Intermodal Competition

The basic principle of first best pricing remains the same for the
case of intermodal competition. Resources are allocated most efficiently when the price charged by each mode in the transport of each
commodity equals the marginal cost for that activity. If all modes
could remain profitable at an equilibrium when marginal cost pricing
is followed, there would be no reason to regulate any of the modes,
at least on grounds of economic efficiency. There would be no need
to look for second best prices since no firm would incur a deficit at
first best prices.

The problem of second best does arise if one or more of the modes
would incur a deficit at first best prices. Several questions about the
second best problem are suggested in this case. Should prices deviate

from marginal costs in all modes at second best, or only in those modes which do not break even with marginal cost pricing? What do the second best pricing rules look like with intermodal competition? Are there any special entry control problems that might be encountered in attempting to achieve second best? These and other questions will be answered shortly. However, in order to resolve the problem, it is important to know which modes operate with economies of scale, and are therefore likely to incur a deficit with marginal cost pricing.

Economies of Scale

Modes of transport have often been placed in two categories on the basis of economic characteristics. According to Pegrum, "railroads and pipelines have the basic economic characteristics of public utilities and are what economists call natural monopolies; motor, water, and air transport exhibit the features of competitive industries" [32]. Freight transportation in the United States has certain distinctive features which lead us to concentrate on the interactions among rail, motor, and water carriers. First, air carriers primarily provide passenger service. The amount of ton miles of intercity freight traffic shipped by air has historically amounted to less than 1 percent [33]. Second, pipelines "constitute a highly specialized form of transportation for the movement of products in liquid or gaseous form" [34]. Because of the special nature of the service they provide and their apparent economies of scale, the regulation of oil and gas pipelines could be treated separately from the other modes, under the jurisdiction of either the Interstate Commerce Commission or the Federal Power Commission [35].

The remaining three modes employ greatly differing technologies which can be viewed as providing services which are imperfect substitutes for one another. Moore shows that since 1940 the loss in the market share for the railroads has been approximately equal to the gains of the motor carriers, while the share of the inland water carriers has remained nearly constant at about 20 percent (see Table 6-4) [36].

The issue of scale economies in railroads is not a closed one. Many empirical studies have been made to test for the existence of economies of scale, with results that have been mixed. For example, Klein used 1936 data to find statistically significant, though modest, economies of scale [37]. However, studies by Borts and Griliches have concluded that scale economies are not prevalent for the larger railroads, although the evidence is less clear for the smaller ones [38].

Table 6—4. National Market Shares for Freight Transported by Railroads, Motor Vehicles, and Inland Waterways, 1940—1974 *(Percentages are of total ton-miles for the three modes)*

Year	Railroads	Motor Vehicles	Inland Waterways
1940	70	10	20
1945	78	7	15
1950	65	18	17
1955	60	20	20
1960	54	26	20
1965	54	27	20
1970	51	27	21
1974*	50	30	20

Source: T.G. Moore, *Trucking Regulation* (American Enterprise for Public Policy Research, 1976), Table U.S.-1, p. 139.
*Preliminary estimates.

Water carriers are the least likely of the three modes to operate with economies of scale. Indeed, water transport markets appear to be quite competitive, and only a small percentage of their traffic is regulated.

Motor carrier activities are probably not characterized by economies of scale, at least for most of their operations. There is some empirical work, such as that of Chow, which suggests that some economies of scale are present in the less-than-truckload segment of general freight motor carriage, and that constant returns to scale are present for the totally loaded segment [39]. However, perhaps the best empirical work on scale economies in motor carriage is that of Friedlaender. She approaches the problem using the most recently developed production theory and econometric techniques to test for economies of scale in the regulated sector of the motor carrier industry, and concludes that:

> Because diverse operating rights permit firms to utilize equipment more efficiently and undertake longer hauls per trip, it is likely that any observed economies of scale are of a regulatory rather than a technological nature. In particular, larger firms have lower costs because they have more diverse operating rights than their smaller competitors. Consequently, in the absence of entry and operating restrictions it is likely that small firms would be able to enjoy the same economies of haul enjoyed by large firms. Thus, it is unlikely that the cost structure of different-sized firms would be significantly different [40].

Friedlaender concludes that with deregulation, motor carriers

> ...could be expected to face U-shaped average cost curves in which the minimum average costs would be reached at a low level of output, [and that] it is likely that the trucking industry would be competitively organized, with the efficiently sized firm being quite small relative to the relevant market [41].

The existence of a healthy, unregulated portion of the industry, particularly for agricultural commodities, lends reinforcement to the conclusions of Friedlaender.

It is not the purpose of this section to critique these empirical studies. Rather, the intent is to show second best pricing rules would have to be set if one of these modes has scale economies (railroads appear to be the most likely candidate) and the other modes (motor and water) do not.

A Model of Second Best

The following model for determining second best prices with intermodal competition has been developed by Braeutigam [42]. The basic assumptions made in that work are as follows:

1. There are m modes which provide transport services between two points. Only one of these modes (mode 1) is characterized by economies of scale. In other words, if the services of mode 1 were all priced at marginal cost, the profits for the firm would be negative.

2. There are many suppliers of transport service in each of the other modes, so that each of the modes $2, \ldots, m$ would be competitive without regulation. It is assumed that with free entry, the supply of transport services in each of these modes is perfectly elastic.

3. Each mode may transport any or all of n commodities. Let i be a modal index ($i = 1, \ldots, m$), j be a commodity index ($j = 1, \ldots, n$), and x_{ij} be the amount of commodity j transported by mode i.

4. All carriers of mode i provide identical service in the transport of commodity j. Restated, this means that there is intramodal homogeneity in the carriage of a particular commodity.

5. There is intermodal service differentiation. In transporting commodity j, carriers of one mode will provide service which differs from the service of carriers of other modes. This recognizes that motor carriers, water carriers, and railroads may differ in the speed of transport, reliability, and in other aspects of service quality.

6. For our purposes, the demand for transportation of commodity j via any mode is independent of the demand for transportation

of commodity $k(k \neq j)$ via any mode. Formally let

$$P_{ij} = P_{ij}(x_{1j}, x_{2j}, \ldots, x_{mj}), i = 1, \ldots, m; \quad j = 1, \ldots, n,$$

where P_{ij} represents the (inverse) demand for transport of commodity j via any mode i.[g]

In addition, let s_{ij} be the price corresponding to the (perfectly elastic) supply function for mode i in the transportation of commodity j, and

$$C^1 = C^1(x_{11}, x_{12}, \ldots, x_{1j}; \text{factor prices})$$ be the total cost function for mode 1. Factor prices are assumed to be constant.

Given these assumptions, second best prices for all modes could be determined by maximizing the sum of consumer and producer surplus for all modes, subject to a constraint that the first mode break even, following the basic approach of Ramsey.[h] Let us refer to this as a totally regulated second best (TRSB), since all modes are regulated both by price and entry controls. In order to achieve TRSB, the following conditions must be satisfied.[i]

---

[g]The model also assumes that there are zero income effects associated with the demand functions, p_{ij}, so that the welfare measure of consumer and producer surplus can be written as a path independent function of the outputs, x_{ij}, $\forall i, j$. Given the assumptions of the model, the sum of consumer and producer surplus can be represented by T, where

$$T = \sum_{j=T}^{n} \left\{ \int_{w=0}^{x_{1j}} P_{1j}(w,0,0,\ldots,0)dw + \int_{w=0}^{x_{2j}} P_{2j}(x_{1j}, w,0,0,\ldots,0)dw \ldots \right.$$

$$\left. + \cdots + \int_{w=0}^{x_{mj}} P_{mj}(x_{1j}, x_{2j}, \ldots, x_{m-1,j}w)dw \right\} - C^1 - \sum_{i=2}^{m} \sum_{j=1}^{n} s_{ij}x_{ij},$$

where s_{ij} is defined below in the text.

[h]Formally, the problem is written

$$\max_{(x_{ij}, \forall i, j)} T$$

subject to: $\sum_{j=1}^{n} P_{1j}x_{1j} - C^1 \geq 0.$

[i]These conditions can be derived from the first order conditions for the problem stated in footnote h. While the detailed derivation is not presented here, it does appear in the Braeutigam paper.

$$R = \left[\frac{P_{1j} - \frac{\partial C^1}{\partial x_{1j}}}{P_{1j}} \right] \left[\frac{P_{1j}}{\frac{\partial P_{1j}}{\partial x_{1j}} x_{1j}} \right] \quad ; \; j = 1, \ldots, n \tag{6.8}$$

$$R = \frac{\frac{P_{ij} - s_{ij}}{P_{ij}}}{\left(\frac{\partial P_{ij}}{\partial x_{1j}} \right) \frac{x_{1j}}{P_{ij}} - \frac{P_{ij} - s_{ij}}{P_{ij}}} \quad ; \; i = 2, \ldots, m; \; j = 1, \ldots, n \tag{6.9}$$

and

$$\sum_{j=1}^{n} P_{1j} x_{1j} - C^1 = 0 \tag{6.10}$$

where R represents a number between zero and minus one, and is the intermodal counterpart to the Ramsey number of Equation (6.6) for the case of the multiproduct monopoly.

These conditions can be interpreted as follows. Equation (6.10) states that at TRSB mode 1 will just break even, as in the case of the multiproduct monopoly. Equation (6.8) displays the extent to which the prices in mode 1 will exceed marginal cost. The first term in brackets represents the amount of this deviation as a fraction of the price level. The second term in brackets is the reciprocal of the quantity (not price) elasticity of demand.[j]

The administration of a TRSB pricing scheme becomes particularly complex because of the condition required by Equation (6.9), which one could think of as the appropriate Ramsey number analog for modes $2, \ldots, m$. The numerator of the right-hand side represents the amount by which price deviates from marginal cost in those modes, stated as a fraction of the price itself. A similar expression appears in the denominator. The first term in the denominator represents the cross-elasticity of the inverse demand, P_{ij}, with respect to the quantity x_{ij}.

It can be shown that under normal conditions, the prices for transport will be held *above* marginal costs in modes $2, \ldots, m$.[k] Since

[j]The quantity elasticity of demand is defined using inverse demand schedules, and is defined as $(\partial p_{ij} / \partial x_{ij}) / (p_{ij} / x_{ij})$.

[k]This follows from normal assumptions about the nature of the inverse demand functions, and can be derived from first order conditions for second best. Specifically, the assumption about demand is that $\partial p_{1j} / \partial x_{ij} = 0$, for $i \geqslant 2$.

this condition would serve as a signal for more firms to enter in those markets absent restrictions, the regulator would have to prevent free entry or else impose a set of excise taxes to achieve TRSB prices. Otherwise entry would occur until the prices were driven down to marginal cost.

Implications for the Administrative Process

There can be little doubt that the execution of the TRSB scheme represents an enormous task for regulators. Some might argue that there is a striking similarity between the outlined program and the one we presently observe for intermodal competition, particularly since regulators presently do control tariffs and conditions of entry. One could even argue that through a consideration of "value of service," regulators attempt to require higher tariffs on commodities with more inelastic demands, and this is generally consistent with the rules of Equations (6.8) and (6.9).

However, it would be difficult to carry the analogy much further. The data requirements for a determination of second best prices are very large. The information required on the numerous cross-elasticities of demand alone might be enough to make the outlined program quite unwieldy.

Even if regulators were committed to a program of totally regulated second best, there are other difficulties at least as important as information-related ones. For example, suppose that mode 2 represents motor carriers, and that a regulator attempts to limit entry in order to hold price above marginal cost for motor carrier services. Then the presence of an unregulated sector of motor carriers, as we have in this country, may present an overwhelming problem related to entry control. If regulated tariffs are held above marginal costs, shippers who would otherwise have used regulated motor carriers will have incentives to buy their own trucks for the private carriage of their own commodities. If private haulage remains unregulated, as it is today, then entry into this activity would not be prevented by the rules applying to regulated carriers. This is not a hypothetical problem. As Professor Paul Roberts has observed, shippers today engage in this practice:

> A typical strategy [of shippers] is to [privately] haul the higher rated commodities and the regular hauls, but to leave the lower-rated commodities and the overflow for the regulated carrier [43].

As a result, although the intent of regulation may be to proscribe entry, the probable effect would simply be to change the form of entry to circumvent the rule.

A Variation: Partially Regulated Second Best

The problems of entry control, data acquisition, and general administration lead us to ask if there is not some modified form of second best which might be of interest. One rather interesting candidate would be a program which allows the modes without economies of scale ($i = 2, \ldots, m$) to clear their markets, and which concentrates on the prices set by the mode with economies of scale. This would release the administrative process from acting on the $n(m-1)$ rates for those modes, and in addition it would not involve itself in the thorny problem of entry controls for modes which would be competitive absent regulation. The administration of regulation under this system would be much simplified.

Let us refer to this variation of second best as partially regulated second best (PRSB). Formally, we could state the PRSB problem as the maximization of the sum of consumer and producer surplus for all modes together, subject to a breakeven constraint for mode 1 and market clearing conditions for all other modes.[1] The market clearing conditions mean that

$$P_{ij} - s_{ij} = 0, \text{ for } i = 2, \ldots, m; \ j = 1, \ldots, n \ . \tag{6.11}$$

It can be shown that the following conditions must be satisfied at PRSB:

$$\sum_{j=1}^{n} p_{1j} x_{1j} - C^1 \geq 0 \tag{6.12}$$

and

$$R \triangleq \left[\frac{P_{1j} - \dfrac{\partial C^1}{\partial x_{1j}}}{P_{1j}} \right] \epsilon_{p_{1j}} \ ; \ j = 1, \ldots, n \tag{6.13}$$

---

[1]The PRSB problem can be represented mathematically as follows:

$$\max_{(x_{1j}, \forall_j)} T$$

subject to: $\sum_{j=1}^{n} P_{1j} x_{1j} - C^1 \geq 0$

and $P_{ij} - s_{ij} = 0; \ i = 2, \ldots, m; \ j = 1, \ldots, n$

where T is as defined in footnote g.

where $\epsilon_{p_{1j}}$, as before, refers to the price elasticity of demand in the market for x_{1j}.

Note that the pricing rules for PRSB, where intermodal competition exists, are the *same* as the ones developed by Baumol and Bradford for a multiproduct monopoly. The Ramsey number of Equation (6.13) must be the same in all markets, and depend only on information about price, marginal cost, and the price elasticity of demand for the first mode.

A Comparison of First Best, Baumol and Bradford, TRSB, and PRSB

Let us step back for a moment to relate the various pricing rules we have discussed in this section to one another. The pricing rules of Baumol and Bradford (Equations 6.6 and 6.7) are conceptually appropriate when the services produced by mode 1 have demands which are independent of one another. If there are other modes, then the TRSB pricing rules imply that it may be efficient (second best) to alter the market clearing outcome for other modes in order to satisfy the break even requirement for the first mode, even if those modes would be quite competitive absent regulation.

There are several reasons why regulators may not attempt to follow a program leading to TRSB. They may perceive the interactions among the services of mode 1 and other modes to be small, or they may simply be unaware of the interaction. They may also recognize the potentially large information and administrative requirements for such a program, or the difficulties in controlling entry as effectively as would be required. There may be other reasons for which regulators may decide to let the potentially competitive markets clear.[m] In any of these cases the rules for PRSB may be of interest.

To illustrate the relationship between several possible pricing schemes with intermodal competition, let us consider a special case which can be represented on a graph. Assume that there are only two modes, mode 1, which has economies of scale, and mode 2, which lacks scale economies. Only one basic service is provided by each mode. The service provided by mode 1 is differentiated from the service of mode 2. However, all firms in mode 2 provide a homogeneous service. Thus, we have retained the assumption of intermodal service

---

[m] The administrative process may be used by affected interest groups to define various equity constraints which may be imposed on certain markets. In principle, these constraints could be appended to a model which maximizes total surplus to find efficient prices given the additional constraints.

differentiation and intramodal service homogeneity from the earlier work. Mode 2 has a supply schedule $s_2(x_2)$, which relates the quantity of service which would be provided, x_2, to the price of that service. The supply schedule need not be perfectly elastic, but we assume that it is always less negatively sloped than the inverse demand schedule in the market, $P_2(x_1, x_2)$. Mode 1 has an inverse demand schedule represented by $P_1(x_1, x_2)$, and a cost function $C^1(x_1)$.

In Figure 6–1 we have placed the quantities of the outputs x_1 and x_2 on the axes. It is possible to represent the set of (x_1, x_2) combinations which satisfy the market clearing condition

$$P_2(x_1, x_2) - s_2(x_2) = 0 \tag{6.14}$$

by the set of points AE. The locus has a negative slope under the assumptions we have made, since

$$\frac{dx_2}{dx_1} = -\frac{\dfrac{\partial P_2}{\partial x_1}}{\dfrac{\partial P_2}{\partial x_2} - \dfrac{\partial s_2}{\partial x_2}} < 0 \tag{6.15}$$

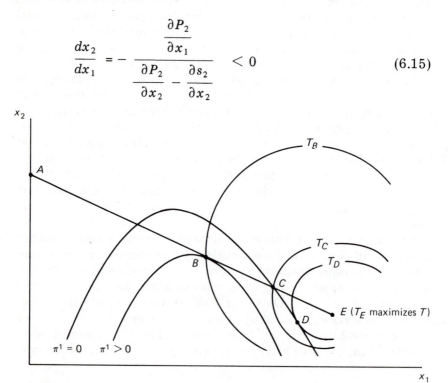

Figure 6–1. Mode 1 Could Be Profitable When Mode 2 Clears

Source: R. Braeutigam, "Optimal Pricing with Intermodal Competition," *American Economic Review* (forthcoming), Fig. 1.

The points on AE can be thought of as a reaction function for mode 2, i.e., given any level of output x_1, then mode 2 suppliers will supply x_2.

It is also possible to represent isoquants of the sum of consumer and producer surplus, shown by the curves T_B, T_C, T_D, and T_E. It can be shown that these isosurplus curves have the slope[n]

$$\frac{dx_2}{dx_1} = - \frac{P_1 - \dfrac{\partial C^1}{\partial x_1}}{P_2 - s_2} \quad . \tag{6.16}$$

Along AE the curves are vertical, since $P_2 - s_2 = 0$. T increases along AE as x_1 increases up to a level of output at which P_1 equals the marginal cost of x_1. E therefore represents a first best point, since both modes are charging prices equal to marginal costs. Therefore T is maximized at E.

The profit for mode 1 can be expressed as

$$\pi^1 = P_1 (x_1, x_2) x_1 - C^1 (x_1) \quad , \tag{6.17}$$

which means that the isoprofit curves for mode 1 will have the slope

$$\frac{dx_2}{dx_1} = - \frac{P_1 + \dfrac{\partial P_1}{\partial x_1} x_1 - \dfrac{\partial C^1}{\partial x_1}}{\dfrac{\partial P_1}{\partial x_2} x_1} \quad . \tag{6.18}$$

Since x_1 and x_2 are imperfect substitutes for one another, the slope will be positive when the marginal revenue exceeds the marginal cost of x_1 (for levels of x_1 less than the profit maximizing level) and negative when the converse is true. The shapes of these curves are as shown in Figure 6–1. The ordering of the curves can be established by noting that given any level of x_1, the profit of mode 1 will

[n]For the case we are studying here

$$T = \int_{w=0}^{x_1} P_1 (w,0)dw + \int_{w=0}^{x_2} P_2 (x_1,w)dw - C^1 (x_1) - \int_{w=0}^{x_2} s_2 (w)dw \quad .$$

Equation (6.16) can be derived by setting $dT = 0$.

increase as x_2 decreases, since

$$\frac{\partial \pi^1}{\partial x_2} = \frac{\partial P_1}{\partial x_2} \, x_1 < 0 \tag{6.19}$$

Figure 6−1 is drawn to illustrate the case in which mode 1 can earn some extranormal profit for some of the market clearing points in the market for x_2. If both modes were unregulated, mode 2 would clear and mode 1 would choose the highest isoprofit curve which comes into contact with AE. Thus, point B represents the point which would occur with total deregulation.

If a regulator wanted to maximize efficiency, it could direct the firms to operate at E, where both modes price at marginal cost. However, the profits for mode 1 would be negative at E because of its economies of scale. A regulator might choose to set tariffs for both modes and control entry so that a totally regulated second best point is achieved. In doing so, it would try to reach point D, where the greatest economic efficiency is achieved while still allowing mode 1 to break even. Note that D lies below the segment AE, so that mode 2 does not clear at TRSB.

For reasons discussed earlier, a regulator might choose a market clearing second best point, such as C. At C mode 1 breaks even, and mode 2 clears its market.

The relationships of the curves would be different if mode 1 could not break even any time mode 2 clears its market. This possibility is reflected in Figure 6−2. There exists no PRSB point and no totally unregulated point where mode 1 avoids a negative profit. Mode 1 can only break even when the market for mode 2 does not clear, and the most efficient operating point at which mode 1 breaks even is the TRSB location at D.

In between the situations of Figures 6−1 and 6−2 is the special case in which mode 1 can just barely break even with total deregulation. This is depicted in Figure 6−3. The unregulated (B) and PRSB (C) solutions coincide in this case. This suggests that if only small profits would be earned by mode 1 without regulation, then an unregulated system would achieve nearly the same economic efficiency as PRSB, and without incurring the administrative costs of the latter.

CONCLUSION

The regulation of intermodal competition has not been an easy task for the ICC. As Congress has extended the hand of regulation during this century, it has instructed regulators to preserve the "inherent

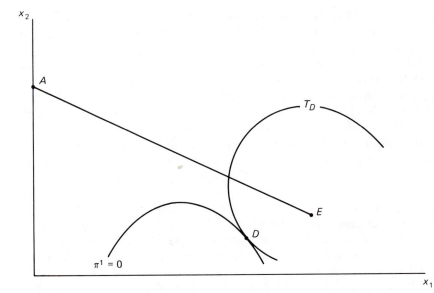

Figure 6−2. Mode 1 Earns Negative Profit When Mode 2 Clears

Source: R. Braeutigam, "Optimal Pricing with Intermodal Competition," *American Economic Review* (forthcoming), Fig. 2.

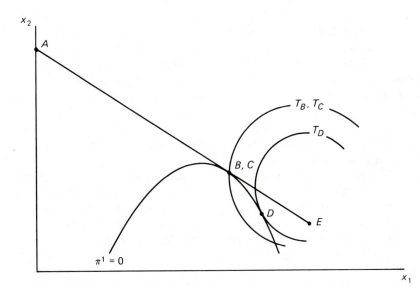

Figure 6−3. Unregulated Mode 1 Just Breaks Even

Source: R. Braeutigam, "Optimal Pricing with Intermodal Competition," *American Economic Review* (forthcoming), Fig. 3.

advantages" of each mode, to insure that "economical and efficient" services are provided, and to foster "sound economic conditions" in interstate transportation.

While these sweeping intentions formed the basis for a national transportation policy, it is not surprising that regulators have faced a series of dilemmas in translating policy into a set of operational regulatory directives. Congressional directives contain phrases which are not well defined and which sometimes appear to conflict with one another. The translation is also difficult because the administrative process is structured to operate on a case-by-case basis, rather than at the industrywide level of congressional mandates.

Our work has focused on the relationship between rate-making and the structure of intermodal competition as two of the levers which regulators have attempted to control. There is no challenge to the proposition that the two are inescapably interdependent. Yet there has been long-standing disagreement over the ways in which regulators ought to coordinate prices and market structure.

The lack of a concretely defined national transportation policy has been indelibly reflected in the resolutions reached through administrative law. The *Ingots Molds* case and ICC Docket 34013 provide clear evidence of this. The central issue in each was the prescription of minimum rates. The ICC recognized that any rule of rate-making would inevitably affect the structure of intermodal competition. Among the cost-based candidates for prescribing minimum rates, it chose fully distributed (or allocated) costs. It has refused to base the determination on any particular formula to define fully distributed costs, arguing that such a formula is neither necessary nor desirable. It has concluded that there is no single method of allocating shared costs (and therefore, determining prices based on fully allocated costs) which is universally applicable in all cases. In short, it has left itself with as much flexibility as possible in rate-making, and continued to struggle with an appropriate calculation of fully allocated costs on a case-by-case basis.

In Chapter 1 we described the emphasis which the administrative process places on the status quo, as various interest groups argue for the protection of their own concerns. One of the consequences of the case approach in calculating fully allocated costs is that the status quo often serves as the benchmark for the comparison of the effects of alternative policies, rather than some notion of overall social benefit such as economic efficiency.

Regarding the notion of economic efficiency, economic theory has been slow to extend many of the basic principles which have been developed for the regulated monopolist to the case of intermodal competition. As a result, regulators have been stranded with comparisons of costs among modes as a measure of economic benefits.

There is obviously more to the story. If two modes provided identical services, then economic benefits would be higher if the lower cost mode were allowed to produce at the lowest price possible (see Chapter 2). But transportation firms do not provide identical services, and it is myopic to compare economic benefits on the basis of costs alone. Consumers value variety, and it may be that economic benefits would be greater if a higher cost mode were also allowed to produce, particularly if its services were differentiated from the services of other modes.

We have shown how the economic principles developed for multiproduct monopolies can be extended to the case of intermodal competition. If there are no modes with economies of scale, then on grounds of economic efficiency there is an important question as to whether any of the modes ought to be regulated. If any of the modes does have economies of scale, then the concept of second best may be of interest to regulators who are interested in economic efficiency, but who either cannot or do not wish to subsidize a mode with economies of scale or to allow price discrimination [44].

There are two kinds of second best concepts we have discussed. In the first, called totally regulated second best (TRSB), regulators would prescribe tariffs and control entry for all modes. The administrative requirements under this form of regulation are unquestionably enormous. Much information about the structure of costs and demands (including cross-elasticities of demand) would be required in order to properly use the pricing rules developed for TRSB. In addition, since prices would generally deviate from marginal costs, even for the modes without scale economies, regulators would have to carefully control entry conditions in those markets. We have argued that entry controls may be largely ineffective in many areas (such as motor carriage) where an unregulated sector of the industry exists.

These potential difficulties led us to explore a modified form of second best. This form, called partially regulated second best (PRSB), does not require the regulation of modes without economies of scale, for either tariffs or entry. Tariffs are specified for a mode with economies of scale, where the tariffs are designed to maximize economic efficiency while allowing that mode to break even. The modes without scale economies would be allowed to clear their markets. The rules for PRSB turn out to be of the same form as the ones developed by Baumol and Bradford for the case without intermodal competition.

If TRSB were costless and effective, efficiency would be greater than for PRSB. However, if the former is costly to achieve (because of large information requirements) or is otherwise difficult to reach (e.g., because entry cannot be effectively controlled), then PRSB may present an attractive alternative.

Both TRSB and PRSB would lead to greater economic efficiency than a totally unregulated system, as long as a mode with economies of scale could earn positive profits absent regulation. However, if profits for such a mode would be near zero absent regulation, then the potential economic efficiency without regulation may be quite close to that which can be achieved under PRSB.

It is appropriate to ask whether regulators are likely to be greatly interested in efficient pricing where intermodal competition exists. Chapter 1 suggests probably not, since considerations of equity will override those of efficiency in the administrative process. Regulators know that the adoption of specific pricing rules will reduce their flexibility in balancing the arguments of various interest groups which participate in the regulatory process.

Perhaps the most important insight that can be gained from an analysis of optimal pricing is a qualitative perspective on the maximum efficiency attainable under alternative regulatory scenarios. This chapter has suggested that the deregulation of a mode with economies of scale, although perhaps motivated out of equity considerations, such as a desire to prevent bankruptcy, may not lead to an allocation of resources as efficient as the deregulation of modes which are essentially competitive. It is not surprising that the administrative process does not emphasize economic efficiency when the legislation that guides this process itself lacks the same emphasis.

Chapter 7

Regulating Prices and Entry:
The Domestic Telephone Industry

INTRODUCTION

Federal regulation of interstate activities in the telephone industry has existed for almost seventy years in this country. During this period regulators have wrestled with many of the problems which are now considered traditional in the regulation of public utilities. Among others, these traditional issues include the measurement of the rate base, the determination of a fair rate of return, the judgment whether production facilities should be constructed, and the determination whether tariffs proposed for telephone services are reasonable.

Problems such as these have not been easy to resolve. Regulators have encountered several features of the industry which have complicated matters. For example, the telephone industry provides many kinds of services. Some telephone services require only local exchange facilities, while others also require transmission over long distance routes (see Table 7—1). Each of these categories can be further subdivided. Most users desire service which gives them access to the general telephone network. At the local level this is usually obtained by subscribing to basic local telephone service. For long distance this general access capability is obtained through the use of message toll services, or through the Wide Area Toll Service (WATS) lines. However, some users desire more specialized transmission capabilities between specified points. In the latter case they may find it less expensive under published tariffs to purchase private line service, particularly if the transmission requirements are large. Private line

Table 7—1.   Selected Types of Telephone Services*

Local Services	Toll Services
Subscriber Station Services	Message Toll Services
Telephone	Telephone
Teletypewriter	Teletypewriter
Public Telephone Services	Other Message Toll Services
Other Nonprivate Line Local Services	Wide Area Toll Service (WATS)
Private Line	Private Line
Telephone	Telephone
Teletypewriter	Teletypewriter
TELPAK	TELPAK
Program Transmission-Audio	Program Transmission-Audio
Program Transmission-Video	Program Transmission-Video
Other Services	Other Services

*The categories displayed in this table are broken down still further in the reports which telephone carriers file with the Federal Communications Commission. For further detail, see *Statistics of Communications Common Carriers*, compiled annually by the FCC.

service enables the user to lease transmission capacity for his own use, in contrast to the public telephone services which are shared jointly with all users. As Table 7—1 shows, there are several types of private line services available, both for local and long distance requirements.

The regulation of firms which provide more than one service has created special problems for regulators of the telephone industry, just as in the case of surface freight transport discussed in Chapter 6. For example, the imposition of a rate of return constraint on the activities of a multiproduct firm does not by itself determine the levels of tariffs for individual services. If a regulator desires to narrow the range of acceptable tariffs, additional rate-making criteria are generally required and developed through the administrative process.

Regulatory matters are further complicated in this industry because a single telephone transmission often travels over facilities owned by different companies, often under the jurisdictions of different regulators. For example, a long distance call may originate in the local facilities of one company, terminate in the local facilities of another, and use the interstate long distance facilities of still a third company (such as AT&T Long Lines) to connect the two. Although tariffs are typically announced to the user only for the overall service (e.g., a long distance call), the revenues which such a service generates must be apportioned among the companies which assist in providing the service. The term "division of revenues" is often used to refer to the allocation of revenues among companies of the Bell System, and "settlements" to refer to the allocations between Bell and independent companies. The process of dividing the revenues among the firms is carried out through "separations" agreements. These agreements have evolved over years of negotiations, and they continue to be a focus of much debate. Local operating companies are typically regulated by state agencies. State regulators generally want the local operating companies to receive larger revenue shares from interstate long distance separations agreements so that less revenue will be required from other local operating company services (such as basic telephone service). On the other hand, if the share of revenues designated for interstate transmission is very low, then a firm such as AT&T Long Lines may claim before the FCC that higher long distance rates are necessary in order for that company to earn its allowed rate of return.

These industry features alone would probably be sufficient to guarantee that the transcripts of rate-making proceedings and other activities of the regulators would be both lengthy and tortuous. However, in the last two decades the Federal Communications Commission has embarked on a course which has added still further complications. In a series of decisions it has moved toward policies designed to allow and even encourage entry by other firms into certain markets previously served only by telephone companies. The markets include the provision of interstate private line services and the supply of terminal equipment. Where entry has been allowed, economic forces have made it necessary for regulators to recognize that market structure and tariff levels are inescapably related.

This chapter focuses on the role of the administrative process in dealing with market structure and pricing decisions in three of the areas where entry has been allowed—the interstate private line market, specialized carriers, and the supply of equipment for customer use by nontelephone companies. The telephone industry provides many excellent examples of strategic use of the administrative process. The second section of this chapter contains some brief historical and structural background about the industry. The following three sections consider each of the three areas in some detail. The reader is encouraged to read Chapter 6 before proceeding with Chapter 7, since an understanding of certain theoretical and structural concepts presented there is assumed.

BACKGROUND AND INDUSTRY STRUCTURE

A brief description of the early development of the telephone industry will facilitate an understanding of the more recent events in private line and terminal equipment markets. While a detailed examination of the technological and corporate growth of the industry is beyond the scope of this chapter, the interested reader can pursue these aspects elsewhere [1].

Alexander Graham Bell invented the telephone in 1876. The roots of the Bell System were established by the patents he secured on his invention in 1877. The American Bell Telephone Company was subsequently organized in Massachusetts, and grew by licensing the use of these patents to local telephone companies operating in selected geographic areas.

During its early years, the Bell System developed in several directions simultaneously. It formed a New York-based subsidiary whose primary responsibility was the direction of the long distance operations of telephone transmission. This subsidiary was called the American Telephone and Telegraph Company. As a part of corporate reorganization during the 1880s, American Bell sold its assets to AT&T, the latter assuming the lead in directing the activities of the Bell System.

Under Theodore Vail, the first president of AT&T, the Bell System began to centralize its control of local exchange and long distance services, and the manufacturing of telephone equipment. Consequently, during the 1880s AT&T began purchasing the stock of Western Electric Manufacturing Company, which had been the largest manufacturer of electrical equipment for Western Union. The Western Electric Company is now a wholly-owned subsidiary of AT&T, and supplies virtually all of the Bell System's equipment needs.

The movement toward a centralized operation of telephone services was facilitated by licensing arrangements between AT&T and the local operating companies which used Bell patents. The patents provided Bell with a monopoly in telephone markets between 1876 and 1894. One of Bell's practices involved the licensing of patents to operating companies through a contract of perpetual duration under which Bell typically demanded a 35 percent equity interest and certain managerial representation in each of the companies receiving licenses. This marked the beginning of the process by which AT&T has acquired nearly complete control of its operating companies.[a]

After the early patents expired in the 1890s, many independent (non-Bell) operating companies and equipment manufacturers entered the telephone business. In some geographic markets the independent operating companies competed directly with Bell compa-

---

[a] The present structure of the operating companies of AT&T will be addressed below.

nies. In some of these areas a duplication of facilities resulted so that a user had a choice among telephone systems. Companies competing in the same area often refused to interconnect with one another, in which case a user had to subscribe to each system [2]. Competition led to a rapid increase in the number of telephones in service, both for the Bell System and the independent telephone companies. Table 7–2 shows that by 1907 the number of Bell system stations was about 50 percent of the total, compared with a 100 percent share in 1894.

While there was competition in the supply of telephone equipment and in the provision of local telephone services, the Bell System maintained its monopoly over long distance during this period. This monopoly position was enhanced during the early 1900s by patents and other technical advances which were achieved in long distance technology. Where a Bell operating company refused to interconnect with a competing independent, the Bell company realized a substantial marketing advantage by virtue of its ability to provide long distance service. This advantage diminished as many state legislatures began requiring interconnection after 1904.

Government Intervention

With the return of Theodore Vail to the presidency of AT&T in 1907 (after a two-decade absence), the Bell System entered a new phase of growth. It was marked by an emphasis on the acquisition of

Table 7–2. Number of Bell System and Independent Telephone Stations
(in thousands, rounded to the nearest thousand)

Year	Bell Stations	Independent Stations	Total
1894*	266	—	266
1900*	836	520	1,356
1905*	2,285	1,842	4,127
1910*	3,933	3,703	7,636
1915*	5,968	4,555	10,523
1920*	8,334	5,079	13,413
1925*	12,035	4,901	16,936
1930*	15,682	4,519	20,201
1934*	13,378	3,511	16,889
1975**	122,188	26,820	149,008

Sources: *Investigation of the Telephone Industry.* Federal Communications Commission, H: Document 340, 76th Congress, 1st Session, 1939, p. 129. Figures are rounded to the nearest thousand.

*Statistics of Communications Common Carriers (FCC, 1975), Table 6. The number of Bell Stations includes 389,000 service telephones (noncompany phones for which service is provided).

independent telephone companies and the purchase of 30 percent interest in Western Union in 1909. Thus, instead of expanding internally to compete with the telephone and telegraph services provided by other companies, AT&T attempted to improve its market position by acquisition.

In 1910 Congress passed the Mann-Elkins Act, extending the jurisdiction of the Interstate Commerce Commission to include those telephone, telegraph, and cable companies (whether wire or wireless) that transmitted messages in interstate or foreign commerce.[b] AT&T did not actively oppose this regulation. In fact it suggested that regulation might serve as a substitute for competition by, among other things, helping to resolve the problems posed by duplicated service [3]. ICC regulation of interstate communications activities continued until 1934, although without noteworthy vigor. During this period, the ICC made no comprehensive studies of the structure of telephone rates, and initiated no inquiries into the practices of the Bell System.

However, the Department of Justice viewed the acquisition and interconnection practices of the Bell System as possible antitrust violations under the Sherman Act. Bell responded to this concern in a letter from H.C. Kingsbury, an AT&T vice president, to the Attorney General of the United States, committing the System to stop some of these practices. First, the Bell System agreed to dispose of its interest in Western Union. It did this in 1914. Second, Bell promised to interconnect its toll lines with local independent exchanges.[c] Finally, AT&T agreed to limit the future acquisition of competing telephone companies to those approved by the ICC. This did not affect the acquisition of operating companies that did not compete with Bell, although AT&T did follow a procedure of informing the Department of Justice and obtaining permission from the ICC.

The part of the Kingsbury Commitment pertaining to the acquisition of competing telephone companies became ineffective with the passage of the Willis-Graham Act in 1921. This legislation permitted the consolidation of competing telephone companies upon the approval of the Interstate Commerce Commission. Between 1920 and 1934, when the Federal Communications Commission was established, the Bell System share of all telephone stations rose from 62 percent to 79 percent (see Table 7-2).

[b] The Mann-Elkins Act also served to extend the jurisdiction of the Interstate Commerce Commission in the railroad industry, as discussed in Chapter 6.

[c] By this time over half of the independent stations were already interconnected with Bell (infra, endnote 2), and several states had already passed laws requiring interconnection.

Structure of the Telephone Industry

The telephone industry in the United States today continues to be dominated by the Bell System. With the establishment of Bell Telephone Laboratories in 1925 to conduct research and development, Bell achieved the basic structure that exists today. It has twenty-three operating companies, serving different geographic areas. Together these companies operate in most of the metropolitan areas of the country and in all states except Hawaii and Alaska. AT&T owns all the stock in seventeen of these operating companies, and at least 80 percent in four others. To bring the total to twenty-three companies in its reports, the FCC includes two "associated" companies (Southern New England Telephone and Cincinnati Bell), in which AT&T owns a minority interest.[d]

AT&T itself is divided into two major departments. The Long Lines Department operates the interstate long distance network that connects the operating companies with one another. It received operating revenues of $2.1 billion in 1975 [4]. The General Department of AT&T provides the operating companies and the Long Lines Department with advice and assistance, much like a centralized consulting service. The General Department revenues for 1975 were $415 million [5].

In addition to its ownership of the operating companies, AT&T owns all of Western Electric, as mentioned earlier. Finally, AT&T and Western Electric jointly own Bell Telephone Laboratories. Thus the Bell System has a structure which horizontally integrates its operating companies, and vertically integrates the operating companies, its equipment manufacturing company, long distance transmission, and research and development, much as Theodore Vail envisioned long ago.

The independent telephone industry includes approximately 1,600 telephone companies. Most of these are small and not affiliated with other telephone companies. However, a few of the larger independents have a holding company structure. General Telephone and Electronics Corporation, United Telecommunications, Incorporated, Continental Telephone Corporation, Central Telephone and Utilities Corporation, and Mid-Continent Telephone Corporation all have subsidiaries which are telephone operating companies. Independent telephone companies provide service to about one-half the land area of the United States [6]. Table 7−3 shows that they generate about

---

[d]The Bell System excludes the two associated companies from its own consolidated reports.

Table 7–3. The Telecommunications Industry of the United States

	Number of Companies				Operating Revenues ($000)			
	1960	1965	1970	1975	1960	1965	1970	1975
1. Telephone								
a) Bell System	25	25	25	25	8,108,806	11,317,928	17,364,639	29,581,647
b) Independents	3,299	2,421	1,841	1,618	1,008,451	1,638,264	2,891,814	5,500,000
2. Telegraph								
a) Domestic	1	1	1	1	262,365	305,615	402,456	504,760
b) International	8	6	6	6	89,976	106,697	193,808	316,070
3. Private Line Microwave								
a) Miscellaneous Common Carriers	—	—	59	45		—	7,347	14,248
b) Specialized Common Carriers	—	—	—	9		—	—	34,944
c) Value added	—	—	—	2		—	—	20
4. Public Land Mobile Radio Service								
a) Telephone Companies	111	281	396	351	11,100	20,900	22,200	61,305
b) Other Firms	409	423	489	434	(combined)	(combined)	(combined)	(combined)
5. Satellite Communications								
a) Domestic	—	—	—	3	—	—	—	16,300
b) International	—	1	1	1	—	2,139	69,598	140,681
6. Nontelephone Company PBX and KTS Equipment	—	—	—	11	—	—	—	143,000
7. Total	3,853	3,158	2,818	2,495	9,477,698	13,391,543	20,951,862	36,312,975

Table 7–3. continued

	Total Communication Plant (Gross in ($000))				
	1960	1965	1970	1975
1. Telephone				
a) Bell System	24,721,830	36,228,981	56,171,376	89,194,378
b) Independents	3,970,578	6,825,867	12,390,327	21,000,000
2. Telegraph				
a) Domestic	398,023	688,757	1,029,149	1,581,052
b) International	163,798	189,242	351,674	645,831
3. Private Line Microwave				
a) Miscellaneous Common Carriers	—	—	23,280	56,191
b) Specialized Common Carriers	—	—	—	166,611
c) Value added	—	—	—	3,020
4. Public Land Mobile Radio Service				
a) Telephone Companies	—	—	—	60,090
b) Other Firms	—	—	—	(combined)
5. Satellite Communications				
a) Domestic	—	—	—	205,000
b) International	—	10,063	188,782	322,679
6. Nontelephone Company PBX and KTS Equipment	—	—	—	Not available
7. Total	29,254,229	43,942,910	70,154,588	133,235,300

Source: *FCC Reports*, 61 F.C.C. 2nd, December 10, 1976, p. 793.

$5.5 billion in annual revenues, compared with $29.5 billion for the Bell System.

In recent years the number of independent telephone companies has declined (see Table 7−3). Mergers among independents and between Bell operating companies and independents have both contributed to this trend. The FCC describes some of the reasons for these mergers as follows:

> In many cases mergers are the result of the passing of the telephone pioneers whose family-operated telephone companies were the mainstays of the independent telephone industry. In other cases neighboring telephone companies have found it expedient to merge as their service areas develop a community of interest. In still other cases, undercapitalized small independents have merged with larger ones in order to acquire the financial resources to improve service. Finally, many independents have rendered themselves prime merger prospects by their higher profitability [7].

The commission notes that, while individual independents are often considered to be weak financially, some of them earn returns on equity in excess of 20 percent, or more than twice the rate of return on Bell's interstate services. The reason for this is that state commissions often set tariffs so that larger telephone companies earn some specified rate of return, and then smaller companies are allowed to charge those tariffs. In fact, the FCC follows such a practice in setting interstate toll rates, resulting in high returns for some independents on their interstate services [8].

The Telecommunications Industry

In addition to the telephone companies, there are several other kinds of firms which contribute to the provision of services which might broadly be classified as telecommunications. These include telegraph carriers, private line microwave firms, public land mobile radio companies, satellite companies, and nontelephone suppliers of interconnect equipment, as listed in Table 7−3. As the table indicates, the telephone companies dominate the telecommunications industry, both in terms of operating revenues and gross plant.

As mentioned earlier, in this chapter we will examine the effects of entry into private line microwave services and the supply of terminal equipment. Within the private line category of Table 7−3 are three groups. The miscellaneous common carriers are engaged mainly in the transmission of television signals to cable television firms and certain broadcast stations, using microwave facilities. The specialized common carriers typically provide point to point transmission of analog (continuous wave) transmission channels, although there have been exceptions. Value added networks (or carriers) typically lease basic communications lines from common carriers, and use their own data processing and switching capabilities to permit different parts of the network to communicate with each other. For example, a value added network might allow two computers or a terminal and a computer to communicate. In our study of private line, we will focus on specialized carriers.

The nontelephone company suppliers of terminal equipment include producers of private branch exchanges (PBX) and key telephone systems (KTS). A private branch exchange is essentially a switchboard which allows for communications within a particular location, such as an office building. Large PBX systems can handle over 100 lines.

Key telephone systems provide for the selection of a number of outside telephone lines from any of the telephones on the system. From the telephone instrument the user may place a call on hold, or switch to another outside line. Small PBX and KTS systems could be substituted for one another for some purposes.

The suppliers of PBX and KTS systems also produce answering systems, recording devices, and a host of other types of terminal equipment. Terminal equipment suppliers are not regulated by the FCC.

TOLL PRIVATE LINE SERVICES

The market for long distance private line services provides an interesting vehicle to study the role of the administrative process in the telephone industry. There are several reasons for this. First, until the end of the 1950s, private line service was provided only by common carriers (primarily the Bell System). Then, with the so-called Above 890 decision, the FCC began to allow other firms to provide long distance private line service in certain markets. A number of subsequent decisions affecting entry and rate-making have been made over the past two decades, giving ample opportunity to observe the continuing interactions of existing carriers, entering firms, communications users, and the FCC itself within the administrative process.

At the outset it is probably worthwhile to describe a particularly difficult problem which has repeatedly confronted the FCC. Toll private line services comprise less than 10 percent of the telephone revenues generated by all toll services (see Table 7-4). This is true whether one considers only the Bell operating companies (that provide almost all of the intrastate toll service in the Bell System), AT&T Long Lines (that provides almost all of Bell's interstate toll

Table 7–4. Toll Service Revenues for Telephone Carriers Reporting Annually to the Federal Communications Commission, 1975 *(millions of dollars, rounded)*

Item	All Companies	Bell System	AT&T (Long-Lines)	Bell Operating Companies
Message Tolls	12,349	11,517	1,701	9,817
Wide Area Telephone Service	1,462	1,427	242	1,185
Toll Private Line Services	1,340	1,280	169	1,111
Telephone	486	438	47	391
Teletypewriter	74	71	10	61
Other Telegraph	3	3	*	3
TELPAK	489	487	71	416
Program Transmission-Audio	19	19	4	15
Program Transmission-Video	63	62	10	52
Other Private Line Services	207	200	26	174
Other Toll Service Revenues	*	*	0	*
Total Toll Service Revenues	15,152	14,224	2,112	12,112

Source: *Statistics of Communications Common Carriers* (FCC, 1975), Table 16.
*Greater than zero, but less than half a million dollars.

service), or all of the companies together that report to the FCC. The problem is this: If a telephone company seeks to reduce its private line rates in response to entry, should it be allowed to do so as a legitimate response to competition, or prevented from doing so on the grounds that such a response is anticompetitive? A telephone company can be expected to argue the former. Prospective entrants are likely to contend the latter, and that low private line tariffs may imply that users of monopoly services are subsidizing private line customers.

Private Line Before Entry

During the 1940s there were two forces which generated increased interest in private line transmission. The first was the development of microwave systems capable of inexpensively transmitting large amounts of information by radio beams. The second was the emerging television industry. The transmission of a television signal requires an information capacity many times the size of a single audio channel.[e] Television networks and other firms were interested in building microwave systems as a potentially cheaper alternative to the use of telephone channels. Several firms had applied for licenses from the FCC in order to provide microwave capacity in the East by the end of the 1940s. However, the plans of these independent firms conflicted with those of the Bell System, which envisioned the development of its own nationwide network capable of providing private line service over microwave facilities.

AT&T advanced its cause along two fronts. First, it created the technical capability to provide radio transmission with the development of the TD−2 microwave system. Second, it successfully argued before the FCC that television signals should be transmitted by common carrier wherever common carrier capacity was sufficient to provide the service [9].

Following this decision in 1948, Western Union remained as the only major common carrier besides AT&T which could have transmitted television channels. In order for Western Union to successfully provide this service, it was necessary that it be able to interconnect its own facilities with the Bell System. In FCC Docket 9539, Bell opposed this interconnection. It contended that a monopoly was necessary to its effort to provide nationwide service, particularly if the FCC desired to have rates averaged over network links so that routes with heavy traffic would generate revenues sufficiently large

---

[e]As an approximation, a television channel requires a channel band width of six megahertz, whereas a telephone channel requires about four kilohertz.

to cover some of the transmission costs incurred over the less profitable routes with lighter traffic. (This creamskimming argument has been raised repeatedly in private line proceedings ever since that time, as we will show below.) The FCC was not convinced that Bell should be forced to interconnect with Western Union in Docket 9539, and therefore did not order compulsory interconnection. Consequently, until the end of the 1950s the Bell System provided a vast majority of the services requiring microwave transmission.

The Above 890 Decision

Toward the end of the 1950s many industrial, commercial, and governmental groups began to recognize the potential cost advantages of microwave transmission. The FCC received many requests for frequency authorization (for the range of frequencies above 890 megahertz) from potential users. The movement was joined by several manufacturers of electronic equipment, who were anxious to fulfill the needs of these customers if frequencies were authorized. Among other groups, the railroads, motor carriers, police authorities, and certain utility companies attempted to persuade the FCC to authorize the use of their own microwave systems.

The Bell System led the way in opposing these applications, using two primary points. First, it argued that the radio spectrum constitutes a scarce natural resource, and can be utilized most efficiently under the control of a common carrier. Without this centralized control, potential congestion and poor service would occur. AT&T also argued that if the commission were to authorize the construction and operation of facilities by anyone who applied, then "the common carriers would stand to lose so much revenue that they would have to compensate for it by increasing their rates to the general public" [10].

The private applicants argued that they could provide their own services at costs considerably lower than the carrier's tariffs if they were permitted to construct facilities. In addition, a number of applicants claimed that the service quality offered by the carriers was not adequate to satisfy their needs. They further emphasized the value of competition as a catalyst in the development of transmission technology, and argued that their entry did not pose the threat to the carriers that the carriers themselves saw [11].

The fundamental question faced by the FCC was whether the public would be better served by free entry or by a common carrier monopoly. The commission ruled in favor of the applicants, noting that:

In many cases, the operation of private users is such that it is not convenient or practicable for common carriers to provide such service. . . . Even in areas where common carrier facilities and personnel are readily available, there appears to be a need for private systems . . . liberalized licensing policies would provide an impetus in the manufacturing of microwave equipment, which, in turn, would result in improvements in the communications art [12].

This decision represented not an end, but only a beginning to proceedings addressing the relationships between the structure of telecommunications markets and the service tariffs. It was not long before Bell responded to the Above 890 decision by filing greatly revised tariff proposals for its private line services. The importance of those proposed tariff changes can best be understood by contrasting the Bell stance on private line tariffs before and after the Above 890 decision.

FCC Docket 11645

In a proceeding separate from the Above 890 case, the FCC began an investigation into the reasonableness of the private line tariffs being charged by Western Union and the Bell System. This investigation, in FCC Docket 11645, began in 1956 and lasted until 1959. During this period Bell offered some private line services which competed with the private line telegraph grade services of Western Union, and other private line services which were then monopolized (the Above 890 decision had not yet been made). Bell argued that "the existing private line telephone rates . . . are not only not unreasonably high, they are too low" [13]. The FCC concluded that Bell was earning 11.9 percent on the private line services which it monopolized, compared with 2.2 percent on services which competed with Western Union.[f]

The TELPAK Tariff

In response to the Above 890 decision, Bell filed new lower tariffs for its private line services. For large users these tariffs represented reductions as large as 85 percent of the prevailing private lines charges. This response was particularly noteworthy in light of the Bell claims in Docket 11645 that private line rates were already too low.

---

[f]There are many problems which arise in attempting to measure the profitability of individual services where there are common costs of production. In making these determinations, the FCC allocates a portion of the common costs to each service sharing a production facility, and the allocation cannot be performed according to any unambiguously derivable rule. This problem was discussed at length in Chapter 6, and will be given still further attention below.

Certain reactions to the TELPAK filing were predictable. Western Union and Motorola, a company which supplied microwave equipment which private entrants might purchase, objected strongly to the new tariff. Despite these objections, the FCC allowed the TELPAK service offering to go into effect. But concern over the question of "proper" tariffs for multiproduct firms, some of whose services were offered in markets where rivals existed, spawned still another docket.

FCC Docket 14650 (Telegraph Investigation)

Shortly after the TELPAK offering began, the FCC launched the Telegraph Investigation to consider allegations that the Bell System was charging tariffs for private line services so low in response to competition that its revenues for these services were not covering a fair share of costs. In other words, the issue was whether Bell was subsidizing its private line markets with revenues generated by its monopoly service offerings.

The key issue here will be familiar to those who have read Chapter 6: How does one define the "fair share" of costs which are to be assigned to each service, particularly since there are production costs which are shared by more than one service? The commission ordered Bell to prepare a study to determine the costs and earnings of seven categories of interstate services. These included message toll telephone, wide area telephone service (WATS), teletypewriter exchange service (TWX), private line telephone service, private line telegraph service, and other services (primarily video transmission).

Although the method of allocating common costs would be the subject of much analysis in the future (in Docket 18128/18684 discussed below), the results of this early "seven way cost study" are of some interest. This represented the first time in the history of the FCC that a full cost allocation was attempted for all of the interstate services of AT&T. It took the advent of entry to turn the attention of the commission from the rate of return for all services together to the services offered individually. Table 7−5 summarizes the results of the earnings based on the fully allocated costs during 1964.

The table indicates that, based on the cost allocation techniques used in the study, the markets in which Bell held a monopoly both had a return of about 10 percent, whereas the markets in which Bell competed either with Western Union or entrants allowed by the Above 890 decision earned a substantially lower return. Although five of the seven markets were characterized by rivalry, these five markets generated less than 15 percent of Bell's interstate revenues.[g]

[g]The share of Bell's interstate service revenues earned by private line services has not changed by much, as shown earlier in Table 7-4.

Table 7—5. Rate of Return on Net Interstate Investment for the Bell System, by Principal Service Categories, Year Ended August 31, 1964

Service Classification	Rate of Return
Message Toll Service	10.0%
Wide Area Telephone Service (WATS)	10.1
Teletypewriter Exchange Service (TWX)	2.9
Telephone Private Line Service	4.7
Telegraph Private Line Service	1.4
TELPAK	0.3
All Other (principally video service)	1.1
Total, All Services	7.5%

Source: FCC Docket 14650, AT&T Exhibit 81, Attachment A, p. 4.

Although no theoretical justification for the allocation method employed in the study was ever offered, the results of the investigation generated predictable responses from Bell, its rival firms, and the FCC. Bell would disavow the relevance of the cost study results, since the cost allocation procedure itself was without theoretical justification. The rivals would point to the results as at least strongly indicative of possible interservice subsidy. And the FCC would launch still other dockets to explore these questions further.

FCC Docket 16258 and Consolidated Docket 18128/18684

The unresolved questions of appropriate interstate rates were considered further through a proliferation of dockets opened by the FCC. An original docket concerning the TELPAK service (FCC Docket 14251) was incorporated in a new docket (FCC Docket 16258) directed to the matter of appropriate rate-making principles which should determine the relationship among the rate levels for Bell's interstate services.

While Docket 16258 was in process, other dockets were opened which addressed the appropriateness of rates for specific services offered by the Bell System. Among others, two of these important proceedings were FCC Dockets 18128 and 18684. The first of these was designed to examine the lawfulness of the tariffs charged for the private line services offered by Bell (except for video and audio program transmission) and Western Union.[h] The program transmission rates were to be examined in Docket 18684.[i]

The issues examined in all of these dockets were quite parallel, and as time passed the commission recognized that they could not be resolved separately. Consequently, on February 18, 1970, before Docket 16258 was completed, the commission decided to incorporate the record of this docket into Docket 18128, along with the record of the earlier TELPAK Docket 14251.[j] In so doing, the FCC terminated the proceedings of Docket 16258, without expressing an opinion on the appropriateness of any rate-making rule. At the same time it consolidated Dockets 18128 and 18684.

The consolidated docket was more than an examination of private line tariffs. The scope included the following issues:

> Whether the rate levels of (1) Message toll telephone service, (2) WATS, (3) private line grade telephone service, (4) private line grade telegraph service, (5) audio and video program transmission services, (6) TWX, and (7) all other service are or will be just and reasonable within the meaning of section 201(b) of the Communications Act of 1934 [14].

Fully Distributed Costs (FDC). From this point on, the record of the administrative process in FCC Dockets 18128/18684 compares remarkably closely with the proceedings in ICC Docket 34013 which were examined in Chapter 6. In both cases there was a dominant-type firm (the railroad and the Bell System), each facing rivalry in some, but not all markets. The rivals argued that the appropriate rate-making rule was some form of fully distributed cost pricing. The dominant carriers argued for a form of incremental cost pricing. The points suggested in support of their views were also quite similar, as we shall see.

Between 1964 and 1971, the FCC had endeavored to find out how the rates of return on Bell services would vary under plausible alternative fully distributed cost allocations. It expanded the initial seven-way cost study in steps. In 1967 it examined nine service categories under four allocation schemes [15]. In 1969 it expanded the four allocation schemes to six [16], and 1971 it examined fully distrib-

---

[h]Bell's private line tariffs are filed as a part of FCC Tariff 260. Western Union files its private line tariffs under FCC Tariff 237. Docket 18128 was instituted on April 10, 1968.

[i]FCC Docket 18684 resulted from the filing of new video rates by the Bell System on August 29, 1969.

[j]More specifically, it was the record of phase I–B of Docket 16258 which was incorporated into Docket 18128.

uted costs for eight service categories using seven methods of allocation [17].

While we do not intend to examine each of these methods in great detail here (a task both tedious and not particularly instructive for our purposes), it is perhaps worthwhile to mention certain basic differences between them. AT&T performed the studies, and characterized the seven methods in two basic groups, Methods 1 and 2 in the first, and the others in the second. According to Bell, the first two methods "are based on averaging techniques that essentially disregard historical cost causation, particularly with respect to the incurrence of costs associated with interexchange circuit plant" [18]. The allocations were generally based "on the embedded cost of the types of facilities available for use by the various services, according to length-of-haul characteristics of the individual services" [19]. Method 2 differed from Method 1 "with respect to the treatment of certain minor investment, certain expense, and miscellaneous revenue items," but still relied on averaging techniques which did not reflect "historical cost responsibility" [20].

In contrast, Bell described the other methods as ones which do attempt to associate individual service costs with the historical pattern in which costs were incurred:

> Methods 3 through 7 were approaches to the allocation of the embedded costs associated with the interchange circuit plant on the basis of historical cost responsibility. The measurement of historical cost responsibility involves determination of the extent to which increases in total embedded costs resulted from the provision of a particular service over the period of years such service was offered [21].

Bell was particularly critical of the first two methods because they did not reflect the fact that many of the facilities used to provide the private line services were newer and less costly than the older facilities built to provide the monopoly services. "These two methods have the effect of assigning a disproportionately large part of the costs of the older types of interexchange circuit facilities . . . to the services other than MTS, although the introduction or major growth of these services occurred well after the bulk of these types of facilities were constructed" [22].

The FCC ultimately decided to place special emphasis on Method 7, as we will see below. This particular approach allocated costs in two steps. First, all of the costs which could unambiguously be identified with the production of a single service were classified as "directly attributable" costs for that service. The remaining costs were called unassigned costs. Then the unassigned costs were allocated to the service categories in approximately the same proportion as the directly attributable costs [23].

The results of the 1971 FDC study are shown in Table 7–6. Two points stand out in this table. First, for reasons noted above in Bell's arguments, the returns on private line services were generally calculated to be lower with Methods 1 and 2 than with the other allocation methods. Second, the two monopoly services usually appeared to be more profitable than the other services, for each of the allocation methods examined in the study.

Bell's Objections to FDC. AT&T opposed the use of FDC as a costing and rate-making standard on several grounds. Bell produced two well-known economists, Dr. William J. Baumol and Dr. James C. Bonbright, who supported Bell's position throughout Dockets 16258 and 18128 [24]. The Bell arguments included: [25]

1. FDC studies are not based on accepted economic principles.

2. FDC analyses attempt to impute costs which are inherently indivisible to individual services.

3. FDC results present a false and misleading measure of the profitability of a service.

4. FDC calculations have no economic basis as a criterion for measuring the existence of interservice subsidies [26].

5. The FDC criterion constitutes an anticompetitive rate-making standard. It does not encourage competition, but rather divides the market "among multiple suppliers rather than competition in which each competitor is doing his best to cut its [sic] costs and to supply service in such amounts as will maximize his own returns" [27]. Dr. Baumol argued that

> Perhaps . . . fully distributed cost is invoked in the cause of protection of competition by those who are really a little afraid of it. . . . There are too many cases in which fully distributed cost and the demand for fairness in competition have been the rallying point for the inefficient and the imposition of umbrella prices requiring consumers to pay considerably more than they would have otherwise, allegedly for their own good. I cannot believe that the Commission can rest content with such a solution [28].

Bells' Proposed Subsidy Test: The Burden Test. Of particular concern in Docket 18128 was the issue of interservice subsidy. As stated earlier, Bell argued strongly that no FDC analysis can adequately

Table 7–6. Fully Distributed Embedded Cost Study, Bell System Interstate Services, Twelve-Month Period Ended July 31, 1971

Summary of Ratio of Net Operating Earnings to Net Investment
Under Various Allocation Methods

Service Category	Method 1	Method 2	Method 3	Method 4	Method 5	Method 6	Method 7
Message telecommunications service	8.6%	7.9%	7.0%	7.7%	7.7%	7.2%	7.3%
Wide area Telecommunications service	9.4	13.8	17.9	15.4	14.9	17.1	16.7
TELPAK	5.4	6.2	11.0	6.9	7.7	10.3	9.6
Private line telephone	4.0	5.0	8.1	5.2	5.0	5.7	5.3
Private line telegraph	5.3	6.3	7.2	6.4	6.4	6.6	5.7
Audio/radio	3.0	5.7	13.9	6.0	5.5	6.4	4.1
Television	4.9	5.1	6.1	5.8	5.8	9.2	8.3
Other*	3.1	2.7	4.4	2.8	2.6	3.2	3.3
Total	7.8	7.8	7.8	7.8	7.8	7.8	7.8

Source: FCC Docket 18128/18684, Common Carrier Bureau Exhibits 23, 24; Bell Exhibit T-9.
*Includes TWX results, prior to the sale of that service to Western Union effective April 1, 1971.

serve to determine if one service is being subsidized by another. Professor Baumol outlined the central point as follows:

> ... the reason no FDC test will do the job is because an FDC test deals only with one circumstance, that is, it deals with the service as it is operated or has been operated. It involves no incremental comparison. It does not compare the circumstances of the user with the service and in the absence of the service [29].

In place of an FDC approach, Bell supported the use of a test which would measure whether the continued provision of a particular service would cause users of other services to pay more than would be the case if the service being tested were not offered. This is the essence of the Burden Test which Bell proposed. The test was presented algebraically by Dr. Baumol.

> Service x does *not* impose a burden on the users of the other company services if

$$R_x \geq p_1 \Delta y_1 + p_2 \Delta y_2 + \ldots + p_n \Delta y_n - \Delta T$$

> where

> R_x is the total revenue yielded by service x, the service to be tested for burden;

> $p_1, p_2, \ldots, p_n$ are the respective current prices of the other company services (service 1, service 2, etc.);

> $\Delta y_1, \Delta y_2, \ldots, \Delta y_n$ are the respective changes in quantity of services 1, 2, etc. that would be demanded if service x were discontinued; and,

> ΔT is the effect on the total revenue requirement without service x, that is, the total revenue requirement if the service were eliminated minus the total revenue requirement if provision of the service were continued [30].

Before further considering certain aspects of the Burden Test, two examples of its application are presented here, both for the TELPAK service at different times. Table 7–7 shows the Burden Test results for TELPAK for the rates in effect on February 1, 1970. In this test, if TELPAK had been discontinued, Bell estimated that it would have lost $355.1 million in TELPAK revenues. However, because some TELPAK users would have switched to other services, other service revenues would have increased by $225.9 million if TELPAK were discontinued. Bell also estimated that its production costs for all services would have declined by $133.9 million if TELPAK were discontinued. As a net figure, this means that TELPAK revenues were less

Table 7−7. TELPAK: Burden Analysis (February, 1970 rates)
**Annual Revenues and Costs Based on End-of-1971 Market Estimate,
Thousands of Dollars**

(1)	R_x: TELPAK revenues (February 1, 1970 rate)		$355,100
(2)	$\sum_i p_i \Delta y_i$: Increased Revenues from cross-elasticities to:		
	Other private line services	$184,000	
	MTS, WATS, TWX	41,900	
			225,900
(3)	$-\Delta T$: Net cost reduction (attributable directly to TELPAK and to cross-elasticities with other services)		133,900
	Result: $R_x \gtreqless \sum_i p_i \Delta y_i - \Delta T$		

Source: FCC Docket 18128/18684, Bell Exhibit SA.

than the sum of the cost savings and increased revenues projected for other services if TELPAK were discontinued. In this case, users of other services would have been required to generate less revenues if TELPAK were discontinued. Hence, TELPAK failed the Burden Test at the February 1, 1970 rates [31].

Following this application of the Burden Test, Bell filed a proposal to raise TELPAK rates to the levels in effect for the analysis of Table 7−8. At the higher rates TELPAK did pass the Burden Test.

A detailed description of the practices followed in applying the Burden Test is not central to our investigation here. However, certain basic points about the Bell proposal should be emphasized. Most importantly, if the commission had adopted the Burden Test, it would have allowed the firm much flexibility in the extent to which prices deviate from marginal costs in various services. This can be emphasized using the simplified two product example of Chapter 6. Recall the example of a firm which produces services 1 and 2 at levels x_1 and x_2, at a total cost represented by

$$C = F + c_1 x_1 + c_2 x_2 \ ,$$

where F is a fixed cost shared in the production of the two services, and the marginal costs of production for each of the services is constant at c_1 and c_2 respectively. To abstract from the effects of cross-elasticities of demand, we further assume that the demands are independent of one another. Suppose service 1 is a monopoly service, while the second service is provided in a market where rival firms

Table 7–8. TELPAK: Burden Analysis (May 1, 1972 rates) Annual Revenues and Costs Based on End-of-1971 Market Estimate, Thousands of Dollars

(1)	R_x: TELPAK revenues (at rates effective May 4, 1972)		$351,800
(2)	$\sum_i p_i \Delta y_i$: Increased revenues from cross-elasticities to:		
	Other private line services	$167,200	
	MTS, WATS, TWX	38,800	
			206,000
(3)	$-\Delta T$: Net cost reduction (attributable directly to TELPAK and to cross-elasticities with other services)		135,500

Result: $R_x \geq \sum_i p_i \Delta y_i - \Delta T$

Source: FCC Docket 18128/18684, Bell Exhibit 21, Attachment A.

exist. Then the Burden Test for service 2 will be passed (among other possible tariffs) when the tariffs for the two services (p_1 and p_2) respectively are:

$$p_1 = (F + c_1 x_1)/x_1$$

and

$$p_2 = c_2 .$$

In this example, the Burden Test would allow the two-product firm to price its competitive service at marginal cost, while recovering revenues from the monopoly service which cover the rest of the costs of the firm. There is a striking similarity between Bell's support of the Burden Test here and the railroads' argument for allowing tariffs which cover out-of-pocket costs, as discussed at length in Chapter 6.[k]

The FCC Decision. Relying on the precedent of *American Commercial Lines* v. *Louisville and Nashville Railroad Co.* (the *Ingot Molds* case) [32], the FCC concluded that "it is within the sound

_____

[k]However, the set of tariffs which pass the Burden Test will not always include a tariff which equals marginal cost for a service, for two reasons. The Burden Test includes an effect for cross-elastic demands which may preclude marginal cost pricing in some cases. Also, the Burden Test is based on the concept of incremental costs, which is different from marginal cost. Incremental costs refer to the difference in costs associated with a specified positive level of service, compared with a zero level of output for that service.

discretion of a regulatory agency to establish appropriate economic policy to effectuate its legislative mandate" and noted "that the Communications Act contains no express direction regarding the choice of a particular costing methodology" [33]. Its decision, adopted on September 23, 1976, included the following points:

1. The commission rejected the use of incremental costing methodologies, including the Burden Test, as "inadequate to allow us to perform our statutory functions" [34]. It argued that in practice "a compelling case can be made for any number of alternative professional approaches to pricing, such as accounting, financial statistical, and legal . . ." and that "policymakers concerned with legislative and other non-economic criteria must well weigh these concerns in reaching yet other pricing policies" [35].

2. The FCC decided to employ FDC Methods 1 and 7 (with some revisions) to define a zone of reasonableness for service tariffs. It ruled that Method 7 costs would "form the primary basis for justifying all tariff filings, in conjunction with Method 1 data which will provide us with a comparative benchmark of present relative use" [36].

3. It judged the TELPAK offering tariffs to be inappropriate on the basis of the FDC standards it adopted, and ordered Bell to terminate the existing TELPAK offering within eight months. Bell would be permitted to file new tariffs, consistent with the accepted FDC guidelines, if it chose to do so [37].

4. The commission required Bell to set rates based on the accepted FDC standards for *all* of its services [38].

FDC pricing rules emphasize several of the characteristics that we have attributed to the administrative process. The rules guarantee that proposed tariff changes will be judged by the commission rather than directly by the impersonal marketplace. Existing interest groups will have a chance to protect their present positions against loss from change, and the judicial nature of the process itself will dampen the rate at which a departure from the status quo can occur.

The tendency of FDC pricing to preserve present market and pricing structure can be stated even more explicitly. To illustrate the circular nature of the FDC mechanism and its emphasis on *existing* tariffs, consider an FDC procedure which allocates unassignable costs in proportion to the levels of costs which are assignable to each service category. In the two service example used earlier, tariffs p_1 and p_2 must each generate revenues which cover assignable costs ($c_1 x_1$ and $c_2 x_2$ respectively) and a fraction (f_i) of the unassignable costs,

F. Symbolically, when the firm earns total revenues which just cover total costs, the tariff in the ith market will be

$$p_i = (f_i F + c_i x_i)/x_i \quad , i = 1, 2 \quad .$$

But if the f_i's are determined in proportion to the assignable costs, as the example assumes, then

$$\frac{f_1}{f_2} = \frac{c_1 x_1}{c_2 x_2} \quad .$$

The circularity is now clear. Tariff levels that are determined to be "appropriate" under this FDC approach depend on the present levels of service, x_1 and x_2, and these in turn depend on existing tariffs. FDC tariffs may change over time as demand and cost conditions are altered, but the FDC mechanism will serve to slow the adjustment of tariffs as long as it depends on recent market history to allocate unassignable costs.

SPECIALIZED COMMON CARRIERS

The Above 890 decision of the FCC allowed large communications users to build microwave systems for their own use, but it did not permit any private owner to sell transmission services to other users as a common carrier. In 1963 Microwave Communications, Incorporated (MCI) applied for FCC certification as a common carrier to provide point-to-point microwave transmission between Chicago, Illinois, and St. Louis, Missouri, including nine intermediate points.

MCI proposed to offer to subscribers a limited common carrier service, which included the long haul transmission between its microwave sites, but leaving each subscriber to supply his own communications link between his place of business and MCI's terminus. While the proposed MCI offering did not include all of the service guarantee and standby support features which have characterized Bell System services, in other ways its offerings would allow more flexibility to users than Bell's services. The MCI proposal imposed fewer restrictions on the types of terminal equipment that could be used, allowed subscribers to subdivide transmission channels into bandwidths not offered by existing carriers,[1] and permitted users to share in the use of channel capacity with other users on a party line basis. In addi-

---

[1] For example, existing carriers leased channels for voice use in a bandwidth no less than 4 kilohertz. MCI proposed to lease and subdivide its channels into increments of 2 kilohertz.

tion, MCI intended to offer its services at rates less than half those of the established carriers.

The application was opposed by Western Union, General Telephone Co. of Illinois, AT&T and its associated companies, and was designated for hearing in February 1966. Those opposing the applications argued that no need for the proposed services had been demonstrated, that MCI was not financially qualified to act as a public common carrier, and that its services would be unreliable. They also objected to the inefficient utilization of the radio spectrum that would result from a grant of the application, and expressed reservations about the technical feasibility of the proposal.

In an initial decision, the hearing examiner recommended the grant of MCI's application [39]. The examiner found that the MCI system would not generate electrical interference with the radio operations of existing carriers, that MCI was financially qualified, and that users of MCI services would be afforded flexibility not offered by existing carriers, at lower rates. He noted that serious questions did exist regarding the reliability of the offering, but found no reason to think that the system would not work. Finally, he concluded that some duplication of facilities already existed over the proposed route, and that MCI's facilities would to some extent increase the duplication. However, he concluded that the duplication resulting from MCI's facilities would not be wasteful or unnecessary because the new facilities would be providing services to users whose needs would otherwise not be fulfilled [40].

The final decision of the FCC was made in 1969, six years after the application of MCI. It adopted the recommendation of the hearing examiner that the application be granted [41]. However, other prospective common carriers had not waited for the final decision to submit their own applications. Within a year of the initial decision of the hearing examiner the FCC received over thirty applications from firms seeking to establish themselves as public common carriers. Most of these proposals were to provide specialized point-to-point private line service, using analog (continuous wave) signals. One applicant, the Data Transmission Company (DATRAN), intended to provide digital transmission over a switched network, which offered certain reliability and accuracy advantages in the transmission of data.[m]

---

[m]Analog signals are transmitted over a continuous wave form. Voice signals are typically transmitted over analog channels. Digital signals are carried as discrete, rather than continuous, wave forms. DATRAN's services offered users the opportunity to transmit discrete data using only digital signals. Existing carrier services involved the translation of digital signals to analog and then back to digital at the receiving end. DATRAN's elimination of this translation reduced the error rate in digital signal transmission.

Some of the applicants were already providing services for themselves as a consequence of the Above 890 decision, and desired to extend their authority to operate as common carriers as well.[n]

As the number of these applications grew, the FCC recognized the need for further examination of the broad policy and procedural issues involved. In 1970 it initiated a public inquiry regarding specialized carriers [42], considering the matter in FCC Docket 18920. Five major questions were addressed in the Inquiry. Would the public interest be served by permitting the entry of new carriers in the specialized communications field? If so, should there be comparative hearings on the various claims of mutual exclusivity among the applicants? What standards should be adopted regarding technical matters, such as the avoidance of interference among carriers in the use of radio frequency? Should some measure of protection for subscribers be taken in the areas of quality and service reliability? What should be the appropriate means for local distribution of proposed services [43]?

The established carriers opposed entry by specialized carriers, following basically the arguments that they offered in the Above 890 and MCI proceedings. The Bell System asserted that the specialized carriers were engaging in creamskimming by proposing to enter the high density markets. The existing carriers' tariffs followed a pattern of rate averaging, so that tariffs were essentially the same for service provided over a given distance, whether on a low density (higher marginal cost) route; or over a high density route. If specialized carriers were to succeed in entering high density markets with tariffs lower than those of the existing carriers, then rate averaging would no longer be tenable.

AT&T also claimed that entry would result in the sacrifice of economies of scale in its own operations, and hence lead to high costs for the services it provided [44]. In evaluating this argument, the commission stated that "an estimate of the proportion of AT&T service that is vulnerable to competitive inroads would be on the order of 2–4 percent of its total business" [45]. In addition, the FCC observed that "competition in the specialized communication field would enlarge the equipment market for manufacturers other than Western Electric, and may stimulate technical innovation and the introduction of new techniques" [46].

---

[n] For example, the Southern Pacific Communications Company, which operated its own microwave system along the railroad right-of-way of its parent company, the Southern Pacific Railway, was one of the firms seeking common carrier status.

The Specialized Carrier Decision

The commission concluded that entry by specialized carriers should be allowed, and that it would not be necessary to restrict entry in any particular area to only one applicant [47]. It admonished applicants to coordinate their use of radio signals prior to application, and "to attempt to resolve technical conflicts in good faith without regard to competitive circumstances" [48]. It also ruled that established carriers should, upon a request from a specialized carrier, permit interconnection of leased channel facilities "on reasonable terms and conditions to be negotiated with the new carriers" [49]. The ambiguity of this language would lead to endless conflict for several years. Finally, the commission deferred the issues of service reliability and quality protection for users until further information could be gathered.

With respect to the creamskimming arguments raised in opposition to the specialized carriers, the FCC recognized that some departures from uniform nationwide practices may be warranted, and would be allowed. It stressed its objective in creating an environment in which all carriers would "have an opportunity to compete fairly and fully in the sale of specialized services" [50]. While the fairness of tariffs was not an issue in this docket, the entry by specialized carriers added to the importance of the later resolution of pricing decisions, including Docket 18128.

As of 1975 a number of specialized carriers had entered communication markets, with annual operating revenues of about $35 million (see Table 7-9). A number of these carriers reported a negative net income for the year, but are still striving to be profitable. However, DATRAN filed a petition for bankruptcy on August 27, 1976, and ceased all commercial operations on September 15, 1976. Table 7-10 shows that the operating revenues of the specialized carriers were about 2 percent of the operating revenues for private line services (including intrastate markets) for telephone companies in 1975. These tables suggest that the specialized carriers are struggling. Among the reasons for this are tariff and technological response of the telephone companies. Two examples of this follow.

Dataphone Digital Service

On October 31, 1972, AT&T filed for authority to offer what it represented as a new private line service, Dataphone Digital Service (DDS). It proposed to establish digital transmission channels over existing microwave routes serving Boston, New York, Chicago, Philadelphia, and Washington, D.C. This was to be expanded to twenty-

Table 7—9. Specialized Common Carriers, December 31, 1975 *($000)*

	Gross Communi-cations Plant	Operating Revenues	Net Income from Micro-wave Services
CPI Microwave, Inc.	10,910	1,876	– 758
Data Transmission Co.	48,733	117	-15,374
MCI Telecommunications Corp.	*	21,319	-24,405
Microwave Communications, Inc.	4,727	1,643	– 1,468
Midwestern Relay Co.**	10,307	2,377	129
N-Triple-C, Inc.	11,871	548	– 2,401
Southern Pacific Communications Co.	71,781	5,088	-14,796
West Texas Microwave Co.**	2,587	871	302
Western Telecommunications, Inc.**	5,695	1,105	265
Total	166,611	34,944	-58,506

Source: *FCC Reports*, 61 F.C.C. 2d, p. 801.
*Parent company is MCI Communications, Corp.
**Operates as both a Specialized Common Carrier and a Miscellaneous Microwave Common Carrier.

Table 7–10.   Operating Revenues: Telephone Company Private Line* and Specialized Common Carriers
(in thousands of dollars)

	1960	1965	1970	1975
Bell System	403,862	543,766	1,030,857	1,479,473
Independent Telephone Companies	14,872	36,782	80,439	133,103
Total Telephone Company	418,734	580,548	1,111,296	1,612,576
Specialized Common Carriers	—	—	—	34,944
Total	418,734	580,548	1,111,296	1,647,520

Source: *FCC Reports*, 61 F.C.C. 2d, p. 802.
*Including intrastate private line.

four cities, and eventually ninety-six cities in a nationwide digital data service network.

AT&T proposed to offer DDS using a new technological development, Data Under Voice (DUV). By adding DUV facilities to existing microwave systems, digital channels could be added to the transmission capability of the system without sacrificing any of the existing analog capacity. AT&T contended that DUV would allow more reliable data transmission than analog techniques, and could provide sizable savings to the customer over the existing private line tariffs.

Several potential users of DDS supported AT&T's applications. However, several objections were filed by other common carriers. DATRAN led the opposition for obvious reasons. DATRAN had originally filed to provide switched digital services over a major network serving thirty-five cities. The technical parameters of the proposed AT&T service were those planned by DATRAN.

In 1973, the commission concluded that "the basic DUV technology is sound and should be introduced into the plant and operations of the AT&T network," but had decided not to permit commercial operations until AT&T submitted descriptions of the exact services to be offered as well as a set of proposed tariffs for these services [51]. On March 19, 1974, AT&T submitted proposed tariffs for DDS, along with supporting cost data.

Importantly, AT&T proposed that DDS rates be filed under a new tariff (Tariff No. 267) rather than under Tariff No. 260 under which analog private line services are listed. The proposed tariffs were quite low, prompting DATRAN to argue that they would effectively preserve the private line data market for AT&T, despite the commission's policy of encouraging competition in specialized communication services [52].

On December 16, 1974, the commission began an investigation of the lawfulness of Tariff No. 267 as proposed by AT&T. However, it did grant AT&T the authority to operate DUV facilities. For the first five cities in the network, DDS services were to be operated at the rates proposed in Tariff No. 267. In the other nineteen cities, tariffs were to be "no lower than those at which AT&T offers data services via its analog facilities under Tariff No. 260" for a period of a year [53]. After the year passed, the Tariff No. 267 rates became effective for the additional nineteen cities as well [54].

During all of these proceedings, the commission had not been able to determine whether Tariff No. 267 rates were predatory, as DATRAN had claimed, or cost-justified, as AT&T had suggested. However, in FCC Docket 20288 the commission examined the tariffs further, and found them unlawful. At the heart of the commission's objections to the tariff were the arguments of AT&T that the DUV portion of the spectrum should be treated as a free good because the existing radio systems could not use it for analog transmission:

> Nowhere are the faulty subjective judgments ... more evident than in AT&T's decision to treat the DUV portion of the spectrum as a "free economic good" ... The digital service market is a competitive market. We find that it is inherently predatory for AT&T to treat the DUV spectrum devoted to that market as a free good. Moreover, not only is such treatment inherently predatory and anti-competitive, that subjective decision is totally inconsistent with Bell's past treatment of spare spectrum. ... Not incidentally, AT&T would derive a competitive advantage by being able to exclude those plant and equipment costs from the investment base upon which its DDS rates are calculated [55].

The commission also objected to the portion of research and development costs which AT&T attributed to DDS.

> Aside from Bell's attempts to treat the DUV spectrum as a free economic good ... nowhere are AT&T's predatory and anticompetitive propensities more evident than in the treatment of R&D expense [56].

The commission was initially unable to elicit a statement about R&D costs for DDS from AT&T, although AT&T later placed the costs at about $715,000. In its own assessment, the FCC Trial Staff estimated these costs at a minimum of $23 million. The commission's review of the findings "convinces us that the Trial Staff is far closer to being correct" [57].

In the end the commission rejected Tariff No. 267, and stated that AT&T must file again if it wished to offer DDS, using an FDC approach as a basis for its tariffs. More specifically, the filed tariffs were to be no lower than for a comparable private line service under Tariff No. 260 [58].

Perhaps the major lesson that can be learned from this docket, regarding strategic use of the administrative process, is suggested succinctly in the decision itself:

> This case involves the adjudication of a rate for a competitive service. DATRAN points out that under the present statutory scheme AT&T can initiate an illegal, noncompensatory rate and by the time that rate is *finally* held to be illegal the competitive damage is done, i.e., the competitor (or competitors) is (are) irreparably crippled or destroyed. This is true. But it does not appear that the Administrative Law Judges have the authority to remedy such anti-competitive conduct [59].

The subsequent failure of DATRAN drives the point home even more clearly.

The Hi-Lo Tariff

Existing carriers have made other tariff responses to entry in reaction to the Above 890 and Specialized Carrier decisions. As discussed earlier, in the Specialized Carrier ruling the commission indicated that some departure from nationwide uniform pricing might be considered a valid response by existing carriers, in light of the cream-skimming arguments raised by AT&T.

A tariff revision of this sort was filed by AT&T in November 1973. AT&T proposed a set of tariffs (for its voice grade private line services) which generally decreased the rates over routes with a high traffic density, and increased the rates over low density routes. This proposal became known as the Hi-Lo Tariff [60].

AT&T selected as its high density locations those rate centers which were served by at least one high capacity radio facility (capable of handling 1,200 voice channels or more), and with multiplexing equipment suitable for producing voice grade channels. In addition, a location qualifying as a high density center would have local distribution facilities to customers' premises, and access to all other high-density centers in the interstate network [61].

Over a transmission from one high density center to another, private line long haul customers would experience rate decreases ranging up to 40 percent under the proposal. Over other long haul routes, rates would generally be higher, ranging up to a 40 percent increase [62].

The tariff changes were opposed by several groups, including certain news services and specialized carriers. At the time the Hi-Lo tariffs would have made the Bell rates lower along certain rates which were also served by MCI. For example, along the 261 mile route from St. Louis to Chicago, MCI's full-time rate per channel was $481.65. The Hi-Lo Tariff proposed a Bell rate of $341.85 [63].

The FCC took two steps. First, on January 9, 1974, it ordered a hearing on the reasonableness of the Hi-Lo Tariff. Among other things, the hearing was to examine whether the rates were discriminatory or not, and in conformity with the Specialized Carrier decision and the then-pending Docket 18128. Second, it suspended the rate until April 14, 1974 [64]. (The tariffs ultimately became effective on June 13, 1974 [65]).

The proceedings in the Hi-Lo case (FCC Docket 19919) were tortuous. For our purposes, we note that a year and a half later the commission still had not concluded the case. In an Interim Decision on September 1975, it reassessed the progress in the case. It described fully distributed cost guidelines by which the tariff would be judged, but noted several deficiencies in the information it required to draw conclusions about the lawfulness of the tariff. It ordered continued hearings [66].

It considered the matter again on January 16, 1976, and still found a number of deficiencies in the record. The commission described the state of the case as follows:

> As a result of these deficiencies, we found in the Interim Decision that AT&T had not satisfied its burden of proof in justifying its tariff. However, in view of the fact that this was the first major competitive response to specialized carrier competition, we felt we should exercise our discretion and remand the case for further hearings while the tariff went into effect. Upon further reflection and reconsideration we believe it inappropriate and not in the public interest to permit t ʼ subject tariff to remain in effect while conducting further hearings into its lawfulness. It appears that much of the operating, cost, and other information which we consider useful for justification of the present Hi-Lo rates, as specified in our Interim Decision, is not readily available either within Bell's books of account or the working papers prepared to support its initial filing. Thus a rehearing of the present case would necessarily involve the development and review of extensive new studies and data, rather than the mere augmentation of existing data. This would, in turn, entail a lengthy proceeding during which the present, unjustified Hi-Lo tariffs would remain in effect [67].

Accordingly, the tariff, which had been in effect for nearly two years was ruled unlawful, and AT&T was ordered to file new tariffs, consistent with the fully distributed cost guidelines that it had described in its Interim Decision [68]. With this action it terminated Docket 19919.

There were important similarities in the DDS and Hi-Lo proceedings. In both cases the response of an existing carrier to entry was at issue. The commission was confronted with the need to make a ruling, but with no guidelines. It did state the importance of conformity with the Specialized Carrier decision and struggled not to prejudge the Private Line case. It recognized the need for allowing a competitive, but not anticompetitive response on the part of existing carriers. And finally, in each case it ruled the proposed tariffs invalid, but only after long delays had harsh effects on the financial pictures of the specialized carriers, and particularly for DATRAN.

In closing the discussion of private line services, we note that there are unresolved questions involving the interactions among private line and the traditional monopoly services. In July 1975, the FCC rejected an MCI proposal to offer its Execunet service [69]. An Execunet customer in one city could call a local MCI office from any telephone in the local telephone exchange, connect with another city via MCI long distance facilities, and reach any telephone at that destination using the facilities of the local telephone company. According to the FCC, Execunet was essentially a switched public message telephone service rather than a private line service. It rejected the tariff proposal for Execunet because MCI was authorized to offer only private line services.

That FCC decision was taken to the United States Court of Appeals for the District of Columbia [70]. The court reversed the FCC decision, primarily rejecting the notion that MTS should be granted the status of a statutory monopoly. In January 1978, the Supreme Court refused to hear the case, reaffirming the decision of the appeals court. This may very well signal a flurry of attempted entry into services in which AT&T previously enjoyed a monopoly status. We can expect the FCC to open new hearings designed to more clearly delineate those services where entry may not be allowed in future applications.

There are still other areas in which entry into markets served by existing carriers permits observation of the administrative process. One of these is the supply of terminal equipment, which we now examine.

CUSTOMER TERMINAL EQUIPMENT

Early Decisions on Entry

Before 1956 AT&T's tariffs prohibited customers from attaching their own terminal equipment to the telephone network. However, in 1956 the United States Court of Appeals for the District of Columbia ruled that this type of tariff restriction was not legal as it applied to a device known as the Hush-a-Phone [71].

The Hush-a-Phone was a cup-like device attached to the mouthpiece of a telephone, designed to allow more privacy for the user and to reduce the amount of room noise in the signal. The FCC had ruled that the Hush-a-Phone could potentially harm the quality of two-party service, and sustained Bell's contention that the device should be proscribed [72]. However the court found that such a tariff restriction represented an "unwarranted interference with the telephone subscriber's right reasonably to use his telephone in ways which are privately beneficial without being publicly detrimental" [73]. The commission subsequently ordered AT&T to rescind the tariff prohibition on any device "which does not injure defendants' employees, facilities, the public in its use of defendants' services or impair the operation of the telephone system" [74].

Over time AT&T has continued to oppose the competitive supply of customer terminal equipment in a number of cases.[o] The case which brought to a head the prohibition of interconnection with foreign attachments involved the Carterfone. The Carterfone was an inductive-acoustically coupled device which allowed mobile telephone users access to the public telephone network using a Carterfone located at the base station of the mobile system. In the Carterfone case, Bell introduced extensive technical and economic arguments to support its case.

> AT&T has urged that since the telephone companies have the responsibility to establish, operate and improve the telephone system, they must have absolute control over the quality, installation, and maintenance over all parts of the system. Installation of unauthorized equipment, according to the telephone companies, would have at least two negative results. First, it would divide the responsibility for assuring that each part of the system is able to function effectively and, second, it would retard development of the system since the independent equipment supplier would tend to resist changes which would render his equipment obsolete [75].

The commission found that the Carterfone did not adversely affect the telephone system. It also acknowledged that the Carterfone was in fact prohibited under the AT&T tariffs in effect. However, instead of enforcing the prohibition in the tariff, the commission concluded "that the tariff has been unreasonable, discriminatory, and unlawful in the past, and that the provisions prohibiting the use of customer-provided interconnecting devices should accordingly be stricken" [76]. The commission allowed the telephone carriers to submit new tariffs which would allow interconnection, but protect the telephone system from devices that might harm the system, including the specification of technical standards for terminal equipment.

This was a landmark decision in the telephone industry. The Carterfone case reaffirmed the Hush-a-Phone principle, allowing entry into the supply of terminal equipment.

Following the Carterfone decision, AT&T filed new tariffs permitting customers to attach their own terminal equipment. However, Bell specified limits on the signal strength and other technical param-

---

[o]For example, it opposed the interconnections of recording devices in FCC Docket 6787, and of answering system devices in Dockets 9383 and 9701.

eters, and required connecting arrangements and network control signalling units provided by the telephone carrier [77]. The FCC allowed these tariffs to go into effect, but instituted a Federal-State Joint Board proceeding to determine whether the network protective device restrictions could be relaxed without causing any harm [78]. The proceeding resulted in the establishment of a registration program which allowed users to connect certain types of equipment providing that the equipment was certified by the commission in meeting certain protective standards [79].

FCC Docket No. 20003

As more entry occurred in telecommunications markets following the Carterfone and Specialized Carrier decisions, the established telephone carriers and some state regulatory bodies raised questions regarding possible adverse economic effects on users of basic telephone services. In 1974 the FCC launched Docket No. 20003 as a fact-finding investigation into the economic effects of interconnection and private line services in the telephone industry. Parties responding to the investigation included AT&T, various independent telephone companies, the United States Independent Telephone Association (USITA), the National Association of Regulatory Utility Commissioners (NARUC), the Office of Telecommunications Policy, and two state commissions.

A central issue in the docket was whether basic telephone service rates would have to rise as a result of competition. AT&T, USITA, and NARUC all took an affirmative position. They claimed that interstate services and terminal interconnection activities not only cover their assignable costs, but also contribute to unassignable costs. If competition diverts part of these markets from the telephone companies, then additional unassignable costs would have to be covered by monopoly services, leading to increased rates.

Other common carriers (including MCI) and the suppliers of terminal equipment argued the opposite position. First, they contended that the competition responses of the telephone companies would prevent any serious erosion of their revenues from private line and interconnect activities. In addition, since AT&T's private line service is noncompensatory (according to these carriers), monopoly service rates need not rise at all as a result of competition.

In September 1976, the FCC released its findings in Docket 20003 [80]. The commission found the telephone industry overall to be quite healthy. Despite the recent inflationary and recessionary trends in the economy, it found that telephone companies had been experiencing a period of record growth in revenues and earnings in 1975 and 1976. "Furthermore, the telephone companies dominate the [telecommunications] industry by a wide margin—receiving $35.1 billion, or about 97% of the total industry revenues, in 1975. Even in the private line and terminal equipment markets—the only areas open to competition—the telephone industry received $4.1 billion, or 95.5% as compared with $194 million, or 4.5% for the competitive industry" [81] (see Table 7−11).

The commission also examined fourteen interstate and intrastate rate increase requests during 1975, and observed that none of these cited the existence of competition as a justification for the request. However, it recognized that the future impact of competition was another matter, and examined a number of studies purporting to show how competition would influence monopoly service rates. The commission expressed disappointment at the general quality of the studies submitted on this point. Although AT&T, USITA, certain independents, and NARUC each submitted reports that supported the contention that competition would lead to losses in the contribution which private line or competitive equipment supply activities presently make toward covering the unassignable costs of the firm, the studies "were found to contain . . . flaws in data, assumptions, and methodologies" [82]. Consequently the commission found no convincing evidence that terminal equipment and private line services are covering their fully distributed costs, much less making any additional revenue contribution. In fact, it suggested that perhaps the rates for those services should be increased in order to cover their fully distributed costs [83].

In short, the FCC found "the record is devoid of justification for the claims of dire consequences to the established carriers" from competition [84]. The commission concluded that there was no need to reexamine or revise its existing policies allowing competition in these two market sectors.

The FCC decision to allow competition in the supply of terminal equipment has now been sustained by the courts [85]. Customers will be allowed to attach their own terminal equipment as long as the equipment is of the type certified as acceptable by the FCC.

CONCLUSION

The telephone industry provides many excellent examples of the strategic use of the administrative process. We can now place the developments in private line, specialized carriers, and terminal interconnection in the perspective of Chapter 1. One of the major points suggested there was that regulated firms and industries operate within the administrative process just as they operate in the market; the

Table 7–11. Selected Telecommunications Industry Statistics

Category	1975 Revenues (in million $)	Percent of Total Industry	Increase Over 1974 (in million $)
1. *Total Industry*	36,313	100.0	3,863
Bell System	29,581	81.5	2,820
Independent Telcos	5,500	15.1	786
Competitive Industries	194	0.5	80
Other (telegraph, public land mobile)	1,038	2.9	150 (est.)
2. *Telephone Industry*	35,081	96.6	3,606
a. *Monopoly Services*	31,004	85.4	3,233
Local Exchange	13,822	38.1	1,213
Interstate Toll (MTX, WATS)	9,176	25.3	1,074
Intrastate Toll (MTS, WATS, private line)	6,868	18.8	854
Miscellaneous Revenues	1,138	3.2	92
b. *Competitive Services*	4,077	11.2	373
PBX and KTS	3,060	8.4	296
Interstate Private Line	1,017	2.8	77
3. *Competitive Industry*	194	0.5	80
Interconnect (PBS and KTS)	143 (est.)	0.4	36
Specialized Carrier	35	0.1	28
Satellite Carrier	16	negligible	16

Source: 61 F.C.C. 2d 810.

environment provides opportunities for strategic behavior in pursuit of economic objectives.

Both existing carriers and prospective entrants have made extensive strategic use of information in the administrative process. These firms have taken virtually every opportunity to make detailed economic and technical filings, understandably in ways which emphasize the strong points in their cases and diminish (or at least obscure) the weaker points. Supporting documents routinely run into the thousands of pages.

Specific examples in this chapter are numerous. Bell has staunchly supported its proposal to use an incremental cost basis for pricing, and developed the Burden Test as a vehicle for translating its market objectives into equity arguments. And, according to the FCC, after the Hi-Lo Tariff was in effect at least on a temporary basis, Bell delayed its presentation of supporting data until the commission ruled that AT&T had not satisfied its burden of proof with respect to the tariff well over a year later.

One of the best examples of strategically stated arguments occurred in the case of Bell's Data Under Voice technology. AT&T presented DUV as a means of delivering portions of the radio spectrum, a scarce economic resource, as a free good. In addition, the commission also found that in trying to justify low DDS tariffs, AT&T had seriously understated the research and development costs of DUV.

The interconnection docket (FCC Docket 20003) provides an example in which both existing carriers and terminal equipment suppliers filed strongly supportive, but widely divergent information. Bell and USITA attempted to show that competition from terminal equipment suppliers would have severely adverse effects on the users of basic monopoly services in the future, while the suppliers argued that monopoly services are presently subsidizing those markets which have been opened to competition.

The three cases examined in this chapter also yield interesting examples of strategic use of litigation. The telephone companies are largely insulated from the effects of extended litigation. However, lengthy proceedings greatly undermined entry attempts in the instances of Hush-a-Phone, Carterfone, and DATRAN. AT&T was also successful in maintaining its TELPAK, Hi-Lo, and DDS rates for long periods of time before they were ultimately found to be unlawful.

On the other side, many potential specialized carriers waited until the Initial Decision in the MCI case was made, only then filing their applications for status as a carrier. Later on, in Docket 18128, they took refuge in the Specialized Carrier decision as a major point in their quest to have tariffs based on fully distributed costs rather than any form of incremental cost.

The telephone industry is also replete with examples of strategically introduced innovation. The Bell System developments of microwave technology in the 1940s and DUV more recently confirm this. Prospective entrants continue to provide new ideas for providing specialized communication services in an effort to carve for themselves a piece of the market.

Chapter 1 also suggests that a multiproduct firm might try to deter entry by showing that entry in one market might destroy an attempt to satisfy some overall objective that a regulator might find desirable. AT&T has contended that rate averaging will be untenable when entry in some markets is allowed. However, the FCC has stated that some departure from uniform nationwide rates would be tolerable in exchange for the specialized services that entrants might provide.

The multiproduct nature of telecommunications firms itself raises a rather fundamental question. What are the criteria for declaring that two services are different, or whether they are essentially identical? There is room for strategy here as well. AT&T contended that TELPAK was a service different from its other private line services, and that different tariffs would therefore be appropriate. It argued the same point when it introduced DDS under a new tariff schedule (Tariff No. 267) instead of under the conventional schedule (Tariff No. 260).

Prospective entrants can play this game, too. If they introduce a service which has some cross elasticity of demand with the basic monopoly services of telephone companies, they will want to argue that the effect is quite small. Telephone companies surely will not agree.

On the basis of the cases we have examined, it could be argued that entrants particularly have sought to use the FCC as a cartel manager. The entrants have claimed that their entry will not adversely affect the telephone companies, emphasizing their own small size and their anticipation that Bell will be allowed to respond so that its market share is not seriously eroded. The private line microwave companies have made three major strides toward success in this respect, including certification as common carriers, the judgment in Docket 18128 that tariffs should be based on fully distributed costs, and the right to gain connection with the local distribution facilities of the telephone companies.

The Administrative Process and Attenuation

A second major effect of the administrative process was described in Chapter 1 as the attenuation of the rate at which market and technological forces impose changes on individual economic agents. At one level, it is easy to point to examples that show how delays are an integral part of the administrative process. It took MCI six years to secure permission to enter. Counting the related proceedings before Docket 18128, it required more than a decade to resolve the private line rate-making question. AT&T was delayed two years in its efforts to construct DUV facilities.

In each of these cases the administrative process imposed delays before it allowed changes. It required some assurance that existing firms and users of communications services would not be "unfairly" treated as a result of the change. The administrative process even institutionalized rate-making rules which slowed departure from the status quo, as we argued in our discussion of fully distributed cost pricing earlier in this chapter. We need not further discuss the obvious preference for equity over efficiency in FDC pricing rules, for a comparison of the kinds of rules that efficient pricing would require and FDC rules were developed at length in Chapter 6.

One could perhaps argue that the decision to allow entry in any market is inconsistent with the proposition that the administrative process protects the property rights of individuals and firms in the status quo. This suggests the query: Why did the FCC allow entry in the first place?

One possible answer to this is that the basic status quo position of monopoly was not altered by the commission, but was changed in a court decision in the Hush-a-Phone case. One could argue that the Hush-a-Phone case in the telephone industry fulfilled the same role as the *Phillips* case in the natural gas industry (see Chapter 3) in dictating a new status quo in which entry would be allowed.

While this is one plausible answer, there are quite probably others. However the important point lies elsewhere. In this book we have not so much attempted to describe the behavior of regulators as to describe the effects of the administrative process. This is a crucial distinction. With the second perspective it becomes clear that the administrative process attenuates not only adjustments which individuals and firms might propose, but even those of the regulators themselves.

❋   *Chapter 8*

Conclusions

Two tentative hypotheses about the regulatory process
were put forward in Chapter 1.

The first hypothesis was that it is useful to think of the administrative process as a strategic game in which regulated entities and
other interested parties struggle to achieve economic rewards. The
legal rules of regulatory activity—administrative law—and the natural
proclivities of regulators combine to create a well-defined environment within which the game is played. The second hypothesis was
that one major purpose of regulation is to protect economic agents—
firms and consumers alike—from too-sudden changes in their economic environment, and that the administrative process achieves this
end by granting implicit legal rights in the status quo. We showed
that it might be rational for individual voters to prefer such a policy
to one of laissez-faire, even at the cost of some economic efficiency,
if they are sufficiently risk-averse.

Several alternative strategic tools for dealing with the administrative process were discussed in Chapter 1. These included the use of
litigation, control of information, the management of invention and
innovation, cross-subsidization among multiple outputs, and among
multiple jurisdictions, along with effective lobbying, the use of the
agency for cartel management, and the cooption of experts. Subsequent chapters provided support for the two hypotheses, showing
how specific strategies have been used in real world cases.

In Chapter 2 we saw how the Federal Communications Commission acted as a cartel manager with respect to the international communication common carrier industry, and how its decisions favor

stability and "fairness" at considerable cost in economic efficiency. We also saw how one firm, AT&T, made successful use of strategic innovation and threats to achieve its ends in the regulation game.

In Chapter 3 we observed that the Federal Power Commission, having once fallen into the practice of keeping natural gas prices below market-clearing levels, found itself unable to deprive consumers of their rights to the low prices, despite the fact that this policy must ultimately lead to shortages, crises, and rationing.

In Chapter 4 we examined the ways in which a tiny service industry—title insurers—has been able to take advantage of the rewards of regulation to achieve protection from competition and antitrust attack.

In Chapter 5 we saw how the cable television industry was faced with continual restrictions in an effort to protect the rights of broadcasters to their existing revenues and of all viewers to their existing levels of service.

In Chapter 6 we showed how the efforts of a firm engaged in intermodal competition will be resisted by other modes that might be adversely affected, and indicated how the flexible pricing rules carved out of equity considerations differ from those designed primarily to lead to economic efficiency. This slows the rate at which prices are adjusted in response to changing market conditions.

In Chapter 7 we saw how existing telephone carriers were able to delay the effects of entry in three areas of telecommunications, and that even programs initiated by regulators themselves can be delayed by strategic uses of the administrative process.

The material in Chapters 2 through 7 provides supporting evidence for the two hypotheses of Chapter 1, but by no means do these illustrations "prove" the validity, or the usefulness, of the hypotheses. Before either hypothesis can be accepted as a reasonable approximation of the truth, it will be necessary to state them as rigorous propositions capable of being rejected by contrary evidence, ideally on the basis of statistical tests. Thus, the first step in future research must be to develop more formal models from which the hypotheses can be derived and tested. This is an extraordinarily difficult task. It is difficult partly because of the enormous richness and variety of regulatory behavior and partly because of the absence of much significant repetitive, commensurate behavior conducive to statistical analysis. In the end it may be necessary to use international comparisons in order to test the hypotheses with any significant degree of rigor.

The piling up of illustrations and examples, while necessary and useful, does not provide a basis for the statistical tests we are suggesting for further research. For example, it is relatively easy to draw contradictory conclusions from the same example by emphasizing different aspects of the case. The creation of the Consumer Product Safety Commission can be seen as an event that introduced significant new risks into the economic environment for consumer product firms, or it can be viewed as a move that provided, because of the standard-setting procedure that was part of the legislation, an important new means of eliminating nonprice competition in such industries, thus reducing economic risk.

The second step in further research, but one that may proceed in parallel with the first, is to ask the obvious normative questions. Does the administrative process actually achieve a reduction in economic risk? At what cost? Are the costs greater or less than the benefits? Are there other policies and devices available to achieve the same benefit at lower costs? What are the effects on incentives for innovation and internal efficiency of the present system of regulation as compared with alternative means of achieving the same ends? These, too, are extraordinarily difficult questions, but ones that must be answered before economists can speak with authority in the public policy debate about regulation.

Notes

NOTES TO CHAPTER 1
STRATEGIC USE OF THE
ADMINISTRATIVE PROCESS

1. See, for instance, *National Broadcasting Co.* v. *United States* 319 U.S. 190 (1943), extending the FCC's authority to television networks, which were not mentioned in the statute; *U.S.* v. *Southwestern Cable* 392 U.S. 157 (1968) and *U.S.* v. *Midwest Video* 406 U.S. 649 (1972), extending FCC authority to cable television, on the grounds that it was "ancillary" to broadcasting. But see *Home Box Office* v. *FCC*—F.2d—, 2 Media Law R. 1561 (D.C. Cir., 1977), *cert. den.*—U.S.—(1977).

2. See *FCC* v. *RCA Communications* 346 U.S. 86 (1953), denying the FCC authority to make a presumption in favor of open entry and competition. But see the "Execunet" decision, *MCI* v. *FCC*—F.2d—(1977), *cert. den.*—U.S.—(1978).

3. See William J. Baumol, Elizabeth E. Bailey, and Robert D. Willig, "Weak Invisible Hand Theorems on the Sustainability of Prices in a Multiproduct Monopoly," *American Economic Review* (June 1977); John C. Panzar and Robert D. Willig, "Free Entry and the Substainability of Natural Monopoly," *Bell Journal of Economics* (Spring 1977); John C. Panzar and Robert D. Willig, "Economics of Scale in Multi-Output Production," *Quarterly Journal of Economics* (August 1977).

4. A much more extensive but still incomplete survey of the literature can be found in Paul L. Joskow, "Regulatory Activities by Government Agencies," MIT Department of Economics, Working Paper 171 (December 1975), which is to appear as Chapter III—14 in the forthcoming *Handbook of Organizational Design*, W. Starbuck, ed. (Elsevier).

5. George J. Stigler, *The Citizen and the State: Essays on Regulation* (University of Chicago Press, 1975).

6. Richard A. Posner, "Taxation by Regulation," *Bell Journal of Economics* (Spring 1971); "Theories of Economic Regulation," *Bell Journal of Economics* (Autumn 1974).

7. Sam Peltzman, "Toward A More General Theory of Regulation," *Journal of Law and Economics* (August 1976).

8. Marvar Bernstein, *Regulating Business by Independent Commission* (Princeton University Press, 1955).

9. See, for instance, Murray Edelman, *The Symbolic Uses of Politics* (University of Illinois Press, 1964).

10. Roger G. Noll and Morris P. Fiorina, "Voters, Bureaucrats, and Legislators," Caltech Working Paper, 1976; Morris P. Fiorina, *Congress, Keystone of the Washington Establishment* (Yale University Press, 1977).

11. Victor P. Goldberg, "Regulation and Administered Contracts," *Bell Journal of Economics* (Autumn 1976).

12. Samuel P. Huntington, "The Marasmus of the ICC: The Commission, the Railroads, and the Public Interest," *Yale Law Journal* (April 1952).

13. See William Wardell's and Louis Lasagna's brief history in *Regulation and Drug Development* (American Enterprise Institute, 1975).

14. Richard E. Caves, *Air Transport and Its Regulators* (Harvard University Press, 1962); Stephen G. Breyer, *Civil Aeronautics Board Practices and Procedures*, Report of the Subcommittee on Administrative Practice and Procedure, Senate Judiciary Committee, 1975.

15. Harvey Averch and Leland Johnson, "Behavior of the Firm Under Regulatory Constraint," *American Economic Review* (December 1962).

16. Edelman, *Symbolic Uses of Politics.*

17. Richard A. Posner, "The Social Costs of Monopoly and Regulation," *Journal of Political Economy* (August 1975).

18. Robert A. Dahl and Charles E. Lindblom, *Politics, Economics and Welfare* (Harper and Row, 1953), p. 498. See also David B. Truman, *The Governmental Process: Political Interests and Public Opinion* (Knopf, 1951), pp. 416–421.

19. For a more detailed look at how ambitious bureaucrats behave, see Gordon Tullock, *The Politics of Bureaucracy* (Public Affairs Press, 1965); or Anthony Downs, *Inside Bureaucracy* (Little, Brown and Company, 1967).

20. Richard B. Stewart, "The Reformation of American Administrative Law," *Harvard Law Review* (June 1975).

21. James Q. Wilson, "The Politics of Regulation," in *Social Responsibility and the Business Predicament*, James W. McKie, ed. (The Brookings Institution, 1974).

22. Michael Porter and Jeffrey Sagansky, "Information, Politics, and Economic Analysis: The Regulatory Decision Process in the Air Freight Case," *Public Policy* (Spring 1976).

23. Paul Joskow, "Inflation and Environmental Concern: Structural Change in the Process of Public Utility Price Regulation," *Journal of Law and Economics* (October 1974); "Pricing Decisions of Regulated Firms: A Behavioral Approach," *Bell Journal of Economics* (Spring 1973); "Regulation and the Financial Condition of Electric Power Companies," *American Economic Review*

(May 1975); "The Determination of the Allowed Rate of Return in A Formal Regulatory Proceedings," *Bell Journal of Economics* (Autumn 1972).

24. See Graham T. Allison, *Essence of Decision: Explaining the Cuban Missile Crisis* (Little, Brown, 1971); J.D. Steinbruner, *The Cybernetic Theory of Decision* (Princeton, 1974); Oliver Williamson, "Franchise Bidding for Natural Monopolies," *Bell Journal of Economics*, Spring 1976.

25. See William A. Niskanen, "Nonmarket Decision Making and the Peculiar Economics of Bureaucracy," *American Economic Review* (May 1968): 293–305; William A. Niskanen, *Bureaucracy and Representative Government* (Aldine-Atherton, 1971).

26. Niskanen, *Bureaucracy and Representative Government*, p. 64.

27. Noll and Fiorina, "Voters, Bureaucrats."

28. Goldberg, "Regulation."

29. Stewart, "Reformation."

30. Roger G. Noll, *Reforming Regulation* (Brookings, 1971).

31. For the history of jurisprudence in this area, see K.C. Davis, *Administrative Law Treatise* (West, 1958; Supplement 1970), and Stewart, "Reformation."

32. *Home Box Office* v. *FCC*—F.2d—2 Media Law R. 1561 (D.C. Cir., 1977), *cert. den.*—U.S.—(1977), is a major step in this direction. The decision banned ex parte contacts in FCC rule-making procedures.

33. See Sam Peltzman, *Regulation of the Pharmaceutical Industry* (American Enterprise Institute, 1974).

34. Henry R. Myers, "Federal Decision-making and the Trans-Alaska Pipeline," *Ecology Law Quarterly* (1975), also see Joskow, "Inflation and Environmental Concern."

35. Mordecai Kurz, "Income Redistribution: Theory and Evidence," IMSSS Working Paper 80, 1977, Stanford University.

36. Owen Phillips, "Legislative v. Administrative Control: A Study of the Determinants of Regulatory Behavior," Studies in Industry Economics, No. 85, 1977, Stanford. A related point is that increasing agency budgets does *not* reduce the amount of delay in decision-making. See Noll, Reforming Regulation; *Study On Federal Regulation: Vol. IV: Delay in the Regulatory Process* (Senate Committee on Governmental Affairs, 1977). The budget power is not, of course, the only way in which congressmen affect agency policy. The Senate confirmation process, oversight hearings, and less formal interactions are also very important. Unfortunately, none of these lends itself to quantitative tests.

37. Susan Wagner, *The Federal Trade Commission* (Praeger, 1971), p. 76.

38. See Bruce M. Owen "Regulating Diversity: The Case of Radio Formats," *Journal of Broadcasting* (Summer, 1977).

39. John Forester, "Toy Bike Syndrome," *Bike World* (October 1973): 24–27. The point here is that the Congress imposed procedural *rules* on the CSPC's standard-setting process that give industry groups an opportunity to manipulate the standards to their own advantage. See Nina Cornell, Roger G. Noll, and Barry Weingast, "Safety Regulation," in Henry Owen and Charles L. Schultze (eds.), *Setting National Priorities: The Coming Decade* (Brookings, 1976).

40. *Cantor* v. *Detroit Edison*, 44 L.W. 5357 (1976).

41. *U.S.* v. *AT&T*, Civil Action No. 74–1698 (District D.C.), *Memorandum Opinion and Order on Jurisdictional Issues*, filed Nov. 24, 1976.

42. *U.S.* v. *NASD* 422 U.S. 694 (1976).

43. F. Harper and F. Jones, *The Law of Torts*, p. 331.

44. *Swift & Co.* v. *U.S.* 196, U.S. 375, 396 (1905); *American Tobacco* v. *U.S.* 328 U.S. 781 (1956); *Continental Ore Co.* v. *Union Carbide*, 370 U.S. 690, 707 (1967).

45. *Lynch* v. *Magnavox* 94 F.2d 883 (9th Cir., 1938); *Steward-Warner* v. *Staley* 42 F. Supp. 140 (W.D. Penn. 1941); *Master Metal Strip Service* v. *Protex* 169 F.2d 700 (7th Cir., 1948); *Forgett* v. *Scharf* 181 F.2d 754 (3rd Cir., 1950); *Kobe* v. *Dempsey Pump Co.* 198 F.2d 416 (10th Cir., 1952). See M.J. Adelman and E.L. Brooks, *J. Pat. Off. Soc'y* 55 (1973): 255, cited in *Trucking Unlimited, infra.*

46. Respectively, 365 U.S. 127 (1961) and 381 U.S. 657 (1965).

47. 365 U.S. 127, p. 135 (1961).

48. 381 U.S. 657, p. 670 (1965).

49. See Note, "Limiting the Antitrust Immunity for Concerted Attempts to Influence Courts and Administrative Agencies; Analogies to Malicious Prosecution and Abuse of Process," *Harvard Law Review* 86 (1973): 715.

50. *Woods Exploration* v. *Alcoa* 438 F.2d 1286, 1297–98 (5th Cir.), *cert. den.* 404 U.S. 1027 (1971).

51. *Hecht* v. *Pro Football* 444 F.2d 931 (1971) *cert. den.* 404 U.S. 1047 (1971); *Israel* v. *Baxter Laboratories* 466 F.2d 272 (1972).

52. 404 U.S. 508 (1972).

53. 410 U.S. 366 (1973).

54. 360 F. Supp. 451, 452 (D. Minn., 1972).

55. M. Rothschild and J.E. Stiglitz, "Increasing Risk: I. A Definition," *Journal of Economic Theory* 2 (September 1970): 225–243.

56. M. Rothschild and J.E. Stiglitz, "Addendum to 'Increasing Risk: I. A Definition'," *Journal of Economic Theory* 5 (October 1972): 306.

57. V. Strassen, "The Existence of Probability Measures with Given Marginals," *Annals of Mathematical Statistics* 36 (1965): 423–439.

NOTES TO CHAPTER 2
REGULATION OF OLIGOPOLY

1. See Kurt Borchardt, *Structure and Performance of the U.S. Communications Industry* (Harvard, 1970); Asher Ende, "International Communications," *Law and Contemporary Problems* (Spring 1969); President's Task Force on Communications Policy, *Staff Papers* (Washington, 1968).

2. All the data used in this chapter refer to information available to policymakers in 1971, the time of the decision we are examining. The picture has not been greatly altered, however, by events since 1971. See FCC Request for Comments on Proposed Policy for Licensing Overseas Facilities, FCC 77–536 Docket 18875 (August 1977).

3. An example is "TASI–B" (for "time assignment speech interpolation, type B"), which derives about 230 circuits from an existing 100–circuit capacity at extremely low cost.

4. Communications Satellite Act of 1962 47 U.S.C. 701 *et seq.*

5. *Authorized User Decision* 4 FCC 2d 421 (1966).

6. 47 U.S.C. 34–39.

7. 47 U.S.C. 151 *et seq.*

8. 14 FCC 523 (1950).

9. 25 FCC 535 (1958).

10. 13 FCC 2d 235 (1968).

11. 4 FCC 2d 421 (1966).

12. 346 U.S. 86 (1953).

13. See Asher Ende, "International Communications," *Law and Contemporary Problems*, (Spring 1969).

14. 4 FCC 2d 421 (1966).

15. 5 FCC 2d 812 (1966).

16. 13 FCC 2d 235 (1968).

17. President's Task Force on Communications Policy, *Staff Papers* (1968).

18. 13 FCC 2d 235 (1968).

19. *Notice of Inquiry* FCC 70–620, Docket 18875, 1970.

20. Office of Telecommunications Policy Staff Papers, *International Facilities Study* (1971) (National Technical Information Service accession number PB 208670). Hereafter, "OTP Staff Report."

21. Ibid., p. 11.

22. Ibid., p. 14.

23. Ibid., p. 23.

24. Ibid., p. 119.

25. FCC 71–659.

26. A similar observation is made in Gerald Jantscher's study of maritime regulation, *Bread Upon the Waters* (Brookings, 1975).

27. "DOMSAT" decisions: 35 FCC 2d 844 (1972); 37 FCC 2d. 184 (1972); 38 FCC 2d 665 (1972).

NOTES TO CHAPTER 3
REGULATING A DEPLETABLE SOURCE

1. Portions of this chapter are a revised version of a paper written for the United States Senate Committee on Governmental Affairs' *Study on Federal Regulation*, Vol. VI (forthcoming).

2. See William K. Jones, *Cases and Materials on Regulated Industries* (The Foundation Press, Inc., 1976), p. 12.

3. See *Gas Facts* (The American Gas Association, 1968), p. 80.

4. See, for example, *Barrett v. Kansas Natural Gas Co.*, 265 U.S. 298 (1924).

5. Alfred E. Kahn, *The Economics of Regulation: Principles and Institutions*, Volume II (Wiley and Sons, 1971), p. 30.

6. Natural Gas Act, 52 Stat 821 (1938), 15 U.S.C.A. 717 *et seq.*, Section 1(a).

7. Ibid., Section 4.

8. *Natural Gas Act*, Section 1(c).

9. *Phillips Petroleum Company v. Wisconsin et al.*, 342 U.S. 672 (1954).

10. See Paul MacAvoy, "The Reasons and Results in Natural Gas Field Price Regulation," in Paul W. MacAvoy (ed.), *The Crisis of the Regulatory Commissions*. (Norton, 1970) p. 154.

11. *Phillips* (1954).

12. *National Gas Survey*, United States Federal Power Commission (1975), p. 85.

13. See *In re Phillips Petroleum Company*, 24 FPC 537 (1960).

14. Kahn, *Economics of Regulation*, Vol. I, p. 43.

15. See The *Permian Basin Area Rate Cases*, 390 U.S. 747 (1968).

16. *Federal Power Commission Annual Report* (FPC, 1974), p. 41.

17. The rate schedule was determined in FPC Opinion Numbers 749 (July 27, 1976), 770–A (November 5, 1976), and 699–H.

18. *Natural Gas Survey* (FPC, 1975), Vol. I., p. 57.

19. See, for example, F.M. Scherer, *Industrial Market Structure and Economic Performance* (Rand McNally, 1970), p. 55.

20. *Sales by Producers of Natural Gas to Interstate Pipeline Companies* (FPC, 1972), Table D.

21. *Natural Gas Survey* (FPC, 1975), Vol. I., p. 57.

22. See the following two references by Paul W. MacAvoy: *Price Formation in Natural Gas Fields* (Yale, 1962), and "The Reasons and Results in Natural Gas Field Price Regulation," in Paul W. MacAvoy (ed.), *The Crisis of the Regulatory Commissions* (Norton, 1970).

23. From MacAvoy, "Reasons and Results," p. 168.

24. See "An Analysis of the Impacts of the Projected Natural Gas Curtailments for the Winter 1975–76," a report of the Office of Technology Assessment, November 4, 1975.

25. Ibid., p. 2.

26. Ibid., pp. 18–23.

27. Paul W. MacAvoy and Robert S. Pindyck, *Price Controls and the Natural Gas Shortage* (American Enterprise Institute for Public Policy Research, 1975).

28. Table 3–8 is compiled as Table 8 in the Braeutigam paper referenced *supra*, n. 1.

29. Paul W. MacAvoy; "The Effectiveness of the Federal Power Commission," *Bell Journal of Economics and Management Science* (Spring, 1970).

30. See MacAvoy and Pindyck, *Price Controls*.

31. See Braeutigam, *supra*, n. 1.

32. Robert B. Helms, *Natural Gas Regulations, an Evaluation of FPC Price Controls* (American Enterprise Institute for Public Policy Research, 1974).

33. As a technical point, the measurement of consumer and producer surplus from a Marshallian demand curve is exact only if there are zero income effects associated with the demand. However, Willig has shown that even if nonzero income effects exist, the measure may serve to approximate the exact measure sought. See Robert D. Willig, "Consumer Surplus Without Apology," *American Economic Review* (December 1976).

34. See MacAvoy and Pindyck, n. 27. The figures cited actually underestimate the efficiency loss CGJ (in Figure 3–1) because the authors do not appear

to include profits which producers make on the additional gas they would supply in the absence of regulation. See the footnote on p. 54 of the MacAvoy and Pindyck work.

35. See Braeutigam, *supra*, n. 1.

36. See Kahn, *Economics of Regulation*, Vol. II, p. 31.

37. See the House of Representatives Report No. 94—732 (94th Congress, 1st Session), p. 6.

38. See *Phillips* (1954).

NOTES TO CHAPTER 4
REGULATION OF SERVICE INDUSTRIES

1. The material in this chapter is based on Bruce M. Owen and Joseph Grundfest, "Licensing Real Estate Brokers As Underwritten Title Agents: A Report to the State of California," Stanford, April 1976 (hereafter cited as "Report"); and Bruce M. Owen and Joseph Grundfest, "Kickbacks, Specialization, Price Fixing and Efficiency in Residential Real Estate Markets," *Stanford Law Review* (May 1977). These two sources provide considerable legal and institutional background material omitted here.

2. See generally, Senate Committee on Banking, Housing, and Urban Affairs, 92nd Cong. 2d Session, Mortgage Settlement Costs: Report of the Department of Housing and Urban Development and Veteran's Administration (1972) (Hereafter, "HUD/VA Report.")

3. Ibid.

4. Kickbacks and rebates are prohibited by section 4 of RESPA (the federal Real Estate Settlement Practices Act of 1974) and by "Bulletin 74—2" of the California Department of Insurance.

5. See Owen and Grundfest, "Report," pp. 108, 115.

6. George Stigler, "A Theory of Oligopoly," *Journal of Political Economy* (Feb. 1964).

7. See "HUD/VA Report," pp. 15—16; Bulletin 74—2 has a long list of payments in kind that fall under the rebate prohibition.

8. Bulletin 74—2 was promoted by the California Land Title Association, the industry trade group. Similarly, section 8 of RESPA was supported in the congressional hearings by the American Land Title Association.

9. *United States* v. *South-Eastern Underwriters Association* 322 U.S. 533 (1944).

10. 15 U.S.C. 1011—1015 (1970).

11. *Mitgang* v. *Western Title* 1974—2 Trade Cases at Par. 75, 322 (N.D. Cal., Oct. 16, 1974).

12. *Chicago Title Insurance Company* v. *Great Western Financial Corp.*, 69 Cal. 2d 305, 322 (1968).

13. Ibid., p. 323.

14. Cf. Alex Maurizi, "Occupational Licensure and the Public Interest," *Journal of Political Economy* (March/April 1974).

15. *Goldfarb* v. *Virginia State Bar* 421 U.S. 773 (1975).

NOTES TO CHAPTER 5
REGULATION OF A NEW TECHNOLOGY

1. Portions of this chapter are a revised version of a paper written for the U.S. Senate Committee on Governmental Affairs' *Study on Federal Regulation* Vol. VI (forthcoming). For additional material on the recent debate over deregulation of cable see Paul A. MacAvoy (ed.), *Deregulation of Cable Television* (American Enterprise Institute, 1977).

2. The preceding statistics are from *Broadcasting Yearbook* (1975), and *Broadcasting* magazine (August 29, 1977).

3. Or was until the recent decision of the D.C. Circuit is *Home Box Office* v. *FCC*—F.2d—2 Media Law R. 1561 (D.C. Cir., 1977), *cert. den.*—U.S.—(1977), which struck down the FCC's pay-TV rules on numerous grounds. See the discussion in MacAvoy, *Deregulation*, Chapter 4.

4. For more extensive histories of broadcast regulation see Roger G. Noll, Merton J. Peck, and John J. McGowan, *Economic Aspects of Television Regulation* (Brookings, 1973); Bruce M. Owen, Jack Beebe, and Willard Manning, *Television Economics* (D.C. Heath, 1974).

5. Radio Act of 1927; Communications Act of 1934. See Title 47, United States Code.

6. For a critical economic analysis of the effects of the localism policy, see Noll, Peck, and McGowan, *Economic Aspects of TV.*

7. For reviews of the FCC UHF policy, see Douglas Webbink, "The Impact of UHF Promotion," *Law and Contemporary Problems* (Summer 1969); Noll, Peck and McGowan, *Economic Aspects of TV*; Erwin G. Krasnow and L.D. Longley, *The Politics of Broadcast Regulation* (St. Martin's Press, 1973).

8. *Report and Order*, Docket 12443, 26 FCC 403 (1959).

9. *Carter Mountain Transmission Corp.* v. *FCC* 32 FCC 459 (1962) *aff'd* 321 F. 2d 359 (D.C. Cor. 1963) *cert. den.* 375 U.S. 951 (1963). *First Report and Order* 38 FCC 683 (1965); *Second Report and Order* 2 FCC 2d 725 (1966).

10. *U.S.* v. *Southwestern Cable* 392 U.S. 157 (1968); *U.S.* v. *Midwest Video* 406 U.S. 649 (1972).

11. *Forthnightly* v. *United Artists* 392 U.S. 390 (1968); *Teleprompter* v. *CBS* 415 U.S. 394 (1974).

12. See, for instance, Ralph Lee Smith, "The Wired Nation" *The Nation*, (May 18, 1970).

13. The "compromise" is discussed in Richard O. Berner, "Constraints on the Regulatory Process: A Case Study of Regulation of Cable Television," Harvard University Program on Information Technologies and Public Policy, Publication P–75–5 (August 1975); Stanley M. Besen, "The Economics of the Cable Television Consensus," *Journal of Law and Economics* (April 1974); and House Subcommittee on Communications, U.S. Congress, Staff Report, "Cable Television: Promise versus Regulatory Performance," Committee Print, January 1976.

14. 36 FCC 2d 143 (1972).

15. The details of the existing rules and their relaxation appear in FCC, *First Report and Order*, Dockets 19554 and 18893, 40 F.R. 57, 15546–15578

(April 7, 1975). Commissioner Robinson's separate statement in this proceeding provides an extensive and highly critical analysis of the FCC's pay-TV policies, an analysis supported by the D.C. circuit's action striking down the rules in the *HBO* decision (*supra*, n. 3).

16. See Bruce M. Owen, *Economics and Freedom of Expression* (Ballinger 1975).

17. Communications law recognizes the link between the welfare of the audience and the economic interests of broadcasters. See *Carroll Broadcasting* v. *FCC* 258 F. 2d 440 (D.C. Cir. 1958).

18. See Owen, *Economics and Freedom of Expression*, Chapter 3, for an extensive discussion.

19. *Broadcasting Yearbook* (1974): 70.

20. 392 U.S. 157 (1968).

21. 406 U.S. 649 (1972).

22. See R.E. Park (ed.), *The Role of Analysis in the Formation of Cable Television Policy* (D.C. Heath, 1973), Chapter 2.

23. FCC, letter to the Hon. Roy Ash, Director, OMB, adopted October 3, 1974, FCC 24100.

24. See 47 C.F.R., Chapter 1, part 76.

25. R.E. Park, "The Exclusivity Provisions of the FCC's Cable Television Regulations," *Rand*, June 1972.

26. *Wall Street Journal*, April 5, 1976.

27. FCC Rules and Regulations § 76. 251(a)(8).

28. See 49 F.R. 34608 (1975).

29. R.E. Park, "Cable Television, UHF Broadcasting, and FCC Regulatory Policy," *Journal of Law and Economics* (April 1972).

30. B.M. Mitchell and R. Smiley, "Cable, Cities, and Copyrights," *Bell Journal* (Spring 1974); Noll, Peck, and McGowan, *Economic Aspects of TV*.

31. For a critical review of the literature, see Stanley M. Besen et al. in MacAvoy (ed.), *Deregulation*, Chapter 3.

32. Besen et al., in MacAvoy (ed.), *Deregulation*.

33. Noll, Peck, and McGowan, in *Economic Aspects of TV*, provide econometric evidence of consumer surplus for TV channels which can be used to estimate the welfare loss to *potential subscribers* of the FCC's anticable policies. However, it is not easy to estimate the benefits, if any, to viewers *protected* by these policies.

34. See Owen, Beebe, and Manning, *Television Economics*, Chapters 2, 4.

35. Ibid., Chapter 4, where it is pointed out that this number must be viewed with some suspicion.

36. Michael Spence and Bruce Owen, "TV Programming, Monopolistic Competition, and Welfare," *Quarterly Journal of Economics* (February 1977).

37. See *House Subcommittee Report*; Cabinet Committee on Cable Communications, *Cable: Report to the President* (GPO, 1974); Sloan Commission on Cable Communications, *On the Cable* (McGraw-Hill, 1971); and Committee for Economic Development, *Broadcasting and Cable Television: Policies for Diversity and Change* (CED, 1975).

38. MacAvoy (ed.), *Deregulation*.

NOTES TO CHAPTER 6
SURFACE FREIGHT TRANSPORTATION

1. *Wabash, St. Louis and Pacific Railway Company* v. *Illinois*, 188 U.S. 557(1886).

2. A.E. Kahn, *The Economics of Regulation: Principles and Institutions*, Vol. 2 (John Wiley and Sons, Inc., 1971), p. 26.

3. G. Kolko, *Railroads and Regulation, 1877–1916* (Princeton University Press, 1965).

4. For an interesting discussion of the efforts made by the railroads to cartelize the industry, see P.W. MacAvoy, *The Economic Effects of Regulation: The Trunk-line Railroad Cartels and the Interstate Commerce Commission Before 1900* (M.I.T. Press, 1965).

5. See, for example, *Interstate Commerce Commission* v. *Cincinnati, New Orleans and Texas Pacific Railway Company*, 167 U.S. 479(1897), in which the courts ruled that the commission could not prescribe maximum rates.

6. Section 4 of the Interstate Commerce Act of 1887 contains the long-and-short-haul clause. The clause did permit the commission to make exceptions to the rule.

7. 168 U.S. 144.

8. D.F. Pegrum, *Transportation Economics and Public Policy* (Richard D. Irwin, Inc., third ed., 1973), p. 64.

9. See A.F. Friedlaender, *The Dilemma of Freight Transport Regulation* (The Brookings Institution, 1969), p. 21.

10. Pegrum, *Transportation Economics*, p. 315.

11. Paul Roberts, "Some Aspects of Regulatory Reform of the U.S. Trucking Industry," forthcoming in the conference volume for the Workshop on Motor Carrier Economic Regulation, April, 1977, to be published by the National Academy of Sciences.

12. Pegrum, *Transportation Economics*, Table 2–3.

13. These objectives were stated in the preamble to the Transportation Act of 1940.

14. This directive was part of the amendment to Section 15(a) of the Interstate Commerce Act.

15. For example, see the *California-Oregon Lumber* case, 308, ICC 345 (1959), *Ingot Molds, Pa. to Steelton, Ky.*, 323 ICC 758 (1965), and *Grain from Idaho, Oregon and Washington to Ports in Oregon and Washington*, 319 ICC 534 (1963).

16. L. Weiss and A. Strickland, *Regulation: A Case Approach*, McGraw-Hill, 1976, pp. 118–121. This reference contains a good summary of the Supreme Court decision in the *Ingot Molds* case.

17. From *New Automobiles in Interstate Commerce*, 259 ICC 475, 513 (1945), quoted in Weiss and Strickland, *Regulation*, p. 116, fn 1.

18. For more detail see the decision of the Supreme Court, which ultimately had to resolve the case, in *American Commercial Lines, Inc. et al.* v. *Louisville and Nashville Railroad Co. et al.* 392 U.S. 571 (1968).

19. Ibid., part I of the opinion.

20. Ibid., part I of the opinion.
21. 392 U.S. 571 (1968).
22. Ibid., part II of the decision.
23. Ibid., part II of the decision.
24. Note the consistency of this position with *Federal Power Commission et al.* v. *Hope Natural Gas Co.* 320 U.S. 591 (1944).
25. 337 ICC 298, July 30, 1970. See particularly pp. 325–327, containing the findings and order. The ICC pursued the problem of rate-making with intermodal competition further in ICC Docket 34013 sub 1, which was terminated in 1976 with the passage of The Regulatory Reform and Railroad Revitalization Act of 1976, discussed below. The sub 1 proceedings led to no substantial conclusions.
26. See the comments made by Professor Noll as a discussant at the Workshop on Motor Carrier Economic Regulation, April, 1977, in the conference volume to be published by the National Academy of Sciences.
27. 337 ICC 298 (see n. 25, *supra*).
28. G.R. Faulhaber, "Cross Subsidization: Pricing in Public Enterprises," *American Economic Review* (December 1975).
29. G.R. Faulhaber, "On Subsidization: Some Observations and Tentative Conclusions," and E.E. Zajac, "Some Preliminary Thoughts on Subsidization," both papers delivered at the Office of Telecommunications Policy Conference on Communications Policy Research, Washington, D.C., November 17–18, 1972.
30. F.P. Ramsey, "A Contribution to the Theory of Taxation," *The Economic Journal* (March 1927), and W.J. Baumol and D.F. Bradford, "Optimal Departures from Marginal Cost Pricing," *American Economic Review* (June 1970).
31. In the paper by Baumol and Bradford, "Optimal Departures," the authors assert that the form of the utility function being maximized was "unspecified." However, Mohring later demonstrated that the unspecified utility function had the same properties as the sum of consumer and producer surplus. See H. Mohring, "The Peak Load Problem with Increasing Returns and Pricing Constraints," *American Economic Review* (September 1970). For more on the measure of consumer and producer surplus, see R.D. Willig, "Consumers' Surplus Without Apology," *American Economic Review* (September 1976).
32. Pegrum, *Transportation Economics*, p. 25.
33. Ibid., Table 2–1. See also Friedlaender, *Dilemma of Freight*, Table C.3. The revenues for air cargo (including air freight, air express, and postal service by air) account for about 16 percent of intercity freight revenues. It is noted here that the exclusion of air freight is primarily for simplicity. The arguments about optimal pricing with intermodal competition, which are developed below, could be extended to include a competitive air freight transport industry by letting this mode be included as one of the modes in the model to be developed.
34. Pegrum, *Transportation Economics*, p. 43.
35. For example, Moore suggests the separate regulation of oil pipelines, and describes the natural monopoly characteristics of this mode. See T.G. Moore, "Deregulating Surface Freight Transportation," in A. Phillips (ed.), *Promoting Competition in Regulated Markets* (The Brookings Institution, 1975).

36. T.G. Moore, *Trucking Regulation*, (American Enterprise Institute for Public Policy Research, 1976). p. 139.

37. L.R. Klein, *A Textbook of Econometrics* (Row, Peterson, 1953).

38. G.H. Borts, "The Estimation of Rail Cost Functions," *Econometrica* (January 1960), and Z. Griliches, "Cost Allocation in Railroad Regulation," *Bell Journal of Economics and Management Science* (Spring 1972).

39. See Garland Chow, "The Cost of Trucking Revisited," forthcoming in the conference volume for the Workshop on Motor Carrier Economic Regulation, April 1977, to be published by the National Academy of Sciences. Chow further suggests that not all less-than-truckload operations are characterized by economies of scale. Scale economies for less-than-truckload operations "appear to be strongest in the short and medium haul, and weakest, if they exist at all, in the long haul." (See Table 4 of his paper for a summary of his regression results.)

40. A.F. Friedlaender, "Hedonic Costs and Economies of Scale in the Regulated Trucking Industry," forthcoming in the conference volume for the Workshop on Motor Carrier Economic Regulation, April 1977, to be published by the National Academy of Sciences. (See the first paragraph of section five of her paper.)

41. Ibid., section five. Friedlaender's "average cost" is a function of ton-miles of freight and factor prices, and parametrically depends on three other variables which describe different kinds of motor carrier technology, (1) a variable to distinguish between the totally loaded and less-than-truckload technology, (2) average length of haul, and (3) weight of haul. She treats the firm as a single product enterprise, and thus her references to "an average cost" function are unambiguous.

42. R. Braeutigam, "Optimal Pricing with Intermodal Competition," *American Economic Review*, forthcoming.

43. See Roberts, "Some Aspects of Regulatory Reform," p. 14. As we note below, it may be possible to prevent unprofitable entry by imposing excise taxes to hold prices above marginal costs in modes $2, \ldots, m$. This is a power presently beyond the jurisdiction of regulatory authorities, however.

44. It should be noted that current research is under way which discusses the application of Ramsey price theory to multipart tariffs. This unpublished research is being performed by G. Faulhaber of Bell Laboratories, and is quite relevant as an avenue for potential application to freight transportation.

NOTES TO CHAPTER 7
REGULATING PRICES AND ENTRY

1. See, for example, *A History of Engineering and Science in the Bell System*, (Bell Telephone Laboratories, 1975), and "Investigation of the Telephone Industry," report of the FCC, H: Document 340, 76th Congress, 1st Session, 1939.

2. The failure of local companies to interconnect was not solely a result of the behavior of Bell. In some cases, Bell companies did interconnect with independents, and in a few cases independents refused to interconnect with Bell.

of interstitial radio spectrum, to which the same comment applies (see paragraph 10 at the decision in Docket 20288).

56. Ibid., paragraph 88, footnote 46.

57. Ibid., paragraph 90.

58. Ibid., paragraphs 143–146.

59. Ibid., paragraph 143, footnote 64 of the decision.

60. See FCC Docket 19919, 44 FCC 2d. 697.

61. Ibid., paragraph 5.

62. Ibid., paragraph 7.

63. AT&T proposed Hi-Lo Tariff, Transmittal No. 11891, and MCI Tariff No. 1.

64. 44 FCC 2d 701.

65. 55 FCC 2d 224.

66. 55 FCC 2d 245–248.

67. 58 FCC 2d 366–367.

68. 55 FCC 2d 246–247.

69. FCC Order 75–799, July 2, 1975.

70. *MCI Telecommunications Corporation* v. *FCC.*, 561 F.2d 365 (1977).

71. *Hush-a-Phone* v. *U.S.* 238 F. 2d 266, 269.

72. 20 FCC 391, 425–427 (1955).

73. See n. 71, *supra.*

74. 22 FCC 112 (1957).

75. 13 FCC 2d 424 (1968), (Dockets 16942 and 17073).

76. 13 FCC 2d 423.

77. AT&T Foreign Attachment Tariff Revisions, 15 FCC 2d 605 (1968), and reconsideration 18 FCC 2d 871 (1969).

78. FCC Docket 19528.

79. 56 FCC 2d 593 (1975). This certification program was extended to include private branch exchanges and key telephone systems in 1976, 58 FCC 2d 736. Some court action has been taken to stay the actions of Docket 19528 (*North Carolina Utilities Commission* v. *FCC and USA*, Case No. 76–1002, fourth circuit). However the stay regarding the certification program on customer supplied data and ancillary devices has been lifted.

80. 61 FCC 2d 766.

81. Ibid., p. 769.

82. Ibid., p. 772.

83. Ibid., p. 773. The commission referred to its decision in Docket 18128, showing that private line revenues did not cover fully distributed costs.

84. Ibid., p. 892.

85. *AT&T* v. *FCC*, 537 F.2d 787 (April 14, 1976), upholding the FCC decision to allow entry into the supply of terminal equipment. Before the United States Supreme Court, *cert. denied*, December 13, 1976.

Bibliography

Allison, Graham A. *Essence of Decision: Explaining the Cuban Missile Crisis.* Little, Brown, 1972.

American Gas Association. *Gas Facts* (Annual).

Averch, Harvey and Leland Johnson. "Behavior of the Firm Under Regulatory Constraint." *American Economic Review* (December 1962).

Balestra, Pietro and Marc Nerlove. "Pooling Cross-Section and Time Series Data in the Estimation of a Dynamic Model: The Demand for Natural Gas." *Econometrica* (July 1966).

Balestra, Pietro. *The Demand for Natural Gas in the United States.* North-Holland Publishing Company, 1967.

Baumol, William J., Elizabeth E. Bailey, and Robert D. Willig. "Weak Invisible Hand Theorems on the Sustainability of Prices in a Multiproduct Monopoly." *American Economic Review* (June 1977).

Baumol, William J. and David F. Bradford. "Optimal Departures from Marginal Cost Pricing." *American Economic Review* (June 1970).

Bell Telephone Laboratories. *A History of Engineering and Science in the Bell System.* Bell Telephone Laboratories, 1975.

Bernstein, Marvar. *Regulating Business by Independent Commission.* Princeton, 1955.

Besen, Stanley M. "The Economics of the Cable Television Consensus." *Journal of Law and Economics* (April 1974).

Besen, Stanley M., et al. "Economic Policy Research on Cable Television: Assessing the Costs and Benefits of Cable Deregulation." In P.W. MacAvoy (ed.), *Deregulation of Cable Television.* American Enterprise Institute, 1977.

Berner, Richard O. "Constraints on the Regulatory Process: A Case Study of Cable Television." Harvard University Program on Information Technologies and Public Policy, Publication P−75−5 (August 1975).

Borchardt, Kurt. *Structure and Performance of the U.S. Communications Industry.* Harvard, 1970.

Borts, George H. "The Estimation of Rail Cost Functions." *Econometrica* (January 1960).

Braeutigam, Ronald. "Optimal Pricing with Intermodal Competition." *American Economic Review* (forthcoming).

Breyer, Stephen G. *Civil Aeronautics Board Practices and Procedures.* Committee on the Judiciary, U.S. Senate, 1975.

Breyer, Stephen G., and Paul W. MacAvoy. *Energy Regulation by the Federal Power Commission.* The Brookings Institution, 1973.

Cabinet Committee on Cable Communications. *Report to the President.* Washington, 1974.

Caves, Richard E. *Air Transport and Its Regulators.* Harvard, 1962.

Chow, Garland. "The Cost of Trucking Revisited." (Forthcoming in the conference volume for the Workshop on Motor Carrier Economic Regulation.) National Academy of Sciences, 1977.

Committee for Economic Development. *Broadcasting and Cable Television: Policies for Diversity and Change.* CED, 1975.

Cornell, Nina, Roger G. Noll, and Barry Weingast. "Safety Regulation." In Henry Owen and Charles L. Schultze (eds.), *Setting National Priorities: The Coming Decade.* The Brookings Institution, 1976.

Dahl, Robert A. and Charles E. Lindblom. *Politics, Economics and Welfare.* Harper and Row, 1953.

Davis, Kenneth C. *Administrative Law Treatise.* West, 1958; *Supplement,* 1970.

Downs, Anthony. *Inside Bureaucracy.* Little, Brown, 1967.

Edelman, Murray. *The Symbolic Uses of Politics.* Univ. Illinois Press, 1964.

Ende, Asher. "International Communications." *Law and Contemporary Problems* (Spring 1969).

Faulhaber, Gerald R. "On Subsidization: Some Observations and Tentative Conclusions." Office of Telecommunications Policy Conference on Communications Policy Research, Washington, D.C., November 17–18, 1972.

Faulhaber, Gerald R. "Cross Subsidization: Pricing in Public Enterprises." *American Economic Review* (December 1975).

Fiorina, Morris. *Congress, Keystone of the Washington Establishment.* Yale University Press, 1977.

Friedlaender, Ann F. *The Dilemma of Freight Transport Regulation.* The Brookings Institution, 1969.

Friedlaender, Ann F. "Hedonic Costs and Economies of Scale in the Regulated Trucking Industry." (Forthcoming in the conference volume for the Workshop on Motor Carrier Economic Regulation.) National Academy of Sciences, 1977.

Goldberg, Victor P. "Regulation and Administered Contracts." *Bell Journal of Economics* (Autumn 1976).

Griliches, Zvi. "Cost Allocation in Railroad Regulation." *Bell Journal of Economics and Management Science* (Spring 1972).

Helms, Robert B. *Natural Gas Regulations, An Evaluation of EPC Price Controls.* American Enterprise Institute for Public Policy Research, 1974.

Huntington, Samuel P. "The Marasmus of the ICC." *Yale Law Journal* (April 1952).

Jantscher, Gerald. *Bread Upon the Waters.* The Brookings Institution, 1975.

Jones, William K. *Cases and Materials on Regulated Industries.* The Foundation Press, Inc., Second Edition, 1976.

Joskow, Paul L. "The Determination of the Allowed Rate of Return in a Formal Regulatory Proceeding." *Bell Journal of Economics* (Autumn 1972).

Joskow, Paul L. "Inflation and Environmental Concern: Structural Change in the Process of Public Utility Price Regulation." *Journal of Law and Economics* (October 1974).

Joskow, Paul L. "Pricing Decisions of Regulated Firms: A Behavioral Approach." *Bell Journal of Economics* (Spring 1973).

Joskow, Paul L. "Regulation and the Financial Condition of Electric Power Companies." *American Economic Review* (May 1975).

Joskow, Paul L. "Regulatory Activities by Government Agencies." MIT Department of Economics Working Paper #171 (December 1975).

Kahn, A.E. *The Economics of Regulation: Principles and Institutions.* Vols. I and II. Wiley and Sons, 1971.

Kitch, Edward W. "Regulation in the Field Market for Natural Gas by the Federal Power Commission." In Paul W. MacAvoy (ed.), *The Crisis of the Regulatory Commissions.* Norton, 1970.

Klein, Lawrence R. *A Textbook of Econometrics*, Row, Peterson, 1953.

Kolko, Gabriel. *Railroads and Regulation, 1877–1916.* Princeton University Press, 1965.

Krasnow, Erwin G. and L.D. Longley. *The Politics of Broadcast Regulation.* St. Martins, 1973.

Kurz, Mordecai. "Income Redistribution: Theory and Evidence." IMSSS Working Paper #80, Stanford, 1977.

MacAvoy, Paul W. *Price Formation in Natural Gas Fields.* Yale, 1962.

MacAvoy, Paul W. "The Reasons and Results in Natural Gas Field Price Regulation." In Paul W. MacAvoy (ed.), *The Crisis of the Regulatory Commissions.* Norton, 1970.

MacAvoy, Paul W. and R.S. Pindyck. "Alternative Regulatory Policies for Dealing with the Natural Gas Shortage." *Bell Journal of Economics and Management Science* (Autumn 1973).

MacAvoy, Paul W. and R.S. Pindyck. *Price Controls and the Natural Gas Shortage.* American Enterprise Institute for Public Policy Research, 1975.

MacAvoy, Paul W. *The Economic Effects of Regulation: The Trunkline Railroad Cartels and the Interstate Commerce Commission Before 1900.* MIT Press, 1965.

Maurizi, Alex. "Occupational Licensing and the Public Interest." *Journal of Political Economy* (March/April 1974).

Mitchell, Bridger M. and Robert Smiley. "Cable, Cities, and Copyrights." *Bell Journal of Economics* (Spring 1974).

Mohring, Herbert. "The Peak Load Problem with Increasing Returns and Pricing Constraints." *American Economic Review* (September 1970).

Moore, Thomas G. "Deregulating Surface Freight Transportation." In A. Phillips (ed.), *Promoting Competition in Regulated Markets*. The Brookings Institution, 1975.

Moore, Thomas G. *Trucking Regulation*. American Enterprise Institute for Public Policy Research, 1976.

Myers, Henry R. "Federal Decision-Making and the Trans-Alaska Pipeline." *Ecology Law Quarterly* (1975).

Niskanen, William A. *Bureaucracy and Representative Government*. Aldine-Atherton, 1971.

Niskanen, William A. "Nonmarket Decision Making and the Peculiar Economics of Bureaucracy." *American Economic Review* (May 1968).

Noll, Roger G. *Reforming Regulation: An Evaluation of the Ash Council Report*. The Brookings Institution, 1971.

Noll, Roger G. and Morris P. Fiorina. "Voters, Bureaucrats, and Legislators." Caltech Working Paper, 1976 (forthcoming in *Public Choice*).

Noll, Roger G., Merton J. Peck, and John J. McGowan. *Economic Aspects of Television Regulation*. The Brookings Institution, 1973.

Office of Telecommunications Policy. *International Facilities Study*. Staff paper, 1971.

Olson, Mancur. *The Logic of Collective Action*. Harvard, 1965.

Owen, Bruce M. *Economics and Freedom of Expression: Media Structure and the First Amendment*. Ballinger, 1975.

Owen, Bruce M. "Regulating Diversity: The Case of Radio Formats." *Journal of Broadcasting* (Summer 1977).

Owen, Bruce M., Jack Beebe, and Willard Manning. *Television Economics*. D.C. Heath, 1973.

Owen, Bruce M. and Joseph Grundfest. "Kickbacks, Specilization, Price-Fixing, and Efficiency in Residential Real Estate Markets." *Stanford Law Review* (May 1977).

Owen, Bruce M. and Joseph Grundfest. *Licensing of Real Estate Brokers as Underwritten Title Companies: A Report to the State of California*. Stanford University, Department of Economics, April 1976.

Panzar, John C. and Robert D. Willig. "Economics of Scale in Multi-Output Production." *Quarterly Journal of Economics* (August 1977).

Panzar, John C. and Robert D. Willig. "Free Entry and the Sustainability of Natural Monopoly." *Bell Journal of Economics* (Spring 1977).

Park Rolla E. "Cable Television, U.H.F. Broadcasting, and FCC Regulatory Policy." *Journal of Law and Economics* (April 1972).

Park, Rolla E. "The Exclusivity Provisions of the FCC's Cable Television Regulations." RAND Corporation, June 1972.

Park, Rolla E. (ed.), *The Role of Analysis in the Formation of Cable Television Policy*. D.C. Heath, 1973.

Pegrum, Dudley F. *Transportation Economics and Public Policy*. Richard D. Irwin, Inc., 1973, third edition.

Peltzman, Sam. *Regulation of the Pharmaceutical Industry*. American Enterprise Institute, 1974.

Peltzman, Sam. "Toward a More General Theory of Regulation." *Journal of Law and Economics* (August 1976).

Phillips, Owen. "Legislative v. Administrative Control: A Study of the Determinants of Regulatory Behavior," Studies in Industry Economics, No. 85, Stanford, 1977.

Porter, Michael and Jeffrey Sagansky. "Information, Politics, and Economic Analysis: The Regulatory Decision Process in the Air Freight Case." *Public Policy* (Spring 1976).

Posner, Richard A. "The Social Costs of Monopoly and Regulation." *Journal of Political Economy* (August 1975).

Posner, Richard A. "Taxation by Regulation." *Bell Journal of Economics* (Spring 1971).

Posner, Richard A. "Theories of Economic Regulation." *Bell Journal of Economics* (Autumn 1974).

President's Task Force on Communications Policy. *Final Report.* Washington, 1968.

Ramsey, Frank. "A Contribution to the Theory of Taxation." *Economic Journal* (March 1927).

Roberts, Paul. "Some Aspects of Regulatory Reform of the U.S. Trucking Industry." (Forthcoming in the conference volume for the Workshop on Motor Carrier Economic Regulation.) National Academy of Sciences, 1977.

Scherer, Frederick M. *Industrial Market Structure and Economic Performance.* Rand McNally, 1970.

Scherer, Frederick M. "The Development of the TD—X and TD—2 Microwave Radio Relay Systems in Bell Telephone Laboratories." Harvard University Graduate School of Business Administration, October 1960.

Sloan Commission on Cable Communications. *On the Cable.* McGraw-Hill, 1971.

Spence, Michael and Bruce M. Owen. "Television Programming, Monopolistic Competition, and Welfare." *Quarterly Journal of Economics* (February 1977).

Steinbruner, John D. *The Cybernetic Theory of Decision.* Princeton, 1974.

Stewart, Richard B. "The Reformation of American Administrative Law." *Harvard Law Review* (June 1975).

Stigler, George J. *The Citizen and the State: Essays on Regulation.* University of Chicago Press, 1975.

Stigler, George J. "A Theory of Oligopoly." *Journal of Political Economy* (February 1964).

Truman, David B. *The Government Process: Political Interests and Public Opinion.* Knopf, 1951.

Tullock, Gordon. *The Politics of Bureaucracy.* Public Affairs Press, 1965.

United States Department of Commerce, Office of Telecommunications. "Geographical Areas Served by Bell and the Independent Telephone Companies in the United States." February 1973.

United States Federal Communications Commission. *Investigation of the Telephone Industry.* 1939.

United States Federal Energy Administration. *Natural Gas Curtailments, 1975–76 Heating Season.* Report of the National Gas Task Force, October 1975.

United States Federal Power Commission. *Annual Report of the Federal Power Commission.* 1974.

United States Federal Power Commission. *EPC News* (August 29, 1975).

United States Federal Power Commission. *National Gas Survey* (1975).

United States Federal Power Commission. *Sales by Producers of Natural Gas to Interstate Pipeline Companies* (Annual).

United States Federal Communications Commission. *Statistics of Communications Common Carriers* (Annual).

United States House of Representatives, Subcommittee on Communications. Staff Report, "Cable Television: Promise vs. Regulatory Performance." (January 1976).

United States Office of Technology Assessment. *An Analysis of the Impacts of the Projected Natural Gas Curtailments for the Winter 1975–76,* November 4, 1975.

United States Senate, Committee on Banking, Housing and Urban Affairs. *Mortgage Settlement Costs: Report of the Department of Housing and Urban Development and Veteran's Administration,* 1972.

United States Senate, Committee on Governmental Affairs. *Study on Federal Regulation,* 6 volumes, forthcoming.

United States Senate, Committee on the Judiciary, Subcommittee on Antitrust and Monopoly. *The Natural Gas Industry.* Hearing, June 26–28, 1973.

Wagner, Susan. *The Federal Trade Commission.* Praeger, 1971.

Wardell, William and Louis Lasagna. *Regulation and Drug Development.* American Enterprise Institute, 1975.

Webbink, Douglas W. "The Impact of UHF Promotion." *Law and Contemporary Problems* (Summer 1969).

Weiss, Leonard W. and A.D. Strickland. *Regulation: A Case Approach.* Mc-Graw-Hill, 1976.

Williamson, Oliver E. "Franchise Bidding for Natural Monopolies—In General and With Respect To CATV." *Bell Journal of Economics* (Spring 1976).

Willig, Robert D. "Consumers' Surplus: A Rigorous Cookbook." IMSSS #98, Stanford 1973.

Wilson, James Q. "The Politics of Regulation." In James W. McKie (ed.), *Social Responsibility and the Business Predicament.* The Brookings Institution, 1974.

Zajac, Edward E. "Some Preliminary Thoughts on Subsidization." Office of Telecommunications Policy Conference on Communications Policy Research, Washington, D.C., November 17–18, 1972.

Index

✳

About the Authors

Bruce M. Owen has recently been appointed director of the Center for the Study of Regulation of Private Enterprise in the Graduate School of Business Administration at Duke University, where he will hold a joint appointment in the School of Law. Professor Owen formerly taught at Stanford, and has held fellowships from the Brookings Institution and the Hoover Institution on War, Revolution, and Peace. He is the author of *Economics and Freedom of Expression* (Ballinger, 1975), co-author of *Television Economics* (1974), and author of numerous articles on regulation and related subjects.

Ronald Braeutigam is an economist. He holds undergraduate and master's degrees in engineering, and received his Ph.D. in economics from Stanford University. His background includes work in private industry as a petroleum engineer, in government as an economist in the White House Office of Telecommunications Policy, and as a lecturer at Stanford University. Professor Braeutigam is presently a member of the economics faculty at Northwestern University, where he is also affiliated with the Transportation Center. His primary research interests include the economics of industrial organization and public policy, including antitrust and regulation. His recent research has included examinations of the effects of regulatory reform in the natural gas, transportation, and telecommunications industries, and the relationship between efficient pricing and market structure.